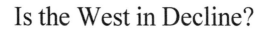
Is the West in Decline?

Is the West in Decline?

Historical, Military, and Economic Perspectives

Edited by
Benjamin M. Rowland

LEXINGTON BOOKS
Lanham • Boulder • New York • London

Published by Lexington Books
An imprint of The Rowman & Littlefield Publishing Group, Inc.
4501 Forbes Boulevard, Suite 200, Lanham, Maryland 20706
www.rowman.com

Unit A, Whitacre Mews, 26-34 Stannary Street, London SE11 4AB

British Library Cataloguing in Publication Information Available

Library of Congress Cataloging-in-Publication Data

Is the West in decline? : historical, military, and economic perspectives / edited by Benjamin M. Rowland.
pages cm
Includes bibliographical references and index.
ISBN 978-1-4985-1852-9 (cloth : alk. paper) — ISBN 978-1-4985-1853-6 (ebook)
1. Balance of power. 2. World politics. 3. International relations. 4. Geopolitics—Western countries. 5. Western countries—Foreign relations. I. Rowland, Benjamin M., editor.
JZ1313.I82 2016
909'.09821—dc23
2015027468

♾️™ The paper used in this publication meets the minimum requirements of American National Standard for Information Sciences Permanence of Paper for Printed Library Materials, ANSI/NISO Z39.48-1992.

Printed in the United States of America

Contents

Introduction

Decline: American Style

David Calleo

For much of the developed world, the decades since World War II have been a time of unparalleled rising production and prosperity. Nevertheless, there is scarcely a single "advanced Western" country that is not troubled by the specter of its own "decline." That decline is gauged and expressed in a variety of forms. It can be seen as absolute when measured against some particular moment in a nation's past. It becomes relative when measured against the rise or fall of significant neighbors. What decline actually measures varies greatly. Easiest are quantitative measurements that lend themselves to facile economic and military comparisons. Of course, since not all growth is good and not all decline is bad, there needs to be a further category of *morbid* decline. Here decline implies some inner sickness of the body politic, regardless of whether the decline is absolute or relative. [1]

Since the nineteenth century, Europeans have got used to seeing their economies surpassed by the Americans. However, since the Cold War, the United States has been challenged by a resurgent and unifying Europe, and, more recently, by the vigorous "rise" of several nations in the "developing" world—China in particular. Current measurements clearly show the United States economy to have been in relative decline vis-à-vis these rising economies. Should America's relative decline also be considered a symptom of *morbid* decline? Does it indicate a wasting sickness of the American economy and body politic? It might well. Nations do rise and fall. Our colleague, Lanxin Xiang, reminds us that China possessed the world's leading economy for the greater part of the previous millennium. In the end, however, its past success did not prevent China from being pillaged throughout most of the nineteenth and twentieth centuries. Is America in danger of a similar fate?

The answer depends on how well the United States manages its still immense patrimony, and how well it recasts its geopolitical position to the realities of the new century.

AMERICAN DECLINE AND WINNING THE COLD WAR

As of now, those realities present a rather confusing picture. American declinists began to flourish in the 1980s. In the era of America's large "twin deficits," declinists were often inspired by the concept of "imperial overstretch." The most popular exposition of that concept was found in Paul Kennedy's *The Rise and Fall of the Great Powers.*[2] Published in 1987, it provided declinists with a geopolitical theory rooted in modern history. As Kennedy read that history, great powers, pursuing hegemony over their neighbors, "overstretch" their national resources to a degree that damages their own internal development. The overstretched hegemon grows weaker internally while its neighbors grow relatively stronger. Professor Kennedy, observing the financial and geopolitical excesses of the Reagan administration, thought that overstretch might well be America's undoing.[3]

There have been numerous other American declinists in recent years, myself included.[4] But few have had Paul Kennedy's blunt message and immediate public impact. Events, however, quickly undermined Kennedy's conclusion. A very few years after his book appeared, the Soviet Union itself collapsed. His analysis thus foretold the fate not of America but of America's principal rival. Thus, a study designed to warn Americans against their own hubris, was easily converted into a triumphant declaration of American global hegemony. This transformation of Kennedy's message was perhaps not as strange as it may seem. Since Kennedy had composed and published his declinist message in the geopolitical climate of the Cold War, it was only natural that his book should present a bipolar view of contemporary great power rivalry. Given this bipolar optic, the collapse of the Soviet Union would almost inevitably be read as a victory for the United States.

My own declinist message had a somewhat different form. For all its brutal military efficiency and nuclear status, or the allure of Marxist dogma, I had difficulty imagining the Soviet Union as America's long-term rival for global hegemony. The Soviets had continued to blight Eastern Europe and a significant part of Asia but never offered a serious alternative to the global Pax Americana, already well into the making as World War II drew to a close. My fear came to be not so much Soviet strength as Soviet weakness. In dying, the Soviet Union might well prove a more serious threat to the United States than while in good health. A moribund Soviet Union would release a swarm of volatile and violent lesser powers. These might prove a fatal distraction for an America already dangerously attracted to the prospect of an imperial Roman future. In the prevailing Cold War climate it was entirely natural to see the Soviet collapse as a decisive victory for American hegemonic ambitions and for the vision of a unipolar capitalist world. As Francis Fukuyama put it, the "end of history" had arrived.[5] I thought his insight was brilliant but wrong-headed.

To begin with, I thought it was reckless to denigrate and humiliate Russia in her own neighborhood. It was most assuredly an ungenerous response to the nation that had done so much to defeat Hitler, and which remained one of the two great continental federations after World War II. It was also unwise. American and Russia states had never opposed each other directly in a major military contest. After World War II, each "superpower" had fought several wars in Asia and the Middle East. The United States engaged in the Korean War and the War in Vietnam. Meanwhile, the Soviet Union fought an undeclared border conflict with its supposed Chinese ally in 1969 and a decade-long war against Afghanistan from 1979 to 1989. In none of these wars could the United States or the Soviets be said to have prevailed decisively.

This was not a record for either "superpower" that lent much support to the fashionable vision of a bipolar world order. Nor did it follow that the defeat of one superpower would ensure the predominance of the other. Thus, while the disintegration of the Soviet Union was obviously a decisive defeat for the Soviets, it was not necessarily a conclusive victory for the Americans. As noted above, the Soviet collapse posed a serious danger for American statecraft. It nourished the unipolar fantasy which was already a powerful incentive for America's continued overstretch. Fortunately, America's presidents at the time, Ronald Reagan and George H. W. Bush, ignored Fukuyama's advice and avoided the trap baited with Soviet disintegration. While Reagan had initially done his best to resume the Cold War, several years in office had made him sensitive to the terrible dangers implicit in constantly relying on a nuclear balance of terror. With unexpected alacrity Reagan welcomed Gorbachev's championing of "glasnost" and "perestroika." This offered a way forward for reducing hostilities between the Soviets and the capitalist West.

Thanks not least to the skilled diplomacy of Reagan's successor, America's good fortune continued. The first President Bush was himself deeply familiar with the course of American diplomacy since World War II. He seemed not overly impressed by the revolutionary possibilities of "rolling back" Russia's Cold War advances into "Eastern Europe." He seemed conscious that America's recent "victories" in freeing the region from Russian occupation were rather passive accomplishments. They sprang neither from an external assault from the West nor from a revolt of restive "captive" nations in the East. Instead, they arose from the cultural collapse of the Russian elites themselves. It was the Russians, after all, who had dissolved the Soviet Union and granted the East European states their freedom. This disintegration of Soviet morale took the advisers around Bush by surprise and many had difficulty believing that it had actually occurred. Bush himself was worried that incendiary disorder might break out in Europe's newly liberated Soviet sphere.[6]

As the scale of the Soviet defeat nevertheless grew overwhelmingly obvious, the pressure increased for the United States to assert its new status as the unipolar super power. With the Soviets fleeing from Europe, and in their death agony at home, Bush was free to reassert Western dominance in the Middle East. He was able to cripple Saddam Hussein's army and eject the Iraqis from Kuwait. But having reestablished the territorial status quo, Bush was prudent enough to disengage and thus control the costs. Assessing his grateful regional allies for contributions in cash, the Bush administration made a profit on the whole expedition.[7] As the Soviet debacle continued, the Soviet withdrawal from Germany and the rest of Central and Eastern Europe was handled calmly. In short, the United States in George H. W. Bush's time avoided pursuing short-term Western victories that could not be sustained. Nor did Bush show any desire to upset the nuclear balance, which he doubtless feared would risk a general catastrophe for Europe, Russia, and America as well.

SQUANDERING THE AMERICAN VICTORY

The Clinton presidency was neither so wise nor so fortunate as its predecessor. In the end, the United States and the new Russia failed to stabilize relations and the United States could find no durable resolution for its fiscal and global imbalances. Things began well. "Clintonomics," combining drastic cuts in American military spending and a stock market boom fueled by Alan Greenspan's expansive monetary policies prompted enough growth in the American economy, and in the government's tax revenue, to make it briefly possible to balance the federal budget.[8] From 1993 to 2000, a United States federal fiscal deficit of $255 billion was gradually replaced by a surplus of $236 billion. But Greenspan's easy money policies gave rise to a different sort of deficit—an external deficit owed by the United States economy as a whole to the rest of the world. Thus, by 2000, the United States was running an annual current account deficit of $416 billion.[9] In my own writing, I saw this external deficit as an alarming symptom of America's imbalance with the rest of the world economy. Clintonomics, however, justified the giant imbalance as the natural and inevitable accompaniment to America's global hegemony. The United States was said to be the world's lender and buyer of last resort. Hence, it would inevitably be a giant exporter of capital. The geopolitical implications of these hegemonic economic assertions grew clearer during the succeeding George W. Bush administration.

In the meantime, the Clinton Administration, enjoying unprecedented prosperity and growth at home, began to acquire a taste for open-ended uses of military force: Somalia in 1993, Bosnia in 1995, missile strikes in Sudan and Afghanistan in 1998, and Yugoslavia in 1999.[10] Occasions for intervention presented themselves in the Balkans, particularly as the retreat of Russian forces awakened the region's slumbering squabbles. Initially, the West European states had seemed eager to use the machinery of the EU and the UN to replace the stabilizing role of Soviet power. But as Western Europe proved unable to provide a replacement for Soviet hegemony in the region as a whole, Clinton's United States began to speak of itself as the "indispensable power" for maintaining order, not only in the Balkans, but throughout the world.[11] The Clinton Administration's flirtation with America's hegemonic visions grew progressively more ardent.

The most ambitious and dangerous flirtation with hegemony came with the increasingly insistent plans for NATO enlargement. Despite the reservations among American policymakers, the alliance was gradually extended not only to the independent states corralled into the Soviet sphere after World War II—like Bulgaria, Czechoslovakia, Hungary, Poland, or Rumania, but also to countries that for centuries had been part of the Russian Empire—such as the Baltic States and Ukraine. By 2008, George W. Bush had grown progressively more inclined to absorb Ukraine and Georgia into NATO.[12] This extension of America's military alliance into long-standing Russian territories naturally aroused Russian fears and made the long-term prospects for peaceful Pan European relations increasingly implausible.

Clinton at least sought to preserve the appearance of the Russo-American cooperation of the first Bush era, but the younger Bush, unlike his father, showed little enduring concern for fostering a harmonious pan-European relationship that included the Russians. The younger Bush's belligerent approach was much appreciated among America's ascendant neo-conservatives, perhaps because it provided the enemy required for completing a Manichean view of world affairs. Similarly, East European states, recently liberated from the Soviets, were pleased to see the Americans take on military commitments designed to prevent the Russians from resuming their traditional regional sway. But Bush's reassertion of NATO and its Cold War perspectives aroused increasing unease among other major Western powers. Many West Europeans looked forward to cordial diplomatic and close economic relations with Russia, especially as a source of abundant cheap energy.[13] Europe had the capital and technology Russia needed to develop its own national economy. The way seemed open for a mutually prosperous future, with Russia increasingly integrated with what might be seen as a greater Europe. But as Russian-American relations deteriorated over the expansion of NATO and the nature of its interventions in the Balkans, West Europeans themselves began to draw closer to the United States at the expense of the

Russians. Given the increasingly aggressive vagaries of the Putin regime, the dreams of a peaceful and prosperous pan-European region, increasingly integrated economically into the West, began to appear less and less realistic.

Misunderstandings and grievances multiplied. Disappointed and angry Russians resumed their Cold War character as did many Americans, particularly those who favored the views of the second Bush Administration. Meanwhile, the United States ensnarled itself with fresh wars in Iraq and Afghanistan. As the costs mounted and success grew elusive, European support for the American-led interventions was more and more grudging. In short, less than a quarter century after the end of the Cold War, the United States found itself slipping into a series of bloody encounters in the Muslim world and was progressively being drawn into the current quarrel between Russia and Ukraine. As the Bush administration drew to a close, the vision of a unipolar world led by America began to seem more and more a derisory prospect. The hugely expensive American military establishment proved unable to translate its military power into decisive political victories. The new century added to the vast expenses of the American military establishment the costs of "Homeland Security." A hallucinatory level of fiscal deficits was the predictable consequence. From 2002 to 2011, sober estimates of the cost of America's Wars in Afghanistan and Iraq alone come to an astounding 2.8 trillion dollars.[14] The 2008 financial crisis made such heavy spending still more problematic. Thus, during his final years in office, Bush's aggressive foreign policy and abandoned fiscal policy grew progressively unpopular, as the American public seemed to be losing its taste for world management.[15]

Obama's presidential campaign of 2008 seemed to promise a foreign policy governed by strategic restraint. That impression was reinforced by what appeared to be a successful withdrawal from the Iraq War in 2011. Subsequent years, however, began to suggest a return to earlier policies. After 2011, the Obama administration found it difficult to extricate itself fully from inflamed Sunni-Shiite rivalries throughout the Middle East. By 2014, Obama had become the fourth-consecutive United States president to introduce United States military forces into Iraq, this time, against the Islamic State of Iraq and Levant (ISIL).[16] Meanwhile, the administration found itself unable to avoid being drawn into the escalating quarrel over the boundaries of the Ukrainian state, as well as over the constitutional arrangements for the treatment of its Russian-speaking populations. Russia, defying America's warnings, invaded and annexed Crimea, and seemed ready to follow up in the Eastern region of the Ukrainian state. This prompted economic sanctions by the Obama Administration in 2014.[17] So far, there seem to be two major lessons from the Obama years: sanctions alone do not offer an easy way to compel changes in Russia's policies, and secondly, the interventionist policies that held sway under George W. Bush reflected beliefs about America's hegemonic responsibilities in the world that are deeply implanted among

American political elites. Thus, while a foreign policy enthralled to America's neo-conservatives was not easy to sustain either at home or among America's allies, populist opposition to such a policy in the United States itself has so far failed to generate a durable shift toward strategic retrenchment.

Obama's difficulty in reversing Bush's foreign policy suggests what declinists fear: an American political system that has great difficulty adjusting to a world that is rapidly growing more pluralistic. As a result, America's federation is increasingly overstretched, unable to organize its burdens and capabilities to achieve sustainable ends. The unipolar undertow beneath both left and right in America is fostering a delusive misreading of a rapidly changing world. To avoid overstretch the United States will have to adapt to this plural world and reassess its own strength and geopolitical position accordingly. This means refraining from interventions that do not enjoy widespread support at home and among other major powers, willing to support the United States both militarily and financially.

MEASURING DECLINE

In a world of several closely related and integrated states, this means that politicians and historians regularly seek to determine comparative military, diplomatic, and economic prowess. Hence the enduring concern with decline. When considering the rise and decline of American power since 1945, it is worth noting just how unbalanced the Second World War had left the world. In 1945, the United States accounted for roughly half the world's GDP. By 1960, U.S. GDP was 40 percent of the world's output. Gradually readjustment followed. By 2008, the United States share had fallen to 23 percent. By 2014, the World Bank estimated the United States share of world GDP at 16.5 percent.[18] The relative decline in America's national production was further accompanied by a sustained increase in America's federal debt. Customarily, surges in federal debt accompany America's major wars. Debt during the Civil War and World War I rose to 30 percent of GDP while debt in World War II reached 80 percent.[19] Recently, debt has risen from 35 percent of GDP in 2007 to nearly 74 percent in 2014—the highest level since World War II.[20] These figures prompt a basic question: why does the United States now require such an increasingly high level of debt?[21]

Declinists are ready with an answer. Abroad, the United States is trying to combine the imperial role of world leader while at home it competes with other rich societies to be a model for the democratic welfare state. That it should have been thought possible for the United States to combine these two highly expensive roles in the first place was only because of the outsized United States economic and military lead over other great powers as a result of World War II. By the 1980s, America's postwar heritage was being engulfed in debt. The 1990s gave America's outsized aspirations a new lease on life. The Soviet collapse allowed Clinton a window for reducing military spending while the dot-com boom and Greenspan's monetary policies promoted rapid growth that funded the government's income and led to a balanced budget. As a result, it appeared, for a time, that America's dual ambitions could be sustained. By now, however, the dot-com boom has run its course. The huge military expenses of the Cold War are returning with a vengeance, and defense spending has risen in real terms to exceed Cold War levels.[22] Nor has there been a compensatory reduction in America's welfare state. Instead, the costs of the welfare state are rapidly escalating among all Western-style nations. The government's programs for pensions and health care are primarily enshrined in the budgetary category of "mandatory spending."[23] The residual category, comprised of non-mandatory items like education and defense spending, counts as "discretionary spending." When mandatory spending escalates faster than discretionary spending as a percentage of GDP, discretionary spending is squeezed. Discretionary spending's share of total federal spending was 67 percent in 1962 but is projected to be 5.2 percent by 2024.[24] This hardly seems a realistic figure for a modern democracy. Rather, it suggests a political system progressively unable to choose among options and thus control spending. Indecision and indiscipline impose heavy costs. The net interest on United States government debt was 6.4 percent of federal outlays in 2013 and by 2024 is projected to reach 14 percent of total federal outlays.[25] If so, interest payments will surpass baseline defense spending itself.[26] Obviously, such projections are difficult to take seriously. But they should make clear why declinism remains an enduring feature of American political discourse.

RADICAL SOLUTIONS

Professor Kennedy notwithstanding, can great nations be expected to collapse because their governments cannot pay their bills? It certainly seems possible, as the sad fate of Marie Antoinette suggests. In due course, however, politics generally intervenes as fresh power arises to reimpose order. Assuming America's federation does resurrect its political will, how will it save itself? One classic remedy is inflation—the path initiated already by "quantitative easing." Another is depreciation of the dollar—a path followed since the 1970s, but for the moment abandoned. These familiar remedies generally have a serious weakness: they point to a quick decline in living standards for many Americans. And, as the current banking crisis has reminded investors, the powerful can often repudiate what they cannot pay. Ordinary citizens are the usual victims. Declinists hope to control this process by retrenching power away from commitments that require excessive contributions. American declinists also recommend a more intense search for allies and a greater willingness to devolve responsibility to them. How the future actually plays out for America depends greatly on the policies of other major states—notably Europe and China, but also Japan, Russia, India, Brazil, and perhaps Iran.

The declinist conclusion that debt will force the United States to retreat from global hegemony because the costs are too excessive to bear may, however, prove to be an unsustainable hypothesis. The view that an overstretched America cannot "afford" to continue on its present hegemonic course depends on geopolitical presuppositions that postwar history appears to challenge. The Pax Americana has, after all, lasted more than half a century. Possibly a more realistic expectation than an American retreat is an indefinite continuation of the status quo whereby America's economic "partners" go on accepting exported dollars and develop ever more ingenious ways to abstract and sterilize their effects. In short, the international monetary system will continue to be a taxation regime for financing a world empire. Such a system, even as it operates at present, puts immense unchecked power in the hands of America's government. To keep this system tolerable for others will require exceptional self-discipline from American politicians as they become increasingly aware that, thanks to their country's continuing hegemonic position, the supply of credit available to America's economy is virtually unlimited. It may seem improbable that an increasingly plural global system will continue to accept such an exploitative hegemony at the root of international finance. Economists might regard such a privileged American position as an outrageous perversion of the doctrines of balance and fairness that lie at the root of their "science." Others, no doubt, will continue to ignore the exploitation so effectively masked by their academic discipline.

Ultimately, a new view of political economy might evolve, one where today's discordant remnants of natural law and equilibrium, left over from the nineteenth century, make way for models based more frankly on political and military power. This new economics should be familiar to students of the nineteenth century. Instead, Friedrich Nietzsche or Joseph Schumpeter may seem more relevant to our present worldview than Adam Smith or Friedrich Hayek. Followers of Hayek should not be surprised. Arguably, today's quantitative easing is the government-imposed inflation of the money supply that Hayek feared.[27] Whether a new economics based on potential power could inspire a more disciplined, humane, and durable multi-national order would depend on the major states themselves—on their ability to strike a political balance and generate the rules needed for a better civilization. Declinists, busily deflating the unreasonable expectations of new and old great powers, may help the world rediscover the virtues of the balance of power. If so, they may spare the twenty-first century a great deal of pain. This seems a more promising quest than the search for a new way to reconfigure a world of masters and slaves.

NOTES

1. Paul Kennedy, *The Rise and Fall of Great Powers* (New York, New York: Random House, 1987). For others in the "declinist school," please see 1) Peter Schmeisser, "Taking Stock: Is America in Decline?," *The New York Times*, April 17, 1988. Available at: http://www. nytimes.com/1988/04/17/magazine/taking-stock-is-america-in-decline.html. 2) David P. Calleo, *Beyond American Hegemony: The Future of the Western Alliance* (New York, New York: Basic Books), 1987.

2. Paul Kennedy, *The Rise and Fall of Great Powers* (New York, New York: Random House, 1987), 533. Kennedy writes that: "it has been a common dilemma of 'number one' countries that even as their relative economic strength is ebbing, the growing foreign challenges to their position have compelled them to allocate more and more of their resources into the military sector, which in turn squeezes out productive investment and, over time, leads to the downward spiral of slower growth, heavier taxes, deepening domestic splits over spending priorities, and weakening capacity to bear the burdens of defense." In short, global obligations of the hegemonic power become too large to sustain.

3. David P. Calleo, *Beyond American Hegemony, The Future of the Western Alliance* (New York: A Twentieth Century Fund Book, Basic Books, 1987).

4. See: 1) Francis Fukuyama, "The End of History?" *The National Interest* (Summer 1989): 3–18. 2) Francis Fukuyama, *The End of History and the Last Man* (New York, New York: Avon Books, 1992). Fukuyama wrote that we might be reaching "the end point of mankind's ideological evolution and the universalization of Western liberal democracy as the final form of human government." For a discussion of his argument and its critics, see: Victor Gourevitch, *After History? Francis Fukuyama and His Critics*, edited by Timothy Burns (Lanham, Maryland: Rowman & Littlefield, 1994).

5. Robert Legvold, "Russian Foreign Policy During Periods of Great State Transformation," in *Russian Foreign Policy in the Twenty-First Century and the Shadow of the Past* (New York, New York: Colombia University Press, 2007), 77–143. This quote refers to the Camp David meeting (1992) between President Bush and Yeltsin. The United States no longer saw Russia as an adversary. However, the United States also restrained itself from acting like "all of our problems are solved."

6. In 1991, financial support from military allies raised "net unilateral transfers" to $42.5 billion. This allowed the United States to run a trade surplus of $10.2 billion, which at that time, was the first in 9 years. See: 1) Associated Press, "United States Posts a Trade Surplus From Gulf War Payments," *New York Times*, June 12, 1991. For the underlying data on net unilateral transfers see: 2) Sara L. Gordon, *The United States and Global Capital Shortages: The Problem and Possible Solutions* (Westport, Connecticut: Quorum Books, 1995), 18–23.

7. Clinton era real base defense spending declined from 1992 to 2000. For the underlying historical data from 1974 to 2014 on discretionary spending, please see: 1) Congressional Budget Office, *An Update to the Budget and Economic Outlook: 2014 to 2024* (August 2014). Available online at: http://www.cbo.gov/publication/45010/. To adjust the historical data to inflation please use GDP price deflators available in the "FY15 Green Book." 2) Under Secretary of Defense (Comptroller), *Fiscal Year 2015 Green Book*, http://comptroller.defense.gov/budgetmaterials/budget2015.aspx/.

8. United States current account deficits grew progressively more negative from 1992 to 2000. Please see: 1) The International Monetary Fund, "World Economic Outlook Database." Available online at: http://www.imf.org/external/pubs/ft/weo//02/weodata/index.aspx/. Current account data is also available from the Bureau of Economic Analysis. Please see: 2) http://www.bea.gov/iTable/index_ita.cfm/.

9. C. Randall Henning, *Accountability and Oversight of United States Exchange Rate Policy* (Washington, D.C.: Peter G. Peterson Institute for International Economics, 2008), 41.

10. Ryan C. Hendrickson, *The Clinton Wars: The Constitution, Congress, and War Powers* (Nashville: Vanderbilt University Press, 2002). *Project MUSE*. Accessed 2 Dec. 2014, online at: http://muse.jhu.edu/.

11. The first example of this phrase comes from President Bill Clinton's second inaugural address. See: William J. Clinton: "Inaugural Address," January 20, 1997. Available online at: Gerhard Peters and John T. Woolley, *The American Presidency Project*. http://www.presidency.ucsb.edu/ws/?pid=54183/.

12. For the NATO-EU relationship, please see: 1) David Calleo, "Transatlantic Folly: NATO vs. the EU," *World Policy Journal* 20, no. 3 (2003): 17–24. For a Russian-centric analysis of NATO, please see: 2) Richard Sakwa, *Conflict in the Former USSR*, edited by M. Sussex (Cambridge: Cambridge University Press, 2012): 64–90. For contemporary news coverage of this issue, please see: 3) "Bush to back Ukraine's NATO hopes," *BBC News*, April 1, 2008. Available online at: http://news.bbc.co.uk/2/hi/ europe/7322830.stm/.

13. See: 1) David Victor, "The Gas Promise," in *Energy and Security: Strategies for a World in Transition* (Baltimore, Maryland: Johns Hopkins University Press, 2013): 88–104. 2) Stephen Larrabee, "Russia, Ukraine, and Central Europe: The Return of Geopolitics," *Journal of International Affairs* 63, no. 2 (2010): 48.

14. Anthony Cordesman, *The FY2015 Defense Budget and the QDR: Key Trends and Data Points*, Center for Strategic International Studies (CSIS), 19. Available online at: http://csis.org/files/publication/140521_FY2015_Defense_Budget_and_the_QDR.pdf/.

15. Pew Research Center. "Bush and Public Opinion." December 2008. Available online at: http://www.people-press.org/2008/12/18/bush-and-public-opinion/.

16. Dana Allin, "Obama and the Middle East: The Politics, Strategies, and Difficulties of American Restraint," *Middle Eastern Security, The United States Pivot, and the Rise of ISIS*, edited by T. Dodge and E. Hokayem (New York, New York: Routledge, 2014): 166–183. For contemporary news coverage of this issue, please also see: Karen DeYoung and Loveday Morris, "United States Airstrikes Target Islamic State Militants in Northern Iraq," *The Washington Post*, December 2, 2014. Online at: http://www.washingtonpost.com/world/middle_east/islamic-state-militants-seize-christian-town-in-northern-iraq-thousands-flee/2014/08/07/942a553a-1e2b-11e4-ab7b-696c295ddfd1_story.html?hpid=z1/.

17. Jim Nichol, "Russian Political, Economic, and Security Issues and United States Interests," *Congressional Research Service*, March 31, 2014. RL33407. http://fas.org/sgp/crs/row/RL33407.pdf/. A critique of this issue is furthered by: Lee S. Wolosky, "How to Sanction Russia and Why Obama's Current Strategy Won't Work," *Foreign Affairs*, March 19th, 2014. Available online at: http://www.foreignaffairs.com/articles/141043/lee-s-wolosky/how-to-sanction-russia/.

18. GDP is measured in current United States dollars (PPP) in both World Bank and IMF data sets. For global GDP share data see: 1) The World Bank, "World Development Indicators (WDI) databank." Available online at: http://data.worldbank.org/data-catalog/world-development-indicators/. For the IMF data set see: 2) The International Monetary Fund, "World Economic Outlook Database." Available online at: http://www.imf.org/external/pubs/ft/weo/2012/02/weodata/index.aspx/.

19. Congressional Budget Office, *Federal Debt and the Risk of a Fiscal Crisis* (July 27th, 2010). Available online at: https://www.cbo.gov/sites/default/files/07-27_debt _fiscalcrisis_brief.pdf/.

20. Congressional Budget Office, *An Update to the Budget and Economic Outlook: 2014 to 2024* (August 2014), 3–9. Available online at: http://www.cbo.gov/publication/45010/.

21. United States Department of Commerce. Bureau of Economic Analysis, "United States Net International Investment Position: End of Third Quarter 2014." Available online at: http://www.bea.gov/newsreleases/international/intinv/intinvnewsrelease.htm/.

22. Defense spending, of course, is a discretionary category of spending. Real base defense spending spiked during major combat operations in Iraq and Afghanistan and has begun to decline. However, in 2014, the United States still spends more in real terms (adjusted to inflation) than it did during the cold war. This "real spending" figure needs to be distinguished from the popularly used "defense spending as a percentage of GDP." Percentage of GDP figures decline more dramatically because growth in mandatory spending is higher than discre-

tionary spending. Thus, the United States technically does spend more in "real terms" on defense since the cold war while also spending less in "percentage of GDP terms." This phenomenon is caused by the dramatic growth of mandatory-spending categories (such as healthcare). See the historical data from 1974 to 2014 in: 1) "An Update to the Budget and Economic Outlook: FY2012 to FY2022, August 2012. Available at http://www.cbo.gov/sites/default/files/cbofiles/attachments/43539-08-22-2012-Update_One-Col.pdf. Also see: 2) FY15 Green Book: Under Secretary of Defense (Comptroller/), *Fiscal Year 2015 Green Book*, http://comptroller.defense.gov/budgetmaterials/budget2015.aspx/.

23. In 2013, United States federal spending was 20.8 percent of GDP, with discretionary spending accounting for 35 percent of total outlays and mandatory spending for 59 percent of total outlays. Andrew Austin, "The Budget Control Act and Trends in Discretionary Spending," *Congressional Research Service* RL34424. Available online at: http://www.senate.gov/CRSReports/crs-publish.cfm?pid='0E percent2C*QLK9 percent23P++ percent0A/.

24. Andrew Austin, "The Budget Control Act and Trends in Discretionary Spending," *Congressional Research Service* RL34424. Available online at: http://www.senate.gov/CRSReports/crs-publish.cfm?pid='0E percent2C*QLK9 percent23P++ percent0A/. For the underlying data please see three sources: 1) Congressional Budget Office (CBO), An Update to the Budget and Economic Outlook: FY2014 to FY2024, April 2014. Available online at http://www.cbo.gov/sites/default/files/cbofiles/attachments/45229-UpdatedBudgetProjections_2 .pdf/. For the data set see: 2) The Congressional Budget Office, "data underlying figures." Online at: http://www.cbo.gov/publication/45229/. For data needed to adjust the CBO data to inflation, please see: 3) FY15 Green Book: Under Secretary of Defense (Comptroller/Chief Financial Officer), *Fiscal Year 2015 Green Book*. Available online at: http://comptroller.defense.gov/budgetmaterials/budget2015.aspx/.

25. Andrew Austin, "The Budget Control Act and Trends in Discretionary Spending," 1–42.

26. Andrew Austin, "The Budget Control Act and Trends in Discretionary Spending," 22.

27. David P. Calleo, "American Decline Revisited," *Survival* 52, no. 4 (2010): 215–227. Friedrich Hayek, *The Constitution of Liberty* (Chicago, Illinois: University of Chicago Press, [1960] 2011), 451–466. In short, Hayek linked government control of monetary policy to the risk of inflation. Hayek stated, "With the government in control of monetary policy, the chief threat in this field has become inflation . . . every one of the chief features of the welfare state which we have considered tends to encourage inflation."

BIBLIOGRAPHY

Allin, Dana. *Middle Eastern Security, The U.S. Pivot, and the Rise of ISIS*. Edited by T. Dodge and E. Hokayem. New York, New York: Routledge, 2014.

Austin, Andrew. "The Budget Control Act and Trends in Discretionary Spending." *Congressional Research Service*. November 26, 2014. RL34424.

Calleo, David P. "American Decline Revisited." *Survival* 52, no. 4 (2010): 215-227.

Calleo, David P. *Beyond American Hegemony: The Future of the Western Alliance*. New York: Basic Books, 1987.

Calleo, David P. "Transatlantic Folly: NATO vs. the EU." *World Policy Journal* 20, no. 3 (2003): 17-24.

Congressional Budget Office. *An Update to the Budget and Economic Outlook: 2014 to 2024*. August 2014. Available online at: http://www.cbo.gov/publication/45010/.

Congressional Budget Office. *Federal Debt and the Risk of a Fiscal Crisis*. July 2010. Available online at: https://www.cbo.gov/sites/default/files/07-27_debt_fiscalcrisis_brief.pdf/.

Cordesman, Anthony. *The FY2015 Defense Budget and the QDR: Key Trends and Data Points*, Center for Strategic International Studies (CSIS). Available online at: http://csis.org/files/publication/140521_FY2015_Defense_Budget_and_the_QDR.pdf/.

Fukuyama, Francis. "The End of History?" *The National Interest*. Summer 1989.

Fukuyama, Francis. *The End of History and the Last Man*. New York, New York: Avon Books, 1992.

Gordon, Sara L. *The United States and Global Capital Shortages: The Problem and Possible Solutions*. Westport, Connecticut: Quorum Books, 1995.

Gourevitch, Victor. *After History? Francis Fukuyama and His Critics*. Edited by Timothy Burns. Lanham, Maryland: Rowman & Littlefield, 1994.

Hayek, Friedrich. *The Constitution of Liberty*. Chicago, Illinois: University of Chicago Press, [1960] 2011.

Hendrickson, Ryan C. *The Clinton Wars: The Constitution, Congress, and War Powers*. Nashville: Vanderbilt University Press, 2002.

Henning, Randall C. *Accountability and Oversight of U.S. Exchange Rate Policy*. Washington, D.C.: Peter G. Peterson Institute for International Economics, 2008.

Kennedy, Paul. *The Rise and Fall of Great Powers*. New York, New York: Random House, 1987.

Larrabee, Stephen. "Russia, Ukraine, and Central Europe: The Return of Geopolitics. " *Journal of International Affairs* 63, no. 2 (2010): 48.

Legvold, Robert. *Russian Foreign Policy in the Twenty-First Century and the Shadow of the Past*. New York, New York: Colombia University Press, 2007.

Nichol, Jim. "Russian Political, Economic, and Security Issues and U.S. Interests." *Congressional Research Service*. March 31, 2014. RL33407. Available online at: http://fas.org/sgp/crs/row/RL33407.pdf/.

Sakwa, Richard. *Conflict in the Former USSR*. Edited by M. Sussex. Cambridge: Cambridge University Press, 2012.

Schmeisser, Peter. "Taking Stock: Is America in Decline?" *The New York Times*. April 17, 1988.

The International Monetary Fund, "World Economic Outlook Database." Available online at: http://www.imf.org/external/pubs/ft/weo/2012/02/weodata/index.aspx/.

Under Secretary of Defense (Comptroller). *Fiscal Year 2015 Green Book*. Available online at: http://comptroller.defense.gov/budgetmaterials/budget2015.aspx/.

United States Department of Commerce. Buereau of Economic Analysis. "U.S. Net International Investment Position: End of Third Quarter 2014." Available online at: http://www.bea.gov/newsreleases/international/intinv/intinvnewsrelease.htm/.

Victor, David. *Energy and Security: Strategies for a World in Transition*. Baltimore, Maryland: Johns Hopkins University Press, 2013.

Wolosky, Lee S. "How to Sanction Russia and Why Obama's Current Strategy Won't Work." *Foreign Affairs*. March 19th, 2014.

I

Systems in Decline

Chapter One

Spengler's Decline of the West Revisited

Benjamin M. Rowland

Oswald Spengler's *Decline of the West* appeared in two volumes in 1918 and 1922. The question that runs through this paper is whether Spengler's work, written nearly a hundred years ago, still holds relevance for readers today, particularly, whether it helps to explain whether or not the West today is in decline. Spengler defines decline in his own way. It might be summarized in brief as the state of affairs, which he calls Civilization, when *noblesse oblige* is dead, when democracy reigns, and when money has *de facto* captured politics and most other human interactions. My working hypothesis is that the West today—Europe and the United States—is likely in decline and at least in part for reasons Spengler develops.

When it was published, *Decline* met with mixed reactions. A bestseller, it was said to comfort Germans because it seemed to rationalize their downfall as part of a larger world historical process. On the other hand, its intuitive, polemical, frequently mocking style put many off. Its sheer scope left it vulnerable to specialist scholars. One reviewer observed that Spengler's work was not considered reputable scholarship, being too metaphysical and too dogmatic. "Yet there it sits, a massive stumbling block on the road to true knowledge."[1] It was still a book to be reckoned with through the interwar period. In 1928, *Time* magazine wrote, "Cultivated European discourse quickly became Spengler-saturated. It was imperative to read Spengler, to sympathize or revolt. It remains so."[2]

Many famous people acknowledged the influence of Spengler's work. The Romantic scholar, Northrop Frye, claimed to have slept with it under his pillow, saying the work was "a grand piece of poetry." Reacting to Spengler's determinism, G.K. Chesterton wrote, "The pessimists believe the cosmos is a clock that is winding down. The Progressives believe that it is a clock that they themselves are winding up. But I happen to believe that the world is what we choose to make it."[3] Spengler met Hitler in 1933 but was not impressed, calling him "a heroic tenor when what we need is a hero." He did not share Nazi anti-Semitism. In his private papers he wrote, "When one would rather destroy business and scholarship than see Jews in them, one is an ideologue, i.e., a danger for the nation, idiotic."[4] He wrote that:

> I see world history as a picture of endless formations and transformations, of the marvelous waxing and waning of organic forms. The professional historian, on the contrary, sees it as a sort of tapeworm, industriously adding onto itself, one epoch after another.[5]

Whereas most historians, in Spengler's view, approach their work in linear, "ancient-medieval-modern," cause-and-effect fashion, Spengler argues to the contrary that history is composed of cultures whose main characteristic is that they are organic. Cultures are born, mature, and die in a manner more like organisms than lifeless cause-and-effect science. A Culture typically lasts around a thousand years. In his scheme there are eight cultures in all. Three of these receive close attention: first, by the culture of the West, called "Faustian," marked, like Goethe's character, by eternal longings and infinite horizons. Second, the culture of classical Greece and Rome, called "Apollonian."[6] Third was a cultural composite of Arab, early Christian, and Judaic called "Magian," whose signifier is a great mystical cave. "Every great Culture begins with a mighty theme that rises out of the pre-urban countryside, is carried through in the cities of art and intellect, and closes with a finale of materialism in the world cities."[7] Cultures are born from a land-based peasantry and end in a religion-crazed urban rabble,[8] the "fellaheen," which is ruled by a "Caesar" who serves no interests but his own.

Cultures are divided into epochs. An event is epoch-making when it marks a "necessary and fateful turning point" in a culture.[9] Analogy is Spengler's main analytical tool, a technique, he says, that is easily misused in the wrong hands. Cultures are analogous in various ways that only a true Historian—a person with intuition and a poetic sensibility—can know.[10] Using analogy, Spengler moves freely among Cultures, time periods, and modalities of expression such as architecture, statue, portrait, music, or statecraft. Epochs divide cultures into stages that can be compared. They allow the Historian to get under the surface of history, beneath the world of mere events. Among other things, they permit predictions of the future, a "venture of predetermining history, of following the still untraveled stages in the destiny of a culture."[11]

Cultures pass through seasons, with analogous springtimes, summers, autumns, and winters. One gets a small taste of Spengler's wit in his calling a culture's last, dying stage "civilization." Culture is to civilization "as the living body of a soul is to the mummy of it."[12] Man is a product of the season or epoch he happens to inhabit, as much as he is also a product of his culture. Thus, the season we live in determines the tasks we can undertake. Spengler's West has been in civilization since the French Revolution and the rise of Napoleon. Civilization determines our life and sets boundaries on what we can aspire to. Under civilization's influence "we have to reckon with the hard cold facts of late life, to which the parallel is to be found not in Pericles' Athens, but in Caesar's Rome. Of great painting or great music there can no longer be for Western people, any question."[13] Art, no less than politics and the State, succumbs to a final state of exhaustion. "We go through all the exhibitions, the concerts, the theatres, and find only industrious cobblers and noisy fools who delight to produce something for the market, something that will 'catch on' with a public for whom art and music have long ceased to be spiritual necessities."[14]

SPENGLERISMS

The purpose of this section is to help understand Spengler's main terms and concepts. They will come into play in the latter part of this paper, which focuses on Spengler's analysis of the State.

Ptolemaic v. Copernican

The world does not revolve around Europe and the West. For most historians "the ground of West Europe is treated as a steady pole, a unique patch chosen on the surface of the sphere for no better reason, it seems, than because we live on it."[15] This "quaintly conceived system of sun and planets" is the Ptolemaic system of history. It needs to be replaced by a Copernican version "that admits no sort of privileged position to the Classical or the Western culture as against the cultures of India, Babylon, China . . . separate worlds of dynamic being which in point of mass count for just as much in the general picture of history."[16]

Nature v. History

"Nature is to be handled scientifically; history poetically."[17] Nature, for Spengler, is *not* the "nature as mystery" associated with Romantic poets like Wordsworth or Keats, or his own favorite, Goethe. Spengler's Nature is quite the opposite. It is the world of science, of things mechanically defined, things that *are* subject to rules of cause and effect, and that are correct once and for all. Nature is the world of "things become," whereas history is the world of "things becoming." In History everything that happens, happens only once. It exists in time. Nature, like science, consists of things that can be replicated. In contrast, "every happening (in history) is unique and incapable of being repeated. It carries the hallmark of Direction ("time"), of *irreversibility*. That which *has* happened is thenceforth counted with the become and not with the becoming, with the stiffened and not the living."[18]

Who experiences history? For the ordinary man, "the sum of his experiences, inner and outer, fills the course of his day merely as a series of facts. Only the outstanding man feels behind the commonplace unities of the history-stirred surface a deep logic of becoming."[19] Indeed, it takes a poet to see history's larger patterns. "That which Dante saw with his spiritual eyes as the destiny of the world, he could not possibly have arrived at by ways of science, any more than Goethe could have attained by these ways to what he saw in the great moments of his Faust studies."[20]

Physiognomic v. Systematic

All modes of comprehending the world "may, in the final analysis be described as *Morphology.* "[21] There is a morphology of science and a morphology of history. The morphology of science and causal relations is called "systematic." The morphology of "the organic, of history, of life and all that bears the sign of direction and destiny, is called "physiognomic." According to Spengler, the use of systematic thinking took hold during the Enlightenment and peaked in the nineteenth century, exemplified by Darwinism. In the end, however, it is the physiognomic and not the systematic that will come to dominate. "In a hundred years all sciences that are still possible on this soil will be parts of a single vast Physiognomic of all things human."[22] This is so because, beneath their surface, the categories of systematic thought, for example, mathematics, are subject to their own "life history of ripening and withering" just like Culture itself. The systematic method of thinking can be taught. Historians, however, must be born to their task, "guided by a feeling which cannot be acquired by learning or affected by persuasion, but which only too rarely manifests itself in full intensity."[23] The historian, artist that he is, can see the becoming of a thing, whereas the systematic spirit, "whether he be physicist, logician, evolutionist, or pragmatic historian, learns the thing that has become."[24] It is the sure eye of the artist, his physiognomic sense, that allows the Historian to see patterns in the randomness of history:

> Countless shapes that emerge and vanish, pile up and melt again, a thousand-hued glittering tumult, it seems, of perfectly willful chance—such is the picture of world history when first it deploys before our inner eye. But through this seeming anarchy, the keener (i.e., historical) glance can detect those pure forms which underlie all human becoming, penetrate their cloud mantle, and bring them unwillingly to unveil.[25]

Culture v. Civilization

As noted above, high Culture needs to be understood through intuition rather than analysis. The essence of a culture in high bloom is that it is "in form," where doing the "right" thing comes effortlessly and naturally:

> There are streams of being which are "in form" in the same sense in which the term is used in sports. A field of steeple chasers is "in form" when the legs swing surely over the fences and the hooves beat firmly and rhythmically on the flat . . . . An art period is in form when its tradition is second nature, as counterpoint was to Bach . . . Practically everything that has been achieved in world history has been the product of living unities that found themselves in form.[26]

Similarly, "the great statesmen are accustomed to act, immediately and on the basis of a sure flair for facts. . . . But the professional thinkers (i.e., men without a sense of form) have been so remote, inwardly, from these actions that they have just spun for themselves a web of abstractions—abstraction myths like justice, virtue, freedom—and then applied them as criteria to past and, especially future, historical happening. Thus, in the end, they have forgotten that concepts are only concepts, and brought themselves to the conclusion that there is a *political science* whereby we can form the world according to an ideal recipe." Rousseau and Adam Smith are two of the prime purveyors of abstraction myths in Western culture.

Civilization is what happens to a culture when its critical impulses overwhelm its creative impulses. Specialization flourishes. Mathematical and statistical analysis come to the fore and smother a culture's creative spark. Moreover, "civilized history is 'superficial history,' directed disjointedly to obvious aims, and so become formless in the cosmic, dependent on the accident of great individuals, destitute of inward sureness, line and meaning."[27] It takes a special event to give rise to a culture:

> A Culture is born in the moment when a great soul awakens out of the proto-spirituality of ever-childish humanity, and detaches itself, a form from the formless, a bounded and mortal thing from the boundless and enduring. It blooms on the soil of an exactly definable landscape to which plant-wise, it remains bound. . . . It dies when this soul has actualized the full sum of its possibilities in the shape of peoples, languages, dogmas, arts, states, sciences, and reverts into the proto soul.[28]

"Great souls" are often religious figures like Buddha or Mohammed. Spengler places the birth of the Faustian soul of the West in the early Gothic period starting around 1000, when millennial fears of a judgment day helped it spring into life.[29]

Destiny v. Causality

> He who regards the world systematically in the end comes to believe that
> everything can be explained by cause and effect. Causality is the reasonable,
> the law-bound, the describable . . . But Destiny is the word for an inner
> certainty that is not describable . . . imparted only by the artist working
> through media like portraiture, tragedy and music. [30]

Destiny, to use terms introduced earlier, is the "becoming," while causality is the "become." People in touch with Destiny can be "in form"; while
causality bears no direct relationship to this special inner quality. "The
physiognomic flair which enables one to read a whole life in a face or to sum
up whole peoples from the picture of an epoch—and to do so without deliberate effort or "system"—is utterly remote from all cause and effect." [31] Yet
the two concepts, destiny and causality, are intertwined in other ways. The
practice of physics, chemistry, mathematics, falls in the domain of causality," but it was destiny that the discoveries of oxygen, Neptune, gravitation
and spectrum analysis happened as and when they did." [32] In different stages
an object or concept can undergo a becoming, while in another stage it can be
"become." Time exists in opposition to space:

> For primitive man the word "time" can have no meaning. He simply lives
> without any necessity of specifying an opposition to something else. All of us
> are conscious, as being aware, of space only, and not of time. Space "is" (i.e.,
> exists in and with our sense world). . . . "Time", on the contrary, is a discovery
> which is only made by thinking. We create it as an idea or notion and do not
> begin till much later to suspect that *we ourselves are Time*, inasmuch as we
> live." [33]

There is always a "subtle hatred" when anything leaves the world of
becoming and is "forced into the domain and form-world of causality." [34] For
example, freedom (becoming) is inevitably sacrificed when one opts for the
rule of law (become). "(W)ith birth is given death, with fulfillment, the
end." [35] Also "what is named, comprehended, measured, is, *ipso facto*, over-
powered. Once more, 'knowledge is power." [36] Different cultures, such as the
Western and Classical cultures, have different senses of "being" and "becoming." People who inhabit the different cultures can have only a distant understanding of the other. How, then, are cultures made comprehensible to one
another?

> The historical environment of another is a part of his *essence*, and no such
> other can be understood without the knowledge of his time-sense, his destiny
> idea and the style and degree of acuity of his inner life. Insofar therefore as
> these things are not directly confessed, *we have to extract them from the
> symbolism of the alien culture*. And as it is thus and only thus that we can

approach the incomprehensible, the style of an alien culture and the great time-symbols belonging thereto acquire an immeasurable importance.[37]

The "great time symbols" are refreshingly mundane. They include clocks, bells, funeral practices. Observing their role and conduct in different cultures offers a common denominator for understanding our own culture and the other. Time symbols can also be more abstract, including the institution of the State. What is Destiny and what is mere incident? "The spiritual experience of the individual soul—and of the Cultural soul—decide . . . (Indeed,) the very attempt to grasp them epistemologically defeats its own object . . . For without the inward certainty that destiny is something entirely *intractable* to critical thought, we cannot perceive the world of becoming at all . . . and he who approaches history in the spirit of *judgment* will only find "data."[38] No culture is free to choose *how* it will evolve. It can, however, foresee the way that Destiny has chosen for it. But this, to repeat, "presupposes the eye of an artist who can feel the whole sensible and apprehensible environment dissolve into a deep infinity of mysterious relationships. So Dante felt, and so Goethe felt."[39]

THE STATE

"A people in the style of a culture are called a Nation. A Nation, as a living and battling thing, possesses a State."[40]

Pre-cultural

In Spengler's scheme, a State, mirroring the Culture itself, goes through four main stages of rise and decline, preceded by a stage called the "pre-cultural," the undifferentiated world of a peasant culture, unaware of time other than seasonal time, rooted in its native soil. The peasant is:

> the eternal man, independent of every culture that ensconces itself in the City. He precedes it, he outlives it, a dumb creature propagating himself from generation to generation, limited to soil-bound callings and aptitudes, a mystical soul, of dry, shrewd understanding that sticks to practical matters, the origin and the ever-flowing source of the blood that makes world history in the cities."[41]

The Peasant is the bloodstock, the *materia prima* from which nobility springs.

Springtime

The earliest stage of a culture is springtime, "formed by awakening souls joined in a unity of self-awareness." In its political formation, feudalism and a warrior aristocracy characterize springtime. Governance is divided between two primary estates, Nobility and Priesthood. The nobility is the "estate proper," and contains within it the highest aspirations of which a culture is capable. It shares with peasantry its plantlike and instinctive quality, deep-rooted in its ancestral land, but unlike peasantry, its family-based self-awareness forms the basis of the dynastic principle. Property is fundamental to the noble estate in a way that can only be captured poetically. "When, in a wood, one feels all about one the silent, merciless battle for the soil that goes on day and night, one is appalled by the depth of an impulse that is almost identical with life itself." Hence, "the negation of property is never race-impulse, (i.e., emanating from the noble estate) but the doctrinaire protest of the purely intellectual, urban, uprooted, anti-vegetal waking consciousness of saints, philosophers and idealists."[42]

Priesthood, the second prime estate, arises, intellectual and systematic, in opposition to the first. Its defining mission and path to primacy is to subordinate nobility through the practice and example of asceticism. It is also the "middleman" between man and the eternal.[43] In comparison to nobility, "priesthood is essentially the counter-estate, the estate of negation, of non-race, of detachment from earth—of free, timeless, and historyless waking consciousness."[44] Priesthood leads to universities, scholarship, intellect, science and the cause-and-effect reasoning that increasingly characterizes a State in decline. Given the two world outlooks "there arise in the end (in every Culture) two sorts of moral (*sic*), of which each looks down upon the other—namely, noble custom and priestly askesis (religious discipline), reciprocally censored as worldly and as servile."[45] Indeed, "Spiritual and worldly power are so different in structure and tendency that any reconciliation, of even understanding, between them seems impossible."[46] "War proper" develops by the end of the feudal period, "the great war with the acquisition of land and people as its object."[47] To ask why a culture awakens is not a question Spengler can, or chooses to answer. It simply "does." However, "when we find in *all* cultures the same occurs in exactly the same form . . . then it is evident that the meaning of the facts must be looked for in the *deepest foundations* of Life itself."[48] The "deepest foundations" are:

> An idea that arises at (their) base and only in these (estates). It gives them the potent feeling of a rank derived from a divine investiture and therefore beyond all criticism—a standing which imposes self-respect and self-consciousness, but the sternest self-discipline as well (and death itself if need be) as a duty and imbues both with the historical superiority, the soul-magic, that does not draw upon power *but actually generates it.*"[49]

Summer

With the beginning of an urban civil society and the rise of critical, secular thought, the second phase of the state/culture is "summer, characterized by absolutist states, dynasties, and rising conflicts between aristocracies and monarchies. The political center shifts from castles and estates to cities and palaces.

Autumn

Autumn is the cultural high point of a state, for example, Rembrandt in painting, Bach in music. The State sees the rise of a bourgeoisie and experiences struggles between it and the aristocracy. The bourgeoisie is the "Third Estate," or sometimes the "Non-Estate," free from the land, drawing on features of both the Nobility and the Priesthood, even as the two prime estates grow outmoded by the rise of the city. In the autumn of the state/culture, "Nobility and clergy, so far as they are still extant, appear rather markedly as *privileged classes*, the tacit significance of the emphasis being that their claim to prescriptive rights on the ground of historical status is . . . obsolete nonsense."[50] All components of the Third Estate are "liberal." "Economy is freed to make money, science to criticize."[51] In sum, the city opposes to the aristocracy of birth the notion of an aristocracy of money and an aristocracy of intellect.

With the close of the late period of every culture, the history of its estates also comes to "a more or less violent end." Finance sheds every trace of feeling for earth-bound, immovable values, and scientific criticism every residue of piety.[52] Money also turns land, the basic stuff of peasantry and the old nobility alike into mere "moveable property," in the sense that finance makes land as "liquid" as mundane goods and services. Thus, money puts in play the foundations of the Culture itself.

Autumn is also a time of revolutions and of "Napoleonism." Shifting alliances among the monarchy, the two estates (nobility and priesthood), and the "non-estate"—the bourgeoisie—account for the turmoil. In response to the "fronds"—nobles arising against the monarchy, the bourgeoisie effectively shifts sides, aligning its interest with the monarchy. But with the Revolution, all parties become aware that the sole winner is the Bourgeoisie itself. Napoleonism, the rise of a strong leader unrooted in the state's cultural traditions, brings about the end of this period.

Winter (Civilization)

Civilization not only destroys the class structure of preceding seasons, it also gives rise to a "Fourth Estate, *the Mass,* which rejects the culture and its measured forms lock, stock, and barrel. It is the absolute of formlessness, persecuting with its hate every sort of form, every distinction of rank, the orderliness of property, the orderliness of knowledge."[53] Around the year 1800, Napoleonism marks the onset of "winter" or civilization for the West. Civilization brings on the exhaustion of the culture-bearing aristocracy, the rise of democracy and the bourgeoisie, parliamentarianism, and looming over it all, a politics captured by money. Money, of course was hardly a stranger to politics. "In England, politicians laid it down as early as 1700 that on the exchange one deals in votes as well as in stocks, and the price of a vote is as well known as the price of an acre of land."[54] Nonetheless, by the later date, Spengler argues, money's role had increased in degree and in kind.

Civilization is the "real return to "Nature," nature meaning the opposite of History. It is the "extinction of nobility—not as a physical stock (which would not matter), but as living tradition—and the supplanting of destiny pulse by causal intelligence. . . . Civilized history is superficial history, directed disjointedly to obvious aims, and so become formless in the cosmic, dependent on the accident of great individuals, destitute of inward sureness, line and meaning."[55] Civilization is marked by pure economic liberalism, the defeat of politics by economics. "Economics likes and intends a state that is weak and subservient to it."[56] In civilization, decline is inevitable but it may be gradual. Spengler suggests a time frame that could run into the twenty-first century. In any event, toward the end of Civilization comes the phenom-enon of Caesarism—named after the Roman soldier-emperors of the third century A.D., strong individuals who attain power usually by seizing it, and act only for themselves. The path to Caesarism includes the capture of politi-cal parties by the unchecked will to power of the race-strong few:

> That the entire mass of the electorate, actuated by a common impulse, should send up men who are capable of managing their affairs—which is the naïve assumption in all constitutions—is a possibility only in the first rush and presupposes that not even the rudiments of organization by definite groups exists.[57]

In the beginning, parties come into existence for the sake of a program. Then they are held onto by their incumbents "for the sake of power and booty. Lastly the program vanishes from memory, and the organization works for its own sake alone."[58] With Caesarism, "history relapses into the historyless, the old beat of primitive life, with endless and meaningless bat-tles for material power."[59]

SPENGLER'S RELEVANCE TODAY

Spengler wrote during and shortly after World War I. Though he claimed his multicultural opus had discovered general, repeating patterns to history it is hard to imagine that War to end Wars had not also colored his theoretical outlook and reinforced his sense of doom. To his many loyal readers, Nazism was evidence of Caesarism, and Hitler, of course, the Caesar.[60] So he was credited with prescience when the Nazis did assume power. In his 1934 volume, *The Hour of Decision,* Spengler warned of a coming world war that could destroy Western culture, the closest he ever came to predicting an apocalyptic event. War was meant to be the basic condition of mankind, peace the exception. Moreover, planning for peace, in his view, merely hastened the opposite. Had he somehow lived until today, how would he have explained the relative absence of "major" war during the postwar years? How would the rise of the United States and the decline of England have colored his views? Spengler has fewer readers today than in the 1920s and 1930s. That would fit his own theories well, since the progress of Civilization calls for more cause and effect reasoning, less room for "liberal arts." This is the difference between history and "nature" explored at an earlier point in this paper.

When he published his work in 1918 and 1922, Spengler reckoned the West had been in decline, in the condition he called "Civilization," since the rise of Napoleon. If he were writing today, would the passage of another hundred years simply be another century of the same? Would the rise of a Caesar figure still be Civilization's climactic event?[61] Or, might the West's Faustian culture itself have "re-booted" following the cataclysm of World War II? Would the new instruments and modalities of governments and societies, the UN institutions, for example, or the EU, or multinational investment, or global warming, or the internet, represent new ideas requiring new theories for their understanding? Could we have put behind ourselves the Faustian culture of limitless horizons for one where, because of global warming and climate change, the limits are all too apparent? Of course there can be no strict answer to these questions. We can never know what Spengler might have thought, but the hypotheticals offer some guidance.

In Spengler's "physiognomic"[62] scheme, civilization, the last stage of a culture, represents the triumph of money over politics. It is the "stage of a Culture at which tradition and personality have lost their immediate effectiveness and every idea, to be actualized, has to be put into terms of money." Democracy, he wrote, "is the completed equating of money with power."[63] Does money exert this kind of power today? In America, at least, money has indeed dominated electoral politics, for example, Citizens United, and is surely one of the important reasons for the paralysis of government institutions today. Moreover, the very forms of finance such as derivative securities and synthetic money are increasingly rootless and barely grounded in an underlying instrument. They would likely be at home in Spengler's "formless world." Civilization is also meant to be marked by a "second religiousness," a role that the current evangelical movement or the Tea Party, could fill very well.

When a culture reaches Civilization, the separation of powers that was present in earlier stages of the culture ceases to exist. Spengler was adamant, too, that the Press was also a captive of moneyed interests. Public opinion could be bought and sold, managed or influenced. "'Contemporary' English-American politics have created through the press *a force-field* of world-wide intellectual and financial tensions in which every individual unconsciously takes up the place allotted to him, so that he must think, will, and act as a ruling personality somewhere or other in the distance thinks fit."[64] The determinism in Spengler's theories underscores not just that there will be an end to Faustian culture, the culture of the West, but that we are all also creatures of the age we live in. It is that age which dictates how we think and what we do, in culture and the arts as well as politics. Stubborn theorists—"political scientists"—may put forth other ideas like socialism, pacifism, and internationalism. They are deluded, Spengler insists, and are building castles in the air. Indeed, "Today all 'philosophy' is nothing but an inward abdication and resignation, or a craven hope of escaping realities by means of mysticism."[65] But the philosophers and scholars are also hastening decline, because they ignore that the basic condition of a society is War. "War is the primary politics of everything that lives."[66] Being "in form" to be at war means that inward oriented reforms must yield to external preparedness.[67] There is little question where Spengler belongs on the "realist—idealist" divide.

War-preparedness helps explain how a country may become over-stretched. But, it is a fact of the stage of the culture and therefore not susceptible to change. Imperialism, says Spengler "is so necessary a product of any civilization that when a people refuses to assume the role of master, *it is seized and pushed into it.*"[68] The inference for today is that the U.S. may be over-extended, but there is little its leaders can do about it. How long will Civilization last? At one point he suggests the end of the twentieth, at another the end of the twenty-first century. What he was certain of, on the basis of his study of eight cultures, and their organic patterns of growth and decay, was that there would be an end. Everything-become is mortal: "Not only peoples, race, languages and Cultures are transient. In a few centuries from now there will no more be a Western Culture, no more be German, English or French than there were Romans in the time of Justinian."[69] As in culture, so also in the arts:

> All art is mortal; not merely the individual artifacts but the arts themselves. One day the last portrait of Rembrandt and the last bar of Mozart will have ceased to be—though possibly a colored canvas and a sheet of notes may remain—because the last eye and the last ear accessible to their message will

have gone. Every thought, faith and science dies as soon as the spirits in whose worlds their "eternal truths" were true and necessary are extinguished. [70]

In summary, the present matches Spengler's prescriptions for decline in at least six ways.

1. Our form of politics is democratic. Democracy is a symptom of decline in part because of what is lost by its rise, that is, *noblesse oblige* (character matters), in part because it is inextricably tied to money.
2. Internally oriented policies come to dominate externally oriented policies. This is a symptom of weakness and decline because war, in Spengler's view, is the natural order of things. In a robust culture, war readiness needs to be the ultimate goal of all policy.
3. The world order is based, in large measure, on liberal internationalism.
4. The United States is, by Spengler's measure, an imperial power, stretched, often against its will, into an excessive international presence.
5. Whether the arts die in Civilization, as Spengler insists, is a matter for subjective judgment, yet a case can be made.
6. Multicultural globalism is a recipe for a failed system. Most of us can't understand cultures other than our own.

There is, in the end, no good way of establishing the relevance of Spengler's theories and convictions to today's circumstances unless, of course, one is a historian, or a poet.

NOTES

1. Oswald Spengler, *The Decline of the West*, edited by A. Helps, and H. Werner (New York, New York: Oxford University Press, 1991). See also: Oswald Spengler, *The Decline of the West: Volume 2*, (New York, New York: Alfred A. Knopf, [1922] 1928).

2. Oswald Spengler, *The Decline of the West: Volume 1* (New York, New York: Oxford University Press, 1991).

3. Oswald Spengler, *The Decline of the West: Volume 1* (New York, New York: Oxford University Press, 1991).

4. Oswald Spengler, *The Decline of the West: Volume 1* (New York, New York: Oxford University Press, 1991).

5. Oswald Spengler, *The Decline of the West: Volume 1*, translated by C. F. Atkinson (New York, New York: 1927), 21–22.

6. Like Nietzsche, who popularized the term, Spengler uses Apollinian (Apollonian) to mean reason, sobriety, and asceticism.

7. Oswald Spengler, *The Decline of the West: Volume 2* (New York, New York: Alfred A. Knopf, 1928), 308.

8. "A second religiousness arises, unremarked but spontaneous, among the masses, and is likely to take the form of Adventism and suchlike sects." Oswald Spengler, *The Decline of the West: Volume 1*, translated by C. F. Atkinson (New York, New York: 1927), 311.

9. Oswald Spengler, *The Decline of the West: Volume 1*, 148.

10. Spengler frequently quotes Goethe as someone with the sensibility to understand History, as in this passage from the first volume of Faust: "A longing pure and not to be described/ Drove me to wander over woods and fields/ And in a mist of hot abundant tears/ I felt a world arise and live for me." These comparisons notwithstanding, Spengler is hostile to the notion that he might be taken as a Romantic, a movement he refers to as "an imitation of an imitation." Oswald Spengler, *The Decline of the West: Volume 1*, 186.

11. Oswald Spengler, *The Decline of the West: Volume 1*, 3.

12. Oswald Spengler, *The Decline of the West: Volume 1*, 353.

13. Oswald Spengler, *The Decline of the West: Volume 1*, 4.

14. Oswald Spengler, *The Decline of the West: Volume 1*, 293.

15. Oswald Spengler, *The Decline of the West: Volume 1*, 17.

16. Oswald Spengler, *The Decline of the West: Volume 1*, 18. Contrary to these declarations, Spengler does indeed focus on Europe and the U.S. from the seventeenth to the twentieth centuries, and on their classical Greek and Roman analogs from the second century B.C. to the fourth century A.D.

17. Oswald Spengler, *The Decline of the West: Volume 1*, 96. This is not meant to suggest that historians can't use facts and figures. In their place, they are very important, but only as a means to an end.

18. Oswald Spengler, *The Decline of the West: Volume 1*, 95

19. Oswald Spengler, *The Decline of the West: Volume 1*, 138–39.

20. Oswald Spengler, *The Decline of the West: Volume 1*, 96.

21. Oswald Spengler, *The Decline of the West: Volume 1*, 100.

22. Oswald Spengler, *The Decline of the West: Volume 1*, 100.

23. Oswald Spengler, *The Decline of the West: Volume 1*, 102.

24. Oswald Spengler, *The Decline of the West: Volume 1*, 102.

25. Oswald Spengler, *The Decline of the West: Volume 1*, 103.

26. Oswald Spengler, *The Decline of the West: Volume 1*, 331.

27. Oswald Spengler, *The Decline of the West: Volume 2* (New York, New York: Alfred A. Knopf, [1922] 1928), 339.

28. Oswald Spengler, *The Decline of the West: Volume 1*, 106.

29. "Every new culture is awakened in and with a new view of the world, that is, a sudden glimpse of death as the secret of the perceivable world. It was when the idea of the impending end of the world spread over Western Europe (about the year 1000) that the Faustian soul of this religion was born." Oswald Spengler, *The Decline of the West: Volume 1*, 167.

30. Oswald Spengler, *The Decline of the West: Volume 1*, 118.

31. Oswald Spengler, *The Decline of the West: Volume 1*, 118.

32. Oswald Spengler, *The Decline of the West: Volume 1*, 119.

33. Oswald Spengler, *The Decline of the West: Volume 1*, 122.

34. Oswald Spengler, *The Decline of the West: Volume 1*, 123.

35. The tension between "being" and " becoming " central to Spengler's view of the world, is also a key to many of the Romantic poets. See, for example, Keats' "Ode to a Grecian Urn."

36. Oswald Spengler, *The Decline of the West: Volume 1*, 123.

37. Oswald Spengler, *The Decline of the West: Volume 1*, 131.

38. Oswald Spengler, *The Decline of the West: Volume 1*, 141.

39. Oswald Spengler, *The Decline of the West: Volume 1*, 159.

40. Oswald Spengler, *The Decline of the West: Volume 2*, 362.

41. Oswald Spengler, *The Decline of the West: Volume 2*, 96.

42. Oswald Spengler, *The Decline of the West: Volume 2*, 344.

43. "Fear before death is the source, not merely of all religion, but of all philosophy and natural science as well." Oswald Spengler, *The Decline of the West: Volume 2*, 345.

44. Oswald Spengler, *The Decline of the West: Volume 2*, 336.

45. Oswald Spengler, *The Decline of the West: Volume 2*, 341.

46. Oswald Spengler, *The Decline of the West: Volume 2*, 351.

47. Oswald Spengler, *The Decline of the West: Volume 2*, 345.

48. Oswald Spengler, *The Decline of the West: Volume 2*, 334.

49. Oswald Spengler, *The Decline of the West: Volume 2*, 336.

50. Oswald Spengler, *The Decline of the West: Volume 2*, 356.

51. Oswald Spengler, *The Decline of the West: Volume 2*, 356.

52. Oswald Spengler, *The Decline of the West: Volume 2*, 357.

53. Oswald Spengler, *The Decline of the West: Volume 2*, 358.

54. Oswald Spengler, *The Decline of the West: Volume 2*, 402

55. Oswald Spengler, *The Decline of the West: Volume 2*, 339.

56. Oswald Spengler, *The Decline of the West: Volume 2*, 349.

57. Oswald Spengler, *The Decline of the West: Volume 2*, 349.

58. Oswald Spengler, *The Decline of the West: Volume 2*, 452.

59. Oswald Spengler, *The Decline of the West: Volume 2*, 339.

60. At times, Spengler suggests that an individual condition rather than a general condition may represent Caesarism. In the former case, Caesarism is the death of the spirit that animates nations and institutions. It is marked by a government that is "formless," irrespective of its *de jure* structure and constitutional status.

61. Amaury de Riencourt, *The Coming Caesars* (New York, New York: Coward-McCann, 1957). Riencourt argues that American presidents have become the new Caesars, amassing additional powers over the years, relative to other branches of government.

62. Physiognomy involves "looking at things directly in the face or heart, rather than scientifically."

63. Oswald Spengler, *The Decline of the West: Volume 2*, 485

64. Oswald Spengler, *The Decline of the West: Volume 2*, 440.

65. Oswald Spengler, *The Decline of the West: Volume 2*, 430.

66. Oswald Spengler, *The Decline of the West: Volume 2*, 440.

67. "A state directed by idealists is the way to a nullity." Oswald Spengler, *The Decline of the West: Volume 2*, 368.

68. Oswald Spengler, *The Decline of the West: Volume 2*, 472.

69. Oswald Spengler, *The Decline of the West: Volume 1*, 167. The Byzantine Emperor Justinian reined from 527 to 565 A.D.

70. Oswald Spengler, *The Decline of the West: Volume 1*, 168.

BIBLIOGRAPHY

Spengler, Oswald. *The Decline of the West*. Edited by A. Helps and H. Werner. New York, New York: Oxford University Press, 1991.

Spengler, Oswald. *The Decline of the West: Volume 1*. Translated by C. F. Atkinson. New York, New York: 1927.

Spengler, Oswald. *The Decline of the West: Volume 2*. New York, New York: Alfred A. Knopf, [1922] 1928.

De Riencourt, Amaury. *The Coming Caesars*. New York, New York: Coward-McCann, 1957.

Chapter Two

"Hegemonic" Decline, Emerging Powers, and Global Conflict

Some Considerations on the Rise of Germany and the Rise of China

Aaron M. Zack

The dispersal of technology and economic strength is eroding America's capacity to buttress global order. An effective response to emerging threats requires a reliance upon cooperation amongst the global powers, rather than a putatively stabilizing hegemon. However, the rise of China and American decline have resuscitated the recurrent problem of hegemonic conflict. The rise of Germany in the late nineteenth century offers insights relevant to our understanding of the rise of China. The European system's shift away from a relatively fluid, Bismarckian "balance of tensions" to a rigid, bipolar "balance of power" paved the path toward hegemonic war. This implies that refraining from the formation of overt, opposed blocs might diminish the likelihood of a future hegemonic conflict in East Asia. China's maintenance of a relationship of "normality" with the United States and other powers would reduce the trend toward the formation of such blocs. However, geo-economic vulnerability similar to Germany's, as well as America's own political culture, are likely to place China's maintenance of "normality" under strain.

THREATS OLD AND NEW: THE EMERGING GLOBAL ORDER AND DISPERSAL OF POWER

The prevailing global order contains the seeds of its own, rather advanced, decay. Two related developments are undermining it. First, the American-guaranteed system of open markets, freedom of the seas, open access to raw materials, and generally convertible currencies has underwritten the rise of great economic powers—such as Japan, the EU, China, Brazil, India, and perhaps Russia. Second, the continuous and accelerating global dispersal of science and technology is raising the prospect that, for the first time in history, non-state actors, and theoretically even individuals, might soon wield the power to gravely injure or destroy mighty and powerful states. [1] The "old" phenomenon of rising states and "new" phenomenon of threats to the modern state are linked not only in their causes, but also in their effects. [2] They are both rendering increasingly problematic an American-dominated global order.

The dilemmas created by the relative weakening of a beneficent, dominant, global power are not novel. The pax Britannica was the culmination of centuries of political, economic, and military development. [3] However, having achieved naval, financial, and manufacturing primacy, Britain's moderate, restrained, and liberal hegemony facilitated and accelerated the rise of great economic and military powers—among them Germany and the United States. [4] The first challenged and bled white the foundations of British power; the second stepped in and inherited it. Similarly, once the United States assumed the role of guarantor of a renewed liberal order after 1945, its manufacturing and financial supremacy were bound to decline. A successful containment strategy, unless exhaustive, assumed the renaissance of European and Japanese manufacturing and financial prowess in order to restore the shattered Eurasian balance of power. Therefore containment, as the Americans conceived of it, presupposed their own relative decline vis-a-vis their European and Asian allies. Furthermore, even after positions of strength had been established, America's liberal hegemonic ethos arguably compelled the United States to refrain from matching, or even obstructing, its own dependents' predatory mercantilism. Thus Japan, while protecting and organizing its own domestic market, progressively decimated one high value-added manufacturing industry in America after another. It seems problematic to completely assign the causes of this process to comparative advantage alone. In any event, had the American elite forced Japan, South Korea, Taiwan, and others to accept the liberal ethos which the Americans proclaimed and practiced, quotas, tariffs, subsidies, and other mercantilist interventions would have been definitively prevented, in the interest of a liberal system beneficial for all. The United States refused to do this. [5]

Therefore the postwar pax Americana was, in fact, merely a semi-liberal and increasingly semi-hegemonic order. A liberal, military-political, quasi-hegemon guaranteed the conditions within which both liberal and predatory, mercantilist states, in addition to America's own burdens and limitations, eroded its sinews of power. Therefore the "unipolar" moment of full spectrum, true American dominance in fact never existed beyond the first postwar years, even within the "West" itself. Presumably, as Europe and Japan recovered, a coherent American grand strategy would have counseled a gradual relinquishment of its originally necessary hegemony.[6] Instead, from fear, their own sense of political mission and ambition, the Americans largely accepted their waning domination of the global economy, while renewing their embrace of military and political power in order to shape the emerging global order. This was the crucial choice which overextended and therefore diminished America's spirit and material strength, damaged prospects for the emergence of a concert of global powers, and increased the likelihood of future conflict between America and a rising Great Power or Powers.

In contradiction with the beliefs of the preponderant American national security elite, therefore, the collapse of the Soviet Union did not signal the end of the bipolar order and an incipient American hegemony.[7] Instead, it represented a shift from one type of multipolar order to another without significant ideological competition but, rather, intensifying "traditional" identity and raison d'Etat motives for conflict. The reality of an American-dominated political and military system was particularly problematic since, despite its advanced military technology, the United States could not credibly coerce nuclear-armed or nuclear-capable states. The known lethality of nuclear weapons suggested that against a power such as the United States, sensitive to human, material, and moral damage, minimal deterrence would be highly effective.[8] The undoubted capacity of advanced industrial powers to quickly develop these weapons implied that had America pursued a truly Roman avocation, it would have swiftly found itself confronted with well-armed states able to resist coercion.[9] With respect to these states, American power was effective only to the extent it remained limited, non-coercive, and non-threatening. Had America attempted to act as a true hegemon, its already limited usable political and military power would have been swiftly checked. America could deter other states. It could influence and convince them within limits, and, for a time, perhaps compel the weak. But it could not, given its nature and potential or actual material realities, shift the emerging trajectory of the international order toward a real or durable hegemony.

Parenthetically, another development which suggested the illusory nature of American hegemony was the increasingly lethal potential of non-state actors. Just as America's quasi-hegemonic, quasi-liberal order facilitated the rise of great new economic and military powers, the limited liberal ethos of the age also facilitated the dispersal of technologies which engendered the threat of earthshaking terrorist assaults. [10] The trend of increasing power over nature and humanity itself began with, or was significantly accelerated by, the Industrial Revolution, and has maintained its rapid pace. [11] However, unlike the effect of the American-guaranteed global order, the relatively open economic order guaranteed by Britain in the nineteenth century facilitated the dispersal of destructive power to states alone. Therefore, and perhaps significantly, states did not need to intensively cooperate against non-state actors in order to ensure their own security.

The rise of great new economic and military powers in the nineteenth century resuscitated the old problem of hegemonic conflict. However, the dynamics of the subsequent German bids for hegemony significantly differed from the previous Habsburg and French bids, in their specific causes, conduct, and outcomes. [12] Therefore, new factors did not prevent, but rather altered certain aspects of the dynamic and consequences of the "old" problem of hegemony and hegemonic conflict. Similarly, accelerating technological and economic trends in the emerging global order will not dispense with the enduring problem of potential hegemonic conflict, and, indeed, seem to be resuscitating it in a modified form. Relative American decline and the rise of China suggest the importance of considering potential conflict between a global power and the potential hegemon of the decisive regional state system of the future. However, we might expect the vertical and horizontal dispersal of destructive technologies to modify the patterns and dynamic of the developing Sino-American rivalry. Even more so than in the past, chaos, anarchy and entropy will threaten the safety and welfare of China, America, and other major powers. The forces of order, to a greater extent than the Great Powers did after the Napoleonic Wars, are likely to experience the costs of conflict as unendurable. [13] In the modern world after the Peace of Westphalia, the actions of sovereign states were the primary cause of destruction. [14] To the extent that destruction from other actors also threatens to catastrophically disrupt a viable international system, a political or military conflict between a rising China and declining America would exact significant additional costs. In order to effectively address the new types of disorder as well as the old, America, China, and others must effectively manage the enduring and recurrent problem of Great Power rise and decline and its associated hegemonic tension.

This essay will consider some factors which might mitigate or accelerate rivalry between America and China. Since the rise of Germany prior to the First World War offers interesting parallels and lessons useful for an understanding of the emerging geopolitical pattern of Sino-American relations, we will first consider factors which propelled Germany on its aggressive path. The parallels between the rise of China and rise of Germany are particularly apposite, since the German bids for hegemony occurred within the context of an industrial civilization and global economy closer to our own than the admittedly global, but preindustrial, economies within which the Habsburg and French hegemonic bids occurred. We will then consider the implications of the rise of Germany for our understanding of the dynamics of a potential Sino-American hegemonic rivalry.

GERMANY'S RISING POWER: THE DILEMMAS OF "SATIATION"

A number of political theorists and historians have noted similarities between the rise of China and the rise of Germany. However, this comparison, with the exception of naval policy, has not been explored in detail. Furthermore, the comparison is typically limited to the period between 1890 and 1914 when the German Emperor, Wilhelm II, and his advisers conducted German policy.[15] This concentration, however, while illuminating in many respects, obscures certain enduring geopolitical challenges which preoccupied all German actors and theorists, and other states, from the creation of the Reich in 1871 until its "successor's" destruction in 1945.[16] In order to thoroughly understand the implications of Germany's rise for a future Sino-American rivalry, we must comprehend durable geopolitical dilemmas, and distinguish them from the twists and turns of contingent technologies, personalities, and events. This will allow us to consider the implications of the previous hegemonic conflict for our comprehension of a different set of historical, geographic, and technological realities.

Germany in 1871 was a primarily rural nation and did not rival the strongest economic power, Britain, in industry, shipping, finance, or trade.[17] The Reich did not encompass the entire German "nation"—Catholic Germans in the Habsburg Empire were considered by the first German Chancellor, Bismarck, a potential threat to Prussian, Protestant domination, and he had no wish to bring them within a Grossdeutchland or "Greater Germany."[18] Therefore the new Reich's population, in an age when population was a key component of a Great Power's strength, was not much more than France's, even after France lost Alsace and Lorraine. And France's demographic stagnation, and Germany's tremendous population growth, had yet to fully manifest themselves.[19] Germany's Prussian-dominated military had demonstrated undoubted effectiveness and efficiency. However, the historically competitive and mutually adaptive nature of the European state system suggested that the other Great Powers (with the possible exception of insular Britain) would quickly imitate Prusso-Germany's military structure and techniques.

Therefore the Reich in 1871 might be considered a "semi-hegemonic" Continental power—stronger than France or Austria, and probably stronger than Russia.[20] But the Reich could not challenge Britain in its global, naval, element, nor could it again challenge a European Great Power without risking the swift formation of an anti-hegemonic coalition against itself. Indeed, the limits placed upon the new Reich's room for maneuver and power-political expansion were made swiftly apparent. In 1875, fearing that Germany intended to wage a preventive war to crush France's unexpectedly swift recovery, Britain and Russia warned Bismarck that if Germany initiated war they would not stand aside and allow France to be defeated.[21] The "flanking" powers of the state system thus "imperiously" demonstrated to Germany that while they expanded into Asia and across the oceans, Germany would not be permitted to turn its precarious, limited "semi-hegemony" into a real hegemony within Europe. Further Prusso-German expansion would not be tolerated.[22] Therefore, thirty-nine years before war actually broke out, and twenty-nine years before the first steps toward the formation of the Triple Entente, the still-potential threat of German hegemony engendered the specter of that "nightmare of coalitions" which Bismarck feared would endanger the existence of the Reich itself.[23]

Consequently, until his dismissal from office in 1890 Bismarck adopted an increasingly complex and problematic policy of "satiation."[24] He assured the other Great Powers that Germany had no further ambitions for expansion. The policy of "satiation" and Bismarck's consequent alliance "system" were designed to prevent rigid coalitions from forming, and therefore, logically and assuming continual satiation, the formation of an anti-German coalition or war of coalitions from ever occurring. Bismarck's alliance system was designed to prevent war, and, given ties with both Austria and Russia, approached incoherence if war should actually break out.[25] Since a solidifying or immobile balance of power threatened the formation of rigid and mutually fearful coalitions, Bismarck's policy aimed at promoting and preserving a "balance of tensions" rather than a "balance of power."[26]

Yet, four years after Bismarck's dismissal from office, France and Russia formed their anti-German alliance. Four years later, in 1898, Germany embarked on a naval building program, designed to challenge Britain's hitherto unquestioned naval superiority, the necessary buttress of its insular security and power in the extra-European, global system.[27] Beginning in earnest during the first Moroccan crisis in 1905, Germany repeatedly attempted to break apart the somewhat latent yet consistently strengthening Triple Entente, through a policy of increasing armaments, military threat, and diplomatic brinksmanship.[28] Combined with developments in Germany's method of governance, military technology, war planning, and the complications of its alliance system, German policy, and the responses of its fearful and ambitious competitors, shifted the European system, over time, from the "balance of tensions" Bismarckian model, designed to prevent war, to a rigid bipolar alliance system, designed to prepare for and win war.[29] Increasingly perceived by Germans and other Europeans as inevitable, the actual outbreak of war against the Entente swiftly facilitated and unleashed Germany's still partially latent hegemonic ambitions, such that linked defensive and offensive elements, always muddied, merged into a definite German bid for European hegemony and consequent global power.[30]

This movement from a policy of "satiation" to one of global and hegemonic ambition has justly fascinated and preoccupied historians and political theorists.[31] Was hegemonic conflict inevitable in a Thucydidean sense—that is, was the war's true cause the rise in German power and the fear this caused in Britain, France, and Russia?[32] Was conflict primarily due to certain traits in the German national character? Could a hypothetical extension of the already-strained Bismarckian policy of "satiation" and "balance of tensions" have prevented the formation of rigid alliance systems, competition with Britain, and consequent conflict?

A detailed analysis of the proximate causes of the First World War is beyond the scope of this essay. As discussed, we instead seek to consider whether broad historical dynamics might enrich our understanding of our own emerging geopolitical challenges. Given these self-imposed interests and constraints, four linked dynamics are of interest: first, the political economy of German national power; second, the perceived and actual interaction between the European state system and a developing global system; third, Germany's perceived and actual geopolitical options; and fourth, the actual and potential reactions of Germany's competitors to both these global and European dynamics and Germany's particular ambitions, fears, political economy, and rising power.

The new German Reich, as stated, was a primarily agricultural and rural nation, with a population approximately ten percent larger than that of France. Between 1870 and 1914, Germany's population increased from 41 to 65 million, and it industrialized and urbanized.[33] Whereas in 1870 Germany produced 34 million tons of coal and Britain 112 million tons, by 1914 Germany produced 277 million tons and Britain 292 million. In 1880 Britain produced 1.3 million tons of steel, France 0.4 million, and Germany 0.7 million. By 1914 Britain produced 6.5 million tons, France 3.5 million, and Germany 14 million.[34] In 1880, Britain's manufacturing output amounted to 22.9 percent of world manufacturing output and Germany's amounted to 8.5 percent. In 1913 Britain's share amounted to 13.6 percent and Germany's amounted to 14.8 percent.[35] To the extent that we deduce military capacity from such figures (and this is problematic for short wars, although less so for long wars), then Bismarck's anxiety about a "nightmare of coalitions" in 1875 was rational, especially given Austria's uncertain posture, and despite the small size of Britain's standing army. Given Britain's and Russia's refusal to allow Germany to crush France again, Bismarck, even if he had never truly intended a preventive war, had to offer assurances of Germany's continuing satiation.

By 1914, opposing coalitions had clarified themselves, tightened their bonds and, in retrospect, were evenly matched. Germany and Austria-Hungary had a total population of 112 million and the Triple Entente 255 million. However, in 1913 Germany and Austria-Hungary produced a total of 20.2 million tons of steel, and Britain, France, and Russia produced a total of 17.1 million tons. The Austro-German alliance consumed energy equivalent to 236.4 metric million tons of coal, while the Triple Entente consumed the equivalent of 311.8 million tons.[36] The Central Powers held their own in the subsequent conflict due to less tangible factors such as morale, efficiency, and skill—until the United States, with its vast productive power, entered the war.

However, Germany's transformation from a primarily agricultural to an advanced, export-dependent, industrial economy had rendered it vulnerable. In Germany's case, its increasing strength and increasing vulnerability went hand in hand.[37] In 1871, the newly formed Reich's vulnerability was "traditional" for a centrally located power without natural, geographical barriers—the war on two fronts; or, as faced by Frederick the Great, possibly three.[38] This problem suggested a number of responses, given the particular history of the Prusso-German state and ethos of the nineteenth century European state system. As noted, Bismarck chose a complex response dependent upon both satiation and a diplomatic and alliance system which created a balance of tensions rather than a balance of power. The balance of tensions, by allowing for or stimulating Austro-Russian suspicion while moderating that rivalry before it reached a boiling point, and maintaining ties to both powers, allowed Germany to avoid a clear choice between the two while maintaining its freedom of maneuver and pivotal status; both of which would have been at risk, in the event of an already unlikely, truly unified Three Emperors' League, replicative of the antique Holy Alliance. Were Germany to abandon the complex, unstable, yet according to its purpose successful "balance of tensions" policy, then, by clearly opting for either Austria or Russia, the "nightmare of coalitions" would begin. For according to the logic of Machtpolitik and the European system, the spurned former friend would seek security in alliance with the remaining land power of significant strength: France.[39] In this manner the complex, opaque, and somewhat fluid balance of tensions would shift toward a simple, clear and predictable balance of power between two alliance systems.[40] Britain, given its traditional and rational fear of any potential European hegemon, would presumably tilt against the stronger coalition.

The balance of power which developed after the 1894 Franco-Russian alliance possessed the apparent virtues of simplicity and predictability when compared to the nerve-wracking, inchoate balance of tensions. But this simplicity came at a price which increased over time, perhaps in accordance with an inner logic. Despite French talk of revenge, and clamoring within Germany for war against Russia, the two alliance systems were, at their outset, primarily defensive. Not only were significant elements in each of the Great

Powers' governing classes averse to war, but ambitions in the 1890s still radiated outward. Germany turned toward Weltpolitik, and, except Austria, the other imperial powers completed their division of the unclaimed and vulnerable regions of the globe. For the Reich, the Dual Alliance with Austria served as a means of clearly securing its Continental position—a necessary precondition, as it were, while it prepared for a policy of extra-European world power.[41]

Over time, though, Russo-Austrian competition and Austria's inner weakness led to trials of strength in the Balkans between these Powers, and compelled Germany—fearful of Austrian disintegration—to relax the limits previously imposed upon its only military ally.[42] With the development of rigid and opposing coalitions, Germany and France perceived their security as dependent upon the retention of their allies, while Russia and Austria competed for prestige and influence. Since the logic of the new, clarified balance of power suggested that the retention of allies would now take precedence over the avoidance of war, and since therefore the risky ambitions of those allies would now command support, or acquiescence, "offensive elements crept into the defensive alliance system, causing it to degenerate."[43] As in many roughly bipolar alliance structures, each side became highly sensitive to gains or losses relative to the other alliance. Crises and trials of strength became increasingly frequent and, unlike during the Soviet-American Cold War, neither side utterly feared war. For these and other reasons important elements on both sides began to view war as inevitable. The primary question then became not how to prevent war, but rather how to position one's respective alliance system to win it, and, particularly in Germany's case, how to conclude actual war such that the state could wage future power-political conflicts, also judged as inevitable, from a position of unassailable strength.[44]

It might be of interest, at this point, to further consider some of the salient differences between the Bismarckian "balance of tensions" and the post-Bismarckian "balance of power." Traditionally, a well-functioning, multipolar, balance of power system has been thought to require absolute flexibility by its members in forming and breaking alliances. Despite arguments to the contrary, multipolar balance of power systems are not completely deficient in any higher ethos or telos: by facilitating the mobilization of adequate counterforce against potentially dominant states, the multipolar order preserves the independence of all and dynamic interaction within the system itself—a dynamism often contrasted with the senescence of universal empire, and linked to the cultural and intellectual achievements of these plural systems.[45] Of course, the price of such independence and dynamism often lies in constant anxiety, frequent conflict, and hegemonic war. Theoretically and historically, the high risk of conflict implicit in a fluid multipolar order might be mitigated by shared values or interests amongst the major powers, which take precedence over their power-political fears or ambitions. A uniform ethos, in itself, is insufficient to prevent conflict—thus the common, highly competitive culture of the Hellenic states not only failed to prevent conflict amongst them, but, rather, promoted it. [46] A different sort of common interest or ethos—such as the Holy Alliance's determination to prevent further revolutionary upheaval, or the contemporary North Atlantic states' liberal values—often significantly limits traditional security dilemmas, such that a multipolar order is consistent with a limited yet durable harmony.

As noted, a broadly bipolar alliance structure, even within the context of an essentially multipolar state system, presents a different set of challenges. Once the fluidity of a multipolar structure is relinquished, each alliance becomes highly sensitive to its perceived relative power trajectory and gains or losses in comparison with the opposing alliance. In a "loose" bipolar alliance structure, there is a high risk that all the powers will be drawn into a conflict initially begun by a few states—and not necessarily the greatest powers in a particular alliance. [47] In a "tight" bipolar structure, with two clearly dominant powers whose allies have less freedom of action, this is less likely, and the likelihood of overt conflict will primarily depend upon the culture, technology, and perceived relative power trajectories of the two strongest states.

Given his insistence upon formal, yet limited, ties with both Austria and Russia, we can deduce that Bismarck feared the further development of the essentially fluid, multipolar order which had facilitated the rise of Prussia and its vault into preeminence within the new Reich and, perhaps, the Continent itself. The common values and fears of the Holy Alliance and, arguably, Concert of Europe, had, for a time, limited the traditional inclinations of the Eastern Courts to expand through the use of force. As time passed, though, and monarchical solidarity and fears of the consequences of war faded, Bismarck and others were prepared to exploit the disunity of the Powers or their withdrawal from attempts to actively shape the European order. Utilizing nationalism and other ideas as they suited him in the service of Machtpolitik, Bismarck's successful resort to maneuver, deceit, and force harkened back to eighteenth century Frederickian raison d'Etat—but in an age of incipient industrialization, imperialism, and passionate mass politics.

However, having in reality and along with others discarded what little remained of the spiritual or sentimental ties of the Eastern Courts, Bismarck was faced with the adverse consequences of his actions. For among other "limitations" upon the new Reich, Germany was partially "immobilized because of France." [48] Whether it was a result of the annexation of Alsace-Lorraine, or French fear or pride, this seemingly immutable Franco-German hostility suggested that an optimal condition for a successful multipolar order—the complete flexibility of all parties to form or break alliances—was absent. [49]

The German liberals believed that Bismarck perverted the "natural" course of German history by shifting the development of the Reich away from liberal democracy and toward a militarized, unstable, neo-autocracy, dependent upon the manipulation of conflicting interest groups. [50] Presumably, according to the liberals' logic, a more felicitous path within Germany would have smoothed the way to a less rivalrous state system, and, in particular, closer relations with Britain. This, in turn, might have precluded or limited German unease that their global prospects were vulnerable to British hostility, and British fear that Germany would eventually threaten Britain's insular security and power-political status. [51] Whether or not German liberalism would have averted the movement toward conflict is a source of interesting speculation. However, it seems unlikely that Bismarck, and the bureaucratic, military aristocracy he somewhat shiftily championed, had cemented the domination of Prussia and its elite over Germany in order to effect the complete eclipse of that class. Then, too, the liberals themselves were not without their aggressive instincts—first toward Russia, and later toward Britain. [52] In explaining the liberals' aggressiveness, it is unlikely without significance that these two Powers, whether in 1875 or later, appeared to be the decisive obstacles to further German territorial and imperial expansion. While democratic peace theory suggests an alternative domestic course might have precluded the shift to "tension" and then a militarized balance of power, the middle classes themselves, from which the liberals drew their support, were increasingly frustrated with Bismarck's policy of satiation. Perhaps in late nineteenth-century Germany, and not only in Germany, there was arguably a potential tension between an expansion of internal liberty and a restrained foreign policy geared toward the prevention of war. [53]

In retrospect, then, the somewhat precariously managed balance of tensions occupied an interstitial space, distinct from both a purely fluid balance of power and a rigid bipolar alliance system. With a mitigating community of values amongst the Eastern Courts an archaic chimera, and given both the internal resistance to and potentially dynamic, unsettling effects of German liberalism, Bismarck depended upon a tense minuet of alliance, threat, detachment, and maneuver to control and hold in check the natural dynamism and aggression of the European system. [54] A detailed exegesis of the Dreikaiserbund, Dual Alliance, and Reinsurance Treaty are beyond the scope of this analysis. However, given that French disaffection precluded a truly fluid system, the essence of Bismarck's diplomacy lay in his intention to keep both Russia and Austria tied to Germany and each other, although not too closely, while isolating France and accepting, in essence, British flexibility.

The controlled "balance of tensions" can therefore be further distinguished from both a potential, merely relative fluidity, which due to the Franco-German enmity could not match the complete fluidity arguably optimal for a multipolar system, and a clarified bipolarity which would result from an acceptance of the free play of this incomplete fluidity. Therefore unless managed, such a post-1870, incomplete fluidity would be likely to lead to bipolarity and, eventually, systemic war, which Bismarck was determined to prevent. It is unclear whether Bismarck's "system" was a series of "stopgaps," artificial and doomed to failure, or the best that could be expected in a European system suffused with power and ambition, willing to risk war and increasingly in the grip of nationalism.[55] However, it does seem clear that Bismarck's policy depended upon German "satiation." Absent that, it seems difficult to conceive of a diplomacy that could have prevented the formation of an anti-German coalition, and, given the culture of the time, the consequent likelihood of hegemonic war.

THE GLOBAL POLITICAL ECONOMY: EMERGING WORLD POWERS AND GERMAN GEOPOLITICAL OPTIONS

The declared, and, by Bismarck, genuinely held policy of satiation was, however, at odds with Germany's shifting political economy. For an autarkic, primarily agricultural state, a policy of satiation was feasible. However, the transformation of Germany into an advanced industrial economy, which proceeded apace throughout Bismarck's tenure and accelerated thereafter, left Germany dependent upon raw material and food imports and foreign markets for its industrial exports. The German economy was "top-heavy"— that is, its dominant industrial sectors were not primarily geared toward satisfying domestic consumers, but rather produced capital goods for export.[56] Furthermore, the worldwide depression of 1873–96 encouraged a turn to mercantilism by some of the great industrial powers. In order to maintain output and efficiently respond to shifts in demand, German, American, and other firms often consolidated into one or two dominant corporations within each nation, and relied upon tariffs and other types of state support to protect their domestic markets.[57]

The Germans also turned to tariffs for another reason: to protect the agricultural livelihood of their Prussian elite. If the Germans had completely submitted to the logic of comparative advantage, cheaper Russian and North American grain would have ruined the East Elbian Junkers—the dominant element in the army, court, and much of the bureaucracy. Rather than allow this to occur, Bismarck, a member of that class (even if unloved), concluded an alliance with heavy industry—"Iron" would get its state support, and "Rye" would as well. Therefore industrial competition with Germany threatened the hitherto industrial dominance of the British, while limitations on food imports damaged the interests of the Russians.[58] While far from determining the future course of events, and without lapsing into a denial of the relative autonomy of military and foreign policy, it is clear that the German and general turn toward protection and mercantilism placed a policy of "satiation" and therefore "balance of tensions" under increasing strain, both actually and potentially.[59] The swiftly growing German economy faced ruin if the British, in particular, and to a lesser extent the Russians, cut Germany off from its vital export markets and sources of raw materials. While Bismarck perceived the danger of the formation of rival blocs within the European system, great global economic blocs were nonetheless in prospect, rendering Germany's long-term power potential vulnerable.[60] Thus Germany faced a nightmare of coalitions if it attempted to create a space equivalent to these rival blocs, and vulnerability if it chose the path of dependence upon the potential or actual mercantilist, solidifying global powers.[61] Parenthetically, should American or other great economic Powers' commitment to or maintenance of a relatively open, global economy waver, then China will face a similar choice between dependence upon mercantilist Powers, or control over an autarkic space, whether regional or global.

Given these challenging developments, the maintenance of a balance of tensions and prevention of the formation of rival European blocs, if pursued, required, at least, a certain level of diplomatic "normality" amongst most of the Great Powers—that is, a relationship of neither clear alliance, nor clear enmity.[62] Although historically typical, and rational, for many powerful states, the relationship of "normality" is, in fact, often more difficult to maintain than the alternative poles of friendship or enmity—particularly in an actual or emerging age of mass politics. "Normality"—with its disparate mix of cooperation, tension, hope, suspicion, satisfaction, and disappointment—places a psychological strain upon the protagonists that clear friendship or enmity might relieve. Yet the relief at a departure from the persistent ambiguity of normality often exacts a steep price. Under the pressure of events, supposedly unconditional friendship might prove illusory. Clear alliance might lead to the formation of a rival coalition. The certainty and psychic satisfaction of clear enmity might lead to unnecessary conflict, and an inability to explore opportunities and take action in the true national, and systemic, interest.

We can see, in retrospect, that the Franco-German enmity—this departure from "normality"—was the original sin, so to speak, of the post-1870 European system. It partially foreclosed cooperative, Continental solutions to Germany's perceived trajectories of "world power or decline" and rendered problematic a, theoretically, at least, functional multipolar order.[63] If this "fixed" enmity could not have been alleviated, then every German effort was necessary to preserve normality not only with Austria, but also Russia and Britain. A balance of tensions and avoidance of the nightmare of coalitions depended upon such normality, which, while admittedly more precarious than a liberal comity, still might have restrained Germany's burgeoning fear about its long-term economic and power-political prospects. Absent normality, the Germans were most likely on the road to either subordination or war, given that confederal solutions and liberal-legal norms lacked credence within the ethos of the system. That is, the Germans might have opted to shift away from normality and toward a subordinate, junior partnership with one of the actual or developing world powers—Britain or Russia.[64] At least in theory, such a partnership could have supported the territorial integrity of the Reich and guaranteed its access to necessary markets and resources. This was, in fact, the position that the post-War West German state accepted within the pax Americana—partially due to unassailable force, but also due to the benefits of access to markets and resources guaranteed under a reliable, American-protected order.

The Germans of the Kaiserreich, and afterwards, were unwilling to accept such a status. Furthermore, it was far from clear whether the Russians, with ambitions of their own, or the British, aloof and weakening, could or would guarantee that subordination would lead to safety.

As noted, however, maintenance of a complex state of normality with Britain and Russia, and its prerequisite, German acceptance of satiation, were stressed not only by Germany's political economy, but also by the developing mercantilist and imperial competition amongst all the actual or potential world powers. The British maintained their commitment to free trade, were an important market for German exports and maintained freedom of the seas for the Germans and others. However, proponents of the industrial sector in Britain, responding to German and American mercantilism, eventually supported Imperial Preference, which would have tightened the bonds of the British Empire and its Dominions from a somewhat loose political entity into a great, protected, mercantilist bloc.[65]

This proposal was defeated by the financial sector and its allies, who wished to invest and profit from investments anywhere in the world. Nonetheless, the Germans faced the potential disintegration of a British-guaranteed open world economy, and the prospect that, without regard to German policy, giant, closed, autarkic spaces might form around a set of world powers, rendering Germany's economy vulnerable and power-political position overshadowed. Quite late, the Germans had created a national state equal in power to the other great states in Europe. This accomplishment—the shift from an object to a subject in the decisive state system—now seemed threatened by both the dwarfing of the powers, like Germany, trapped within it, and the eclipse of the heretofore decisive European system as a whole. Three world powers, at least, seemed to be taking shape, each subsuming a space large enough to guarantee control over the necessary population, raw materials, food, and markets which were the prerequisites for global power: the British Empire and its Dominions, Russia, and America. Germany, cordoned off within an increasingly dwarfed European system, was blocked from significant extra-European expansion by British sea power and Russian land power. The three potential or actual giants had no need to "break out" to secure necessary markets or resources. For the Germans, however, vaulting forward into the ranks of the emerging global powers would require a break-out by land or sea—unless the Continent itself could cooperatively coalesce to form a potential fourth world power.[66] Given French enmity, the national-ist ethos of the day and, not least, the limitations of the Germans themselves, the formation of a cooperative Continental system was unlikely. For the Germans, then, the geopolitical options seemed clear: a descent into insignif-icance, or an attempt to carve out a military-economic space that could stand aside, or perhaps overshadow, the emerging world powers.[67] "Satiation" and, perhaps, "normality," seemed to promise short-term safety but long-term decline.

The extra-European, imperial path to autarky implied a naval arms race, and probably war, with Britain, while the Continental path implied war with France and Russia. Furthermore, given Britain's historical dependence for its safety upon a European balance of power, the second path implied war with Britain as well. While the first path emerged as Germany's preferred course prior to the First World War, the unresolved and linked animosities within the European system itself led to a conflict that pitted Germany, and its rather unsteady allies, against the Russo-French alliance as well as Britain. During the course of the war the Germans increasingly turned toward the second option: maintaining control over a vast Continental space, extending from the channel ports deep into Russia. The resources and natural strength of this space would allow Germany to confront the "Anglo-American" sea powers in a future conflict from a position of strength, despite their dominance of the oceans and extra-European world.[68]

German Continental visions toward the end of the first war provided some of the intellectual bases of future German ambitions. The German tyrant, Hitler, believed the primary error of the Kaiserreich was to court conflict with both England's sea power and the Continental land powers simultaneously—that is, to unclearly and indecisively follow both the extra-European and Continental paths to world power.[69] Instead, Hitler intended to augment Germany's inadequate natural strength by approaching world power in stages. Initially challenging the Anglo-American sea powers was to be strictly avoided. Instead, by temporarily renouncing naval and extra-Euro-pean ambitions, Hitler hoped that England would stand aside and America lie dormant, while he pushed aside France and conquered an autarkic, racially based empire out of East-Central Europe and the Soviet Union. Then, its power augmented by populations (reduced to the status of helots) and re-sources that stretched across Europe to the Urals, Hitler expected a German world power to eventually challenge America for global mastery.[70]

FROM AUTARKY TO VULNERABILITY: CHINA'S "PEACEFUL RISE" AND GEOPOLITICAL OPTIONS

Like Germany in 1871, until the late 1970s China was a largely autarkic economy, generally self-sufficient in food and raw materials and with little impact upon the international economy.[71] Since then, though, China has transformed itself into an industrial and economic powerhouse. Whereas in 1990 it accounted for 3 percent of global manufacturing, it now accounts for 19.8 percent. The United States, which emerged as the largest global manufacturer around 1895, currently accounts for 19.4 percent.[72] If current trends continue, China will overtake the United States as the world's largest economy by approximately 2020, although it will remain poorer in per capita terms.[73] Extrapolation and a quantitative focus are both undoubtedly problematic and too blunt to predict Great Power policy, yet nations such as Germany prior to the First World War have either courted or, despite trepidation, risked conflict based upon them.[74] In 2003, in constant 1990 dollar values and assuming purchasing power parity, China had a GDP of $6,188 billion and a per capita GDP of $4,803, while the United States had a GDP of $8,431 billion and a per capita GDP of $29,037. Extrapolating from current trends in growth and population, and assuming certain constants, in 2030 China will have a GDP of $22,983 billion and a per capita GDP of $15,763, while the United States will have a GDP of $16,662 billion and a per capita GDP of $45,774 (1990 dollar values.)[75] In relative terms, China is rising and America declining, although whether the United States fears China's rise will also depend upon the credence given to and accuracy of extrapolation, China's policies and the power trajectories of other states such as India, Japan, Russia, and a (possibly) unified Europe.

As in Germany's case, China's development of vast productive power and accrued wealth have left it increasingly vulnerable to disruptions in trade or foreign markets. Autarky is a thing of the past.[76] While still self-sufficient in certain critical food categories (although this might not persist, given the increasing scarcity of water), China is now a voracious importer of oil, iron-ore, copper, and other raw materials necessary to fuel its industrial production.[77] Its economy is trade-oriented: it is the largest merchandise exporter in the world, the second largest importer and its trade to GDP ratio is 55.4 percent.[78] The livelihood of millions of Chinese now depends upon sea traffic between China and its markets and suppliers in the Western Hemisphere, Europe, the Middle East, and Africa. Like Germany before it, the rise in China's power has gone hand in hand with the development of far greater vulnerability to economic dislocation, and, in particular, an unwelcome dependence upon the dominant sea power of the day, which also views China's rising power with some trepidation.

As the Germans initially did before them, the Chinese have therefore chosen a world-oriented economic strategy, although with a different dynamic in a post-imperial age. And, as in Germany's case, China's distinct discomfort with a growing geo-economic dependence upon the global power whose military undergirds that world economic strategy has led China to shift its ambitions, toward the capacity to project outwards significant maritime and air power. Initially justified as necessary to deter a Taiwanese move toward independence, it is now clear that China is developing military capabilities designed to deny American forces unchallenged access to an area demarcated by the "second island chain" in the Western Pacific.[79] Presumably, however, were China to insist upon the capability to defend and control its trade routes, logic suggests that its power projection capabilities will continue to develop, and, by their nature, challenge American dominance in its long-unchallenged global element.[80]

It might be of interest, at this point, to compare Bismarck's policy of "satiation" with the policy of "peaceful rise" advanced by the Chinese Communist Party.[81] Satiation, by reassuring the other European Powers that Germany abjured hegemony, was designed to preclude the formation of an anti-German coalition similar to the anti-hegemonic coalitions that had defeated the Habsburgs and French.

If we were to partially detach Machtpolitik from dynamic economic development, as, according to his critics, Bismarck did, then the differences between Prusso-Germany's position in the emerging global order of its time and China's in the twenty-first century order seem salient. China possesses the natural endowments of a true Great Power, and therefore its rise did not require the aggressive wars attendant with the rise of Prussia and creation of Germany. However, the doctrine of "peaceful rise" leaves open the compelling question—what then? Unlike Imperial or Nazi Germany, China is large and populous enough that it need not fear its eclipse by actual or putative "world powers"; even without dominating East Asia or dependencies abroad, China possesses natural prerequisites, such as population and space, for global power in its own right. And, to be sure, in a post-imperial age the other global or potential global powers seek to strengthen themselves through internal development and economic expansion, rather than territorial aggrandizement. The ethos of the contemporary global system differs from that of the early twentieth century, such that the maintenance of China's power-political status need not require an overt Chinese "breakout" or territorial expansion, since the other Powers (generally) refrain from territorial expansion themselves.

Therefore, in purely geopolitical terms, the historical, linked, and specific dynamics between a multipolar European system facing eclipse and an emerging set of expanding global powers which partially determined the rejection of Bismarckian restraint and rise of the German problem would not seem to apply to the rise of China. Rather, China's rise and likely emergence as one of a set of global powers suggest that the historical, combustible dynamics between two systems—European and global—might not be replicated in a transposed form. China, according to this (perhaps) "neo-Bismarckian" perspective, need not challenge the plurality of the East Asian system or the established, global sea power in order to advance or maintain China's own status.

As discussed, however, China's internal development, like Imperial Germany's, has rendered it increasingly dependent upon Powers and economic events beyond its control. The temptation to exert some influence over these factors is understandable, and therefore the durability and continuation of "peaceful rise" might prove as problematic as the endurance of Bismarckian "satiation." The Germans, once their Weltpolitik proved implausible in the face of superior British sea power, shifted their efforts toward the formation of an autarkic, Continental bloc invulnerable to British or American interdiction. Should China, too, find that its global, overseas necessities are under subtle or overt threat—due to military force or mercantilism—then it might logically opt for a "Continental" sphere of influence in the East, similar in logic to the German "Continental" option or Imperial Japan's plans for a continental (and, necessarily, partially maritime) East Asian Co-Prosperity Sphere.[82] Indeed, the rise of mercantilism and post-Depression breakdown in the relatively open, global economy influenced the Japanese to reject the liberal Washington Conference System, and renew their movement toward autarky, empire, and conflict.[83] To be sure, we enter here into the realm of interesting speculation. We can be certain though, that the Chinese, as the Germans before them, cannot return to the relative autarky which preceded their "peaceful rise," and Chinese geopolitical options will reflect this. In this sense, to prematurely respond to China's rising maritime strength with subtle or overt plans for blockade or exclusionary trade blocs might merely shift and intensify conflict into a continental arena, rather than mitigate it.[84]

However, America is, geopolitically speaking, an island off the far larger and more populous Eurasian landmass.[85] Despite America's greater distance from China than Britain's from Germany during the historical Anglo-German rivalry, and perhaps lesser vulnerability, the potential displacement of American power out of the Western Pacific, and its potential eclipse globally, present certain threats similar to those the British faced when Germany moved toward world power. America, although in possession of a large and varied landmass, is no longer an autarkic economy. It imports a great deal of energy and manufactured goods (although advances in drilling and extraction technology have improved its energy posture, albeit at a potentially high ecological cost). It is also a large exporter of both primary and manufactured goods, and its trade as a ratio of GDP has increased from 10.76 percent in 1960 to 27.7 percent in 2008–2010.[86] Furthermore, the globally dispersed and specialized nature of contemporary manufacturing suggests that an array of goods vital to the American economy will depend upon suppliers located abroad. If the United States continues to acquiesce to comparative advantage, its dependence upon imported goods is likely to continue. America depends upon sea traffic for its welfare, and a superior maritime power would therefore present a threat to that welfare.

And, even if the United States were to reverse its increasing economic and consequent geopolitical dependency, China's rising maritime and power projection capabilities present another dilemma. The rise of German naval power not only threatened Britain's vital trade routes, but also threatened to cut Britain's globally derived power off from the decisive, European state system. Absent Britain's historical balancing effect against the potential Continental hegemon—whether German, French or, to a lesser extent, Habsburg—the European system as a whole would have been far more likely to fall under the durable hegemony of one of these powers. [87] Similarly, although the United States, despite its dissipation of industrial strength and autarky, is arguably less vulnerable to interdiction than Edwardian Britain, the dilemma of hegemony remains relevant. Were China to dominate the Western Pacific and Indian oceans, America's Asian allies might consider accepting their incorporation into a possibly restrained, yet undeniable Chinese hegemonic bloc as their only reasonable alternative. Should this include a stagnant yet advanced Japan, in particular, the United States might reasonably fear that such a bloc would wield power incompatible with American security.

Traditionally, the United States has considered the domination of Eurasia or one of its significance spheres by a single power as a threat to American security. Had a hegemon emerged in either Europe, East Asia, or Eurasia as a whole, then that hegemon would have likely wielded sufficient economic and military power to project force into the Western Hemisphere, and probably overshadowed the United States in long-run military potential. [88] Until 1914 the Americans were relieved of the burdens of maintaining plurality in Eurasia, and its significant spheres, by Britain's management of the balance of European and global power. Thus the congruence of American isolation and American security was historically specific. In truth, though, the power-political links between the Western Hemisphere and struggles for hegemony in the previously decisive state system—the European—were a reality long before British ascendance. The resources of the New World were often both an object of the aspiring European hegemon's ambition, and a factor that supported or frustrated the potential hegemon's bid for mastery in Europe itself. [89] If this dynamic of a Western Hemispheric system linked in power-political terms with the decisive, power-suffused Eurasian system endures, then it is unlikely that the United States could consider the rise of a potential East Asian hegemon with equanimity. The likely response, given America's political and military traditions, will be the construction of an effectively uniform anti-Chinese coalition, which would consequently create a relatively overt, bipolar power system in East Asia, with both sides highly sensitive to gains or losses in material or prestige vis-a-vis each other.

Some scholars claim that the developing Sino-American rivalry might be dissolved or mitigated by interdependence.[90] The American economy, though, while presently complemented by China's labor-abundant production, could, should strategic tension grow, turn to alternative producers of labor-intensive goods (although some time would be required for adjustment). Mechanization will also "reshore" some manufacturing back into the United States. The Chinese, however, are not content to languish indefinitely as a low-cost producer of labor-intensive goods. Given that their ambitions extend to developing technology and entering advanced, capital-intensive sectors, the heretofore complementarity of the two economies will diminish, as China's mercantilist ethos portends greater zero-sum competition with American (and other) advanced sectors.[91] In this sense, the trajectory of China's economy and its emergence as a mercantilist threat would simply follow the path previously trodden by Japan, South Korea, and others. However, these smaller nations were not perceived by the Americans as concurrent economic and strategic threats, and mercantilist tensions were somewhat leavened by the perception of common geopolitical interests. Parenthetically, in the early twentieth century Germany exported a significant amount of capital-intensive goods to the British Empire. As discussed, some British statesmen considered this development a threatening mercantilism, requiring a political response: "Imperial Preference."[92] This proposal was rejected, but the Germans had been warned, and their response was to aggressively reduce their dependence through the creation of an autarkic space. Similarly, rather soon, two advanced economies—one highly mercantilist—will both compete and cooperate amidst geopolitical rivalry and strategic suspicion.

CONCLUSION: SOME THOUGHTS ON "NORMALITY"

Is there a way out? The prevailing trends do not seem promising. The history of the German problem demonstrates the importance of "normality," among other factors, in preventing the emergence of rigidly opposed blocs locked into a mutually destructive dynamic. However, world political-economic trends placed the congruence of normality and Germany's long-term power potential under strain. Bismarck attempted to maintain, in the last resort, normality with Britain, Russia, and Austria, and perhaps belatedly recognized the advantages, and perhaps necessity, of a return to normality with France.[93] Bismarck's successors, though, sought the absolute security and unlimited sovereignty of a truly defensible and autarkic geopolitical space, and, along the way, jettisoned the complex, inchoate tension of normality for clear allies and enemies.[94] In retrospect, though, the Germans were not the sole power that rejected normality. After its defeat in 1871, France might have rejected revanche and, eschewing the historical policy of the French minister, Richelieu, accommodated itself to the unity and limited preeminence of its newly powerful neighbor. This, to be sure, would have entailed significant risks, particularly given the ethos and historical dynamic of the European system. By precluding an attempted return to normality, though, the French also partially precluded, for a time, a logical geopolitical alternative to German Weltpolitik or Continental hegemony and their attendant conflicts: a broadly cooperative European bloc, able to hold its own in the world of emerging economic and military giants.[95] Perhaps this was too much to ask of the French, or the Germans, in an age of nationalism, mercantilism and mass politics. Whatever the reasons, though, the original departure from normality poisoned the future development of the state system, and, perhaps unavoidably, condemned it to the likely formation of rival blocs, a consequent security dilemma and hegemonic war.

Since the end of the Cold War, the Americans, whether from hubris, Manichean traditions, or hegemonic instincts of their own, have been instinctively uncomfortable with normality. Certain states, particularly democratic and subservient allies, have been idealized, while enemies, disappointing allies, and obdurate nations have been demonized. To be sure, the United States has out of necessity and material interest grudgingly and uncomfortably agreed to a tenuous normality with China and some of the Islamic powers. But, for the Americans, the maintenance of normality (with its uncomfortable ideational and emotional restraint) is an unpleasant struggle. China, however, possesses a leadership class which is fully versed in and at home with the opacity and tension of normality.[96] Normality implies tolerance of both imperfection and constant, manageable ambiguity, as opposed to the (necessarily ephemeral) satisfaction of the quest for absolute clarity in relations. Bismarck illuminated the mature benefits of normality well when he replied, to those who advocated offensive war with a growing yet not necessarily hostile Russia, that "preemptive war is like committing suicide out of fear of death."[97] In other words, the radical cures for geopolitical normality are typically worse than its chronic, yet tolerable tension. The history of Germany's rise further suggests that prospects for European equilibrium amidst normality were, in addition to Germany's growing objective vulnerability, diminished by passionate, subjective antipathies: French commitment to revenge, and Germany's consequent "permanent" enmity toward the French "hereditary enemy." Whether a commitment to a renewed normality by both Germany and France after 1871 would have mitigated the looming nightmare of coalitions is necessarily a matter of speculation. Nonetheless, Germany's rise and the response to it suggest that the nations of Asia and both sides of the Pacific might be better served in the long run by carefully preserving "normality," despite its tension and ambiguity, than by quixotic visions of (apparently) diminished vulnerability resulting from "absolute" friends, enemies, or coalitions, which would invariably elicit a rigid, proportional response.

The decision, then, partially rests with the Chinese themselves. With the Americans increasingly unable to conduct a normal policy, the Chinese will bear the greater burden in maintaining cooperation and normality with the United States and others, in order to prevent a renewed nightmare of coalitions from forming despite China's geo-economic vulnerability. Perhaps this asks too much of the Chinese. But, with global order increasingly at risk from old threats and new, and cooperation necessary to maintain it, much will depend upon their decisions.

NOTES

I would like to thank Giulio Gallarotti, David Calleo, and Charles Doran for reading and commenting upon earlier drafts of this paper.

1. Franz Kohout, "Cyclical, Hegemonic, and Pluralistic Theories of International Relations: Some Comparative Reflections on War Causation," *International Political Science Review* / Revue internationale de science politique, xxiv (2003), 55–56, 59–64.

2. Ludwig Dehio, *The Precarious Balance, Four Centuries of the European Power Struggle* (New York: Alfred Knopf, 1962), 117–118.

3. Francois Couzet, "The British Economy at the Time of Trafalgar: Strengths and Weaknesses" in David Cannadine (ed.), *Trafalgar in History: A Battle and its Afterlife* (New York: Palgrave Macmillan, 2006), 8, 16. Peter N. Stearns, "Britain and the Spread of the Industrial Revolution" in C. J. Bartlett (ed.), *Britain Pre-Eminent: Studies of British World Influence in the Nineteenth Century* (London: Macmillan, 1969), 7–30. S. G. E. Lythe, "Britain, the Financial Capital of the World" in Bartlett, *Britain Pre-Eminent*, 31–53.

4. David Calleo, "Twenty-First Century Geopolitics and the Erosion of the Dollar Order" in Jonathan Kirshner and Eric Helleiner (eds.), *The Future of the Dollar* (Ithaca: Cornell University Press, 2009), 165–74.

5. G. Kennan, "Containment Then and Now," *Foreign Affairs*, lxv (1987), 887-8.

6. David Calleo, *Follies of Power: America's Unipolar Fantasy* (New York: Cambridge University Press, 2009), 7–11.

7. Lawrence Freedman, "The First Two Generations of Nuclear Strategists" in Peter Paret with Gordan A. Craig and Felix Gilbert (eds.), *Makers Of Modern Strategy: From Machiavelli to the Nuclear Age* (Princeton: Princeton University Press, 1986), 778.

8. Kurt A. Raaflaub, "Born to Be Wolves? Origins of Roman Imperialism" in Robert W. Wallace and Edward M. Harris (eds.), *Transitions To Empire: Essays in Greco-Roman History*, 360–146 B.C., in honor of E. Badian (Norman: University of Oklahoma Press, 1996), 275–7.

9. Ikle, *Annihilation*, 65–69. Allison, *Nuclear Terrorism*, 92–98. David Albright and Corey Hinderstein, "Unraveling the A. Q. Khan and Future Proliferation Networks,"*Washington Quarterly*, xxviii (2005), 111–28.

10. Ikle, *Annihilation*, 1–17.

11. David Calleo, *The German Problem Reconsidered: Germany and the World Order, 1870 to the Present* (Cambridge: Cambridge University Press, 1978), 1–7.

12. Henry Kissinger, *A World Restored: Metternich, Castlereagh and the Problem of Peace 1812–1822* (Boston: Houghton Mifflin, 1957), 172–4.

13. William McNeill, *The Pursuit of Power: Technology, Armed Force, and Society since A.D. 1000* (Oxford: Basil Blackwell, 1982), 117–43.

14. Douglas Peifer, "China, the German Analogy, and the New AirSea Operational Concept," *Orbis*, LV (2011), 117–20. Holger Herwig, "Imperial Germany: Continental Titan, Global Aspirant" in Andrew Erickson, Lyle Goldstein and Carnes Lord (eds.), *China Goes to Sea: Maritime Transformation in Comparative Historical Perspective* (Annapolis: Naval Institute Press, 2009), 193–4. Andrew Erickson and Lyle Goldstein, "China Studies the Rise of the Great Powers" in Erickson, *China Goes to Sea*, 413–14. Aaron Friedberg, "The Future of U.S.-China Relations: Is Conflict Inevitable?," *International Security*, XXX (2005), 11, 19. Avery Goldstein, "An Emerging China's Emerging Grand Strategy: A Neo-Bismarckian Turn?" in G. John Ikenberry and Michael Mastanduno (eds.), *International Relations Theory and the Asia-Pacific* (New York: Columbia University Press, 2003), 58, 61–63, 85–86. Richard Baum and Alexei Shevchenko, "Bringing China In: A Cautionary Note," in Richard Rosecrance (ed.), *The New Great Power Coalition* (Lanham: Rowman and Littlefield, 2001), 330–3.

15. Andreas Hillgruber, *Germany and the Two World Wars* (Cambridge: Harvard University Press, 1981), 41–8. Annika Mombauer, *The Origins of the First World War: Controversies and Consensus* (London: Pearson Education Limited, 2002), 176–80.

16. Klaus Hildebrand, *German Foreign Policy From Bismarck to Adenauer: the Limits of Statecraft* (London: Unwin Hyman, 1989), 9–13. Calleo, German Problem, 60.

17. W. N. Medlicott, *Bismarck and Modern Germany* (London: English Universities Press, 1965), 104–12. Lothar Gall, *Bismarck: The White Revolutionary, Volume II, 1871–1898* (London: Allen and Unwin, 1986), 41–43.

18. Medlicott, *Bismarck*, 97.

19. Hillgruber, *World Wars*, 4. Katherine Lerman, *Bismarck* (Harlow: Pearson Education Limited, 2004), 207.

20. Lerman, *Bismarck*, 210.

21. Klaus Hildebrand, "Opportunities and Limits of German Foreign Policy in the Bismarckian Era, 1871–1890: A System of Stopgap?" in Gregor Schollgen (ed.), *Escape Into War? The Foreign Policy of Imperial Germany* (Oxford: Berg Publishers, 1990), 78–82. Gall, Bismarck, 142–3.

22. Hildebrand, "Bismarckian Era," 79. Jonathan Steinberg, *Bismarck: A Life* (Oxford: Oxford University Press, 2011), 355.

23. Medlicott, *Bismarck*, 89. Steinberg, *Bismarck*, 312–14, 355–6.

24. Gall, *Bismarck*, 145, 150–1. Hildebrand, *"Bismarckian Era"*, 84.

25. Medlicott, *Bismarck*, 160.

26. Fritz Fischer, *From Kaiserreich to Third Reich: Elements of Continuity in German History* (London: Unwin Hyman, 1986), 43–44.

27. Fritz Fischer, *From Kaiserreich to Third* Reich, 45–47.

28. Hillgruber, *World Wars*, 5–8.

29. Hillgruber, *World Wars*, 41–48.

30. Gregor Schollgen, "Introduction: The Theme Reflected in Recent German Research" in Schollgen (ed.), *Foreign Policy*, 1–19. Keir Lieber, "The New History of World War I and What it Means for International Relations Theory," *International Security*, xxxii (2007), 155–91.

31. David Grene, *The Peloponnesian War: Thucydides, the Complete Hobbes Translation* (Chicago: The University of Chicago Press, 1989), 50–51.

32. A. J. P. Taylor, The Struggle for Mastery in Europe, 1848–1918 (London: Oxford University Press, 1954), xxv. Paul Kennedy, "The First World War and the International Power System" in Steven Miller (ed.), *Military Strategy and the Origins of the First World War* (Princeton: Princeton University Press, 1985), 10.

33. Taylor, *Struggle for Mastery*, xxix–xxx.

34. Kennedy, "Power System," 12.

35. Taylor, *Struggle for Mastery*, xxxi–xxxii.

36. Calleo, *German Problem*, 37, 206. Fischer, German History, 45, 56–58.

37. Michael Sturmer, "A Nation State Against History and Geography: The German Dilemma" in Schollgen (ed.), *Foreign Policy*, 63–72. Lerman, Bismarck, 208–9.

38. Lerman, Bismarck, 218–19.

39. John Lowe, *The Great Powers, Imperialism and the German Problem, 1865–1925* (London: Routledge, 1994), 44.

40. Fischer, *German History*, 49.

41. Hillgruber, *World Wars*, 32.

42. Hildebrand, "Bismarckian Era," 85.

43. Hillgruber, *World Wars*, 42–43.

44. Aaron M. Zack (2010). *Ludwig Dehio and International Relations: A Theoretical, Historical and Strategic Analysis*. Retrieved from Proquest Digital Dissertations. (AAT 3410152), 98–111.

45. C. M. Bowra, *The Greek Experience* (New York: Praegar Publishers, 1957), 20–24.

46. W. Robert Connor, *Thucydides* (Princeton: Princeton University Press, 1984), 34–35.

47. Hildebrand, "Bismarckian Era," 75.

48. Steinberg, *Bismarck*, 313.

49. Erich Eyck, *Bismarck and the German Empire* (New York: W. W. Norton, 1968), v, 323. Steinberg, Bismarck, 398, 467.

50. Henry Kissinger, *Diplomacy* (New York: Simon and Schuster, 1994), 192–4.

51. Hildebrand, "Bismarckian Era," 84. Fischer, *German History*, 43–44. Wolfgang Mommsen, *Imperial Germany, 1867–1918: Politics, Culture, and Society in an Authoritarian State* (Arnold: London, 1995), 196, 201–4.

52. Hildebrand, "Bismarckian Era," 91–92.

53. Steinberg, *Bismarck*, 329. Lerman, *Bismarck*, 214.

54. Hildebrand, "Bismarckian Era," 91–92.

55. Fischer, *German History*, 41. Calleo, *German Problem*, 57–84.

56. Calleo, *German Problem*, 62–73.

57. Ibid., 13–18. Lowe, *Great Powers*, 70–71.

58. Lerman, *Bismarck*, 219.

59. Kenneth Fielden, "The Rise and Fall of Free Trade," in Bartlett, *Britain Pre-Eminent*, 94–9. Lowe, Great Powers, 77–81.

60. Calleo, *German Problem*, 69–73.

61. Hildebrand, *German Foreign Policy*, 64–83.

62. Calleo, *German Problem*, 116–17.

63. Gall, *Bismarck*, 145. Hillgruber, *World Wars*, 11. Lowe, *Great Powers*, 148.

64. Fielden, "Free Trade," 94–99. Donald Southgate, "Imperial Britain" in Bartlett, *Britain Pre-Eminent*, 163–4.

65. Lowe, Great Powers, 164.

66. Ibid., 196. Calleo, *German Problem*, 116–17. Dehio, Precarious Balance, 228–32. Hillgruber, *World Wars*, 50–53.

67. Michael Epkenhans, "Wilhelm II and 'his' navy, 1888 -1918" in Annika Mombauer and Wilhelm Deist (eds.), *The Kaiser: New Research on Wilhelm II's role in Imperial Germany* (Cambridge: Cambridge University Press, 2003), 21–23.

68. Hillgruber, *World Wars*, 43–45, 53–54.

69. Calleo, *German Problem*, 89–90.

70. Hillgruber, *World Wars*, 50.

71. Rebecca Karl, *Mao Zedong and China in the Twentieth-Century World: A Concise History* (Durham: Duke University Press, 2010), 83–84.

72. "China Noses Ahead as Top Goods Producer," *Financial Times*, 13 March 2011.

73. "China or the US? Make Your Choice," *Financial Times*, 3 Oct. 2011.

74. Charles Doran, "World War I as existential crisis amidst the shifting tides of history," *International Relations*, 28(2) (2014), 263–266. Kohout, "War Causation," 59–60.

75. Angus Maddison, *Contours of the World Economy, 1–2030 AD: Essays in Macroeconomic History* (Oxford: Oxford University Press, 2007), 343.

76. Karl, *China*, 174.

77. "China Sows Seeds of Food Self-Sufficiency," *Financial Times*, 16 April 2009. "Water: Shortages Threaten to Hamper Growth," *Financial Times*, 25 Oct. 2011.http://stat.wto.org/CountryProfile/WSDBCountryPFView.aspx?Country=CN&

78. http://stat.wto.org/CountryProfile/WSDBCountryPFView.aspx?Country=CN&
79. Richard Halloran, "AirSea Battle," *Air Force Magazine*, xxviii (2010), 44–48.
80. "Chinese Military Seeks to Extend its Naval Power," *The New York Times*, 24 April 2010, 1. "Pilotless Planes, Pacific Tensions," *The New York Times*, 13 May 2013, 21.
81. Zheng Bijian, "China's 'Peaceful Rise' to Great Power Status," *Foreign Affairs*, LXXXIV (2005), 18.
82. Fischer, *German History*, 56–8. Akira Iriye, *The Origins of the Second World War in Asia and the Pacific* (London: Longman Group UK Limited, 1987), 67–73.
83. Iriye, *Asia and Pacific*, 2–20.
84. "China left out of Obama free trade party," *Financial Times*, 1 Apr. 2013. "It won't be easy to build 'anyone but China' club," *Financial Times*, 22 May 2013.
85. Zbigniew Brzezinski, *The Grand Chessboard: American Primacy and its Geostrategic Imperatives* (New York: BasicBooks, 1997), 30–36.
86. http://stat.wto.org/CountryProfile/WSDBCountryPFView.aspx?Language=E& Country=UShttp://www.census.gov/foreign-trade/statistics/graphs/gands.html
http://www.databank.worldbank.org
87. Ludwig Dehio, *"Ranke and German Imperialism"* in *Germany and World Politics in the Twentieth Century* (New York: Alfred Knopf, 1960), 49–50.
88. Kissinger, *Diplomacy*, 813. Brzezinski, *Grand Chessboard*, 30–35.
89. Zack, *Dehio*, 112–47.
90. Zhongying Pang. (2013). A "New Type of Great Power Relationship" between China and United States. China-US Focus. Retrieved fromhttp://www.chinausfocus.com/foreign-policy/a-new-type-of-great-power-relationship-between-china-and-us/.
91. Calleo, *Follies of Power*, 94–126.
92. Calleo, *German Problem*, 115–7.
93. Gall, *Bismarck*, 140–3.
94. Hillgruber, *World Wars*, 44–45.
95. Calleo, *German Problem*, 22.
96. Kissinger, *Diplomacy*, 726–30, 830–1.
97. Fred Ikle, *Annihilation From Within: the Ultimate Threat to Nations* (New York: Columbia University Press, 2006), 1–4, 34–37. Graham Allison, *Nuclear Terrorism: The Ultimate Preventable Catastrophe* (New York: Times/Henry Holt, 2004), 61–86. Andrew Krepinevich, *Seven Deadly Scenarios: A Military Futurist Explores War in the 21st Century* (New York: Bantam Books, 2009), 63–91. Robert Cooper, *The Breaking of Nations: Order and Chaos in the Twenty-First Century* (London: Atlantic Books, 2003), viii–x. Lerman, *Bismarck*, 29.

BIBLIOGRAPHY

Allison, Graham. *Nuclear Terrorism: The Ultimate Preventable Catastrophe*. New York, New York: Times/Henry Holt, 2004.
Baum, Richard and Alexei Shevchenko. "Bringing China In: A Cautionary Note." In *The New Great Power Coalition*. Lanham: Rowman and Littlefield, 2001.
Bijian, Zheng. "China's Peaceful Rise to Great Power Status." *Foreign Affairs* LXXXIV, (2005).
Bowra, C. M. *The Greek Experience*. New York: Praegar Publishers, 1957.
Brzezinski, Zbigniew. *The Grand Chessboard: American Primacy and its Geostrategic Imperatives*. New York: BasicBooks, 1997.
Calleo, David P. "Twenty- First Century Geopolitics and the Erosion of the Dollar Order." In *The Future of the Dollar*. Ithaca: Cornell University Press, 2009.
Calleo, David P. *The German Problem Reconsidered: Germany and the World Order, 1870 to the Present*. Cambridge: Cambridge University Press, 1978.
Calleo, David P. *Follies of Power: America's Unipolar Fantasy*. New York: Cambridge University Press, 2009.
Connor, Robert. *Thucydides*. Princeton: Princeton University Press, 1984.

Cooper, Robert. *The Breaking of Nations: Order and Chaos in the Twenty-first Century.* London: Atlantic Books, 2003.

Couzet, Francois. "The British Economy at the Time of Trafalgar: Strengths and Weaknesses." In *Trafalgar in History: A Battle and Its Afterlife.* New York: Palgrave Macmillan, 2006.

Dehio, Ludwig. *The Precarious Balance: Four Centuries of the European Power Struggle.* New York, New York: Alfred Knopf, 1962.

Dehio, Ludwig. "Ranke and German Imperialism." In *Germany and World Politics in the Twentieth Century.* New York: Alfred Knopf, 1960.

Doran, Charles. "World War I as existential crisis amidst the shifting tides of history." *International Relations* 28, no. 2 (2014): 263.

Erickson, Andrew and Lyle Goldstein. "China Studies the Rise of the Great Powers." In *China Goes to Sea: Maritime Transformation in Comparative Historical Perspective.* Annapolis: Naval Institute Press, 2009.

Eyck, Erich. *Bismarck and the German Empire.* New York: W. W. Norton, 1968.

Fischer, Fritz. *From Kaiserreich to Third Reich: Elements of Continuity in German History.* London: Unwin Hyman, 1986.

Freedman, Lawrence. "The First Two Generations of Nuclear Strategists." In *Makers Of Modern Strategy: From Machiavelli to the Nuclear Age.* Princeton: Princeton University Press, 1986.

Friedberg, Aaron. "The Future of U.S. - China Relations: Is Conflict Inevitable?" *International Security* 30, (2005): 11–19.

Gall, Lothar. *Bismarck: The White Revolutionary, Volume II, 1871–1898.* London: Allen and Unwin, 1986.

Goldstein, Avery. "An Emerging China's Emerging Grand Strategy: A Neo-Bismarckian Turn?" In *International Relations Theory and the Asia-Pacific.* New York: Columbia University Press, 2003.

Grene, David. *The Peloponnesian War: Thucydides, the Complete Hobbes Translation.* Chicago: The University of Chicago Press, 1989.

Herwig, Holger. "Imperial Germany: Continental Titan, Global Aspirant." In *China Goes to Sea: Maritime Transformation in Comparative Historical Perspective.* Annapolis: Naval Institute Press, 2009.

Hildebrand, Klaus. *German Foreign Policy From Bismarck to Adenauer: The Limits of Statecraft.* London: Unwin Hyman, 1989.

Hildebrand, Klaus. "Opportunities and Limits of German Foreign Policy in the Bismarckian Era, 1871–1890: A System of Stopgap?" In *Escape Into War? The Foreign Policy of Imperial Germany.* Oxford: Berg Publishers, 1990.

Hillgruber, Andreas. *Germany and the Two World Wars.* Cambridge: Harvard University Press, 1981.

Iklé, Fred. *Annihilation From Within: The Ultimate Threat to Nations.* New York, New York: Columbia University Press, 2006.

Iriye, Akira. *The Origins of the Second World War in Asia and the Pacific.* London: Longman Group UK Limited, 1987.

Kennan, George. "Containment Then and Now," *Foreign Affairs* lxv (1987), 887–888.

Kennedy, Paul. "The First World War and the International Power System." In *Military Strategy and the Origins of the First World War.* Princeton: Princeton University Press, 1985.

Kissinger, Henry. *A World Restored: Metternich, Castlereagh and the Problem of Peace 1812–1822.* Boston: Houghton Mifflin, 1957.

Kissinger, Henry. *Diplomacy.* New York: Simon and Schuster, 1994.

Kohout, Franz. "Cyclical, Hegemonic, and Pluralistic Theories of International Relations: Some Comparative Reflections on War Causation," *International Political Science Review* xxiv, (2003): 55–64.

Krepinevich, Andrew. *Seven Deadly Scenarios: A Military Futurist Explores War in the 21st Century.* New York: Bantam Books, 2009.

Lerman, Katherine. *Bismarck.* Harlow: Pearson Education Limited, 2004.

Lieber, Keir. "The New History of World War I and What it Means for International Relations Theory," *International Security* xxxii, (2007): 155–191.

Lowe, John. *The Great Powers, Imperialism and the German Problem, 1865–1925*. London: Routledge, 1994.

Maddison, Angus. *Contours of the World Economy, 1–2030 AD: Essays in Macroeconomic History*. Oxford: Oxford University Press, 2007.

McNeill, William. *The Pursuit of Power: Technology, Armed Force, and Society since A.D. 1000*. Oxford: Basil Blackwell, 1982.

Medlicott, W. N. *Bismarck and Modern Germany*. London: English Universities Press, 1965.

Mombauer, Annika. The Origins of the First World War: Controversies and Consensus. London: Pearson Education Limited, 2002.

Mommsen, Wolfgang. *Imperial Germany, 1867 - 1918: Politics, Culture, and Society in an Authoritarian State*. Arnold: London, 1995.

Peifer, Douglas. "China, the German Analogy, and the New AirSea Operational Concept." *Orbis* LV, (2011): 117–120.

Raaflaub, Kurt A. "Born to Be Wolves? Origins of Roman Imperialism." In *Transitions To Empire: Essays in Greco-Roman History, 360–146 B.C.* Norman: University of Oklahoma Press, 1996.

Stearns, Peter N. "Britain and the Spread of the Industrial Revolution." In *Britain Pre-Eminent: Studies of British World Influence in the Nineteenth Century*. London: Macmillan, 1969.

Steinberg, Jonathan. *Bismarck: A Life*. Oxford: Oxford University Press, 2011.

Taylor, A. J. P. *The Struggle for Mastery in Europe, 1848–1918*. London: Oxford University Press, 1954.

Zack, Aaron M. *Ludwig Dehio and International Relations: A Theoretical, Historical and Strategic Analysis*. Retrieved from Proquest Digital Dissertations. AAT 3410152, (2010): 98–111.

Chapter Three

Decline and Rise of China

A New Perspective

Lanxin Xiang

ENLIGHTENMENT VS. RENAISSANCE

Until recently, China's "absolute" decline from a top power status was considered irreversible. No one anticipated thirty years ago China's rapid rise from one of the poorest nations to the number two economy in the world. Even with tangible evidence that this might happen, western observers remained skeptical as late as 1998 when the most famous apologist for the supremacy of the west, economic historian David Landes still debunked the Asian economic miracle, calling it rather insignificant.[1] The study of world power has long been blighted by Eurocentric historians who have distorted and ignored the dominant role China played in the world economy between 1100 and 1800. John Hobson's brilliant historical survey of the world economy during this period provides an abundance of empirical data making the case for China's economic and technological superiority over Western civilization for the better part of a millennium prior to its conquest and decline in the nineteenth century.[2]

China's re-emergence as a world economic powerhouse raises important questions about what we can learn from its previous rise and fall and about the external and internal threats confronting this emerging economic superpower for the immediate future. Since the majority of western economic historians (liberal, conservative, and Marxist) have presented historical China as a stagnant, backward, parochial society, an "oriental despotism," some detailed correctives will be necessary. It is especially important to emphasize how China, the world technological power between 1100 and 1800, made the West's emergence possible. It was only by borrowing and assimilating Chi-

47

nese innovations that the West was able to make the transition to modern capitalist and imperialist economies.

A question that has caught imaginations of many intellectuals both in China and the west for decades is "why industrial revolution did not take place in China?" This issue was first raised by Max Weber (1864-1920), the German sociologist, but was popularized by an English scholar on Chinese science and technology, Joseph Needham (1900-1995), and is thus labeled the "Needham Puzzle." There are many theories aimed at answering this question. These theories assert either there was a lack of cultural roots for modern industrialism and capitalism (Weber), or that technical progress only results from a large disequilibrium between supply and demand in the economy. As the Chinese economy at the time of British Industrial Revolution in mid-eighteenth century was too stable and largely in equilibrium, there was no incentive that prompted people to find creative new ways to address the difficulties produced by disequilibrium (Mark Elvin's "High-level-Equilibrium Trap").[3]

But few have asked why was there was an inherent need for a Chinese industrial revolution, if external economic relations played a marginal part in national economy and political legitimating process. This question ultimately concerns the vision of the state. It is important to note that the traditional Chinese view of the state was anti-industrial revolution, very much akin to the Renaissance view, as Machiavelli argued, that political and economic power can never be separated mechanically, for there is no divine guidance from universal truth in politics. The Confucian tradition stresses moral adjustment to the world, but never rational domination of the world. The Renaissance humanists and the Confucianists thus share a vision of politics: every political system acquires its own legitimacy only through a constant legitimating process based on moral adjustment to the society and nature in order to reach and maintain consensus and cooperation. The existence of one type of political legitimacy does not need to depend upon de-legitimating another political system. What is beyond dispute was that not everyone would agree with the ideals of rationality, universality, and national autonomy. Thus, without a return to this Renaissance humanist vision, it is hard to find a ground for compromise between the Chinese vision of politics and that of the contemporary West. Unfortunately, the Enlightenment, typified by Montesquieu, turned out to be a counter-revolution against Renaissance humanist vision of politics, for it transformed politics and state into mechanical compartments and absolute universal values.

GDP-led economic performance became in the twentieth century a critical modern element that justifies and sustains a state's political legitimacy. Indeed, nowhere other than in the economic arena can the Enlightenment orthodoxy of universal principles be readily applied. In this area, however, the genuine conversation between the West and China hardly exists, because the west has been absolutely confident about its possession of the "secret" in economic development, which has allegedly been denied to the rest of the world.

It has long been a dominant theme in the west that economic prosperity is the foundation for political legitimacy, but sustained economic development can only take place in a Judeo-Christian cultural context which has created modern democratic societies. Max Weber pioneered in the cultural interpretations of relative economic performance, providing a most powerful conceptual tool for the west to monopolize the legitimacy debate. Weber in particular offered what he considered ultimate answers to the question of why capitalism could not develop in China. He insisted that Confucianism lacked the necessary tension—that it emphasized only equality, harmony, decency, virtue, and pacifism—so that it was impossible for China to develop capitalist competition. He summarized further five conceptual problems as to why in history capitalism could never develop in China. The first conceptual flaw of Confucianism was that it considered the human world the best of all possible worlds, that is, it lacked the notion of a world after death. Second, human beings were supposed to be innately good and perfectible. The third was the belief that the "right path to salvation" was adapting oneself to Tao (*Dao*) or the cosmic harmony. The fourth mistake was the belief in the ideal of grace and dignity. The fifth and final mistake was considering decency and propriety as the central virtues. This catalogue of "mistakes" committed by Confucianism prevented the development of a capitalist instinct among the Chinese, for they despised the profit motive which was the real foundation for capitalist competition. For Weber, this list, of course, could also be considered a list of the achievements of European Enlightenment and ideals, even though the latter is primarily theistic while the former is not. [4]

Such arguments opened the door for the general theory of economic "backwardness" to expand and acquire new features, for it could be located in the context of geography, culture, and even race. During the twentieth century, "backwardness" and "progress" became two opposing philosophical propositions on economic development. Europe represented a "forward-looking," hence "progressive," civilization, while China became the quintessential model of a "backward-looking" society and static economy.

But China's developmental performance in the past decades surprises even the most hardened Weberian theorists, and raises serious questions about this Euro-centric modernization theory in its entirety. OECD's economic historian Angus Maddison produced a well-established statistical study about the world economy for over a millennium, and it indicates that as late as the 1820s, Chinese economy remained the largest single economy in the world, even though international trade was never a crucial element in Chinese economy until the twenty first century. [5] So the conception of China as a "backward" economic model was a twentieth-century invention out of the imagination of Western cultural superiority rather than historical reality. Moreover, the backward-looking habit had been generally adopted in Europe itself until the French Revolution of 1789. Before that, the concept "revolution" had always retained a dimension of cyclical, rather than "progressive," hence linear, teleological historical perspective.

Weber has continued to exercise a decisive impact on modern sociology and many developmental economic theories. As Weber's leading disciple, Seymour Martin Lipset, asserted, "Since most countries which lack an enduring tradition of political democracy lie in the underdeveloped sections of the world, Weber may have been right when he suggested that modern democracy in its clearest form can occur only under capitalist industrialization."[6] But Weber and Lipset both seem to believe that only Christian culture can allow capitalist industrialization to take place and produce sustained economic development, thus it is evident that the prevailing view in the west is in fact a tautology: that democratic systems are the preconditions for a country's initial economic takeoff as well as for its sustainability and at the same time, the best and most rational political system, democracy, can only take place in western cultural environment. But the extraordinary Chinese economic performance under a one-party system in the past decades seems to have broken the backbone of this argument.

The Weber-Lipset theory is fundamentally wrong because, first of all, it assumes that it is the West that invented the doctrine of free market economy, or the *laissez-faire* principle. But nothing could be farther from the truth. The *laissez-faire* concept was first used by French physiocrat, François Quesnay, founder of modern economics, and a forerunner of Adam Smith's alleged invention of the free trade philosophy. Quesnay was in his lifetime known as "the European Confucius." His book *Le Despotisme de la Chine*, written in 1767, describes his views of the Chinese imperial system. He was supportive of the meritocratic concept of giving scholars political power, without the cumbersome aristocracy that characterized French politics, and the importance of agriculture to the welfare of a nation as a whole. The phrase *laissez-faire*, coined by fellow Physiocrat Vincent de Gournay, is postulated to have come from Quesnay's writings on China.[7] The doctrine and even the phrase of "laisser-faire" had been directly inspired by the Chinese concept of Wu Wei (无为), usually translated as "non-action." But de Gournay's translation of this concept was not accurate, because for him, *laissez-faire* merely meant "non-interference, or let things alone." This may have been a misconstrual of the concept of *Wu Wei* itself, which, as a key concept of Taoism, actually means more than "letting things alone," but "creating action through non-action." In terms of a national economy, it should mean "creating economic action without government intervention in every aspect of the market." Ironically, Adam Smith, deeply influenced by Quesnay on this *laissez-faire* philosophy, may have got right the original meaning of *Wu Wei* with his invention of "invisible hand," suggesting a pro-active rather than passive economic system; for him, the best way to create wealth of nations is active "free trade." The rapid decline of the Chinese state power and the dismal economic development record since the Opium War of 1840s had been the Achilles Heel of political legitimacy for every Chinese government until recent economic "miracle"; hence the Chinese never had a chance in the past 160 years to have a serious voice in the debate over economic development and its link to political legitimacy until now.

Since "modern" times, a most popular theme in the west is that only the western economic system is responsible for creating the first wave of economic "globalization" and only modern Europe is the "unbound Prometheus," to paraphrase the works of David Landes,[8] in his glorified history of the capitalist industrial revolution. From this vantage point, Europe has been the center of the world system and the rest of the world has thus become periphery.

Moreover, concerning the question "why industrial capitalism does not exist in a Chinese cultural context"? Max Weber simply attributed this to the lack of Christian and especially, Protestant ethics, after disparaging the Confucian tradition as being backward, static, and non-innovative. To refute this view, we should start with the question "What does economic development mean for China?" "Economy" (*jingji*, 经济) in Chinese language is a term describing neither pure economic nor even commercial activities. It simply means "managing everyday life of the society and providing sufficient funds for running the state" (经世济国). In this conception, politics and the economy can never be separated into two mechanical spheres. The *body politic* and the *body economic* are organically connected. Also, the maintenance of a fine balance between internal market demand and supply is the best model for any Chinese state to manage its economy. External trade, despite China's active trade with foreign countries through the "Silk Road" was never considered capable of playing a decisive role for the health of national economy. And the need for sustained Gross Domestic Product (GDP) growth is a recently imported concept and an alien vision that has to be supported by a predatory and nationalistic psychology in dealing with foreign economies.

Among many theories of economic development, a popular theory that had long dismissed the possibility for China to take off economically is the "Modernization Theory." It is a theory of development that states that the development can be achieved through following the processes of development that were used in the past by the currently developed countries. Scholars such as Walt Rostow[9] and A.F.K. Organski[10] even postulated clear-cut stages of development that can be applied to every country.

Rostow sees five stages of economic development, and the first and the most difficult is the stage of so-called traditional society. He presented five steps through which all countries must pass to become developed: 1) traditional society, 2) preconditions to take-off, 3) take-off, 4) drive to maturity, and 5) age of high mass consumption. The model asserted that all countries exist somewhere on this linear spectrum, and climb upward through each stage in the development process. Organski sees four stages of political and economic development: the politics of primitive unification, the politics of industrialization, the politics of national welfare, and the politics of abundance. In view of history then, with the phrase "traditional society" or "primitive unification," these scholars were able to lump together what Rostow calls the "whole pre-Newtonian world": the dynasties in China; the civilization of the Middle East and the Mediterranean, and the world of medieval Europe. And to them he adds some post-Newtonian societies, which, for a time, remained untouched or unmoved by man's new capability for regularly manipulating his environment to his economic advantage.

Modernization Theory, in contrast to Classical Liberalism, viewed the state as a central actor in modernizing "backward" or "underdeveloped" societies. Another author who has written extensively on the process of modernization is historian David S. Landes, not so much as a sheer theory but rather as a set of powerful propositions of the predestined direction of world history. A key flaw in Modernization Theory is the belief that development requires the developed countries to patronize developing countries in learning from their own success story of "progress." In addition, it is believed that the lesser developed countries could then grow faster than developed countries and catch up, but *only if* their political systems can be transformed into the similar ones in the developed countries, that is, democracy; and then it is possible for equal development to be reached.

This is a typical "perlocutionary" speech-act that has gone astray: firstly, they fail to see that development and underdevelopment are the two sides of the same coin. The concept of economic and political development in the third world needs to be intertwined with the origins of economic backwardness and dependency brought out by colonialism or foreign domination. Secondly, the concept of economic and political development needs to be evaluated in terms of the existing political orientation of two different political systems, democracy and non-democracy. It cannot be something imposed from above. Thirdly, the stability of a political system remains essential in any type of economic development. Thus, the aspects of nation building as an ethical objective must take along the task of state-building. In the developing world, where the state has not been strong and effective, nation building can only be done by a strong effort to build state power. The Chinese state-building experience has been long and effective for millennia. The recent Chinese experience has emphatically proved that the westernization of internal system of governance is not the pre-condition for a country's economic success.

But the opposing theories to Modernization Theory cannot explain today's China either. Let us take the popular *Dependency Theory* as an example. While Modernization Theory understands development and underdevelopment as a result of internal conditions that differ between economies, Dependency Theory understood development and underdevelopment as relational. It saw the world's nations as divided into a *core* of wealthy nations, which dominate a *periphery* of poor nations whose main function in the system is to provide cheap labor and raw materials to the core. It is held that the benefits of this system accrue almost entirely to the rich nations, which become progressively richer and more developed, while the poor nations, which continually have their surpluses drained away to the core, do not advance. Developed in the 1950s, a most important conclusion of the Dependency theorists holds that for underdeveloped nations to develop, they must break their ties with developed nations and pursue internal growth. One type of policy they advocated from this insight was "import substitution" path to industrialization. But the recent Chinese success in economic development is precisely because it rejected the Dependency Theory and the "import substitution" strategy from the beginning of the reform. Chinese leaders adopted what is known as the "Asian Model" of development, which switched the national economy immediately to the path of export-led growth.

Another opposing theory is the World Systems Theory, according to which the division of periphery and center is further divided into a trimodal system consisting of the core, semi-periphery, and periphery. In this system, the semi-periphery lies between the core and periphery and is exploited by the core while exploiting the periphery. This conceptual division aims to explain the industrialization within lesser-developed countries. World Systems Theory was initiated by Immanuel Wallerstein, and focuses on inequality as a separate entity from growth in development and examines change in the global capitalist system.[11] One distinguishing feature of this theory is distrust for the state and a view in which the state is seen as a group of elites and that industrialization cannot be equated with development. Out of this theory stem anti-systemic movements which attempt to reverse the conditions of the system's inequality through social democratic and labor movements.

Once again, the Chinese economic success in the past decades proves the World System Theory to be wrong. The remarkable growth rate in GDP has been driven by the popular confidence in the efficacy of the state power and its policy elite. The state has played the decisive role not only in design but also in guidance of the national economy. From the Chinese perspective, the idea of a "nation-state in retreat" theme that was popular not too long ago, is as absurd as Francis Fukuyama's "End of History" rhetoric or the assertion by Thomas Friedman that the world is becoming "flat."[12]

In response to the distrust of the state in World Systems Theory, State Theory is based upon the view that the economy is intertwined with politics and therefore the take-off period in development is unique to each country. Development is dependent upon state stability and influence externally as well as internally. State Theorists believe that a developmentalist state is required for development by taking control of the development process within one state. State Theory may have provided us with some analytical tools for interpreting the recent Chinese economic miracle, but its focus is on a very different agenda from that of the Chinese state. State Theory emphasizes the effects of class relations and the strength and autonomy of the state on historical outcomes. Thus, development involves interactions between the state and social relations because class relations and the nature of the state impact the ability of the state to function. The Chinese state, however, has not focused on class relations at all, for the guiding principle is to build a broadly based "socialism with Chinese characteristics." Class struggle, as a political instrument for internal control, as during the period of Mao, has been largely abandoned.

None of the prevailing western theories, however, seems able to explain the Chinese economy in the past three decades. When the Chinese economy was first discussed in Europe 400 years ago as a development model, the Europeans had little doubt that the Chinese economic development level was much higher than that in Europe. At the high point of the Industrial Revolution, Europe began to identify itself as the sole progressive, civilized, and democratic section of the world, while applying all the opposite and negative features to China. Political economist John Stuart Mill and philosopher Georg F. Hegel even began to promote a fatalistic view that China's backwardness derived from its "flawed" civilization and the reason that Chinese economy was in rapid decline in the nineteenth century was its failure to adopt a European model. [13]

A new narrative on Chinese "modern" history is thus needed. Broadly speaking, to understand the story of rise, fall, and re-emergence of China as a global power, we must first of all analyze and discuss the factors and circumstances which led to China's decline since the nineteenth century and its subsequent domination, exploitation, and pillage by Western imperial countries, first England and then the rest of Europe, Japan, and the United States. Secondly, we must also pay close attention to the factors leading to China's emancipation from colonial and neo-colonial rule and analyze its recent rise to becoming the second largest global economic power.

AN ALTERNATIVE VISION OF POLITICS

Most analysis about China in the West is rooted in the Enlightenment value judgments, often disguised as "value-free" universal truths. A most promising alternative is the Renaissance humanist perspective, which was inherited by English Romanticism. The most important contribution made by American scholar David Calleo to the study of politics and international affairs is the revival of the Renaissance humanism based, in my reading, on three principles: multipolarism, interdisciplinarianism, and conservative idealism. Calleo's methodology is rooted in English Romanticism, and in particular, the writings of the great poet and political thinker Samuel Taylor Coleridge (1772-1834). Romanticism arose as a reaction to the Enlightenment and the French Revolution. Instead of searching for universal rules governing nature and human beings, the Romantics searched for a direct communication with nature and treated humans as unique individuals not subject to scientific rules.

But apart from his great imagination about the East in his masterpiece poem *Kubla Khan*, Coleridge had left no systematic comment about China and it is a pity he died in 1834, just a few years before the first British war with China, which elevated his favorite drug, opium, to the level of international *casus belli*. Nevertheless, we may have good reason to believe that Coleridge would not, were he alive in 1840, wave the Union Jack in support for Lord Palmerston's Opium War. This war was legitimized by the British Parliament not, of course, as a noble act defending the state-sponsored international drug trafficking. On the contrary, it was conveniently justified by "universal truths": the Free Trade doctrine of Adam Smith, Christian universalism, and "scientific classifications" of the human races, which led naturally to the civilizing mission of the "white man's burden."[14] Calleo is among the first to recover from the myriad published Coleridge literary works, political commentaries, and unpublished personal notes a coherent idea about politics in general and of modern states in particular. Based on Calleo's discovery, the first morally justifiable principle for Coleridge could be labeled multipolarism with two meanings: first, it is essentially anti-hegemonism, for hegemony or monopoly of power by any single player, in a domestic setting for a nation-state, or in an international setting for a world system, will do more harm than good for the harmony and peace in human societies. Hence for Coleridge, it makes little sense for one human group to impose upon other human groups its own value system or ideology. Second, cultural diversity and tolerance are necessary to maintain the political pluralism and stability of any social and international system. As Calleo points out, "The natural tendency of the Enlightenment was to pick a single cosmopolitan ideal culture and to regard all others as promising or retrograde in terms of their distance to the ideal."[15]

This leads naturally to Coleridge's second principle, interdisciplinarianism, in *accessing* truth in politics, "The greatest weakness of the intellect," Coleridge believed, "is its tendency to seize arbitrarily upon one type of insight and to suppress all others."[16] Coleridge refused to succumb himself to the tyranny of compartmentalized knowledge, which he considered too mechanical. Nothing reflects better the "interdisciplinary" vision and imaginative power on human affairs than Coleridge's *Kubla Khan*, where the seemingly disconnected elements, the "Tartars" (actually Mongols), the "dome of pleasure" (Persian), the River of Alph (Greek), the secret garden (Christian Garden of Eden), and a singing Abyssinian maid are united into a coherent vision about war and peace.

Undoubtedly, Calleo himself is a leading practitioner with this interdisciplinary approach and has produced a dazzling mix of original works covering the seemingly disconnected disciplines such as history, political science, economics, and in subjects such as political philosophy, a theory of political economy, modern German history, transatlantic alliance system, U.S. budgetary policy, decline of great powers, the function or malfunction of international monetary system, and the list is long. Calleo inherited a great tradition of the Renaissance humanism via English Romanticism, which was always skeptical of any disciplinary authority that was put into an absolute form, no matter whether it is labeled cosmopolitanism, rationalism, or universalism.

The third Romantic vision of Coleridge is reflected by his conservatism in its original sense: respecting tradition, recognizing dynamics for change, but disapproving of extremism both in theory and practice. This is conservatism rooted in Idealist tradition. Hence like Coleridge, Calleo is incapable of becoming either a left-wing liberal like John Rawls who thinks that individual rights should be given absolute priority in any society, or a right-wing conservative who appropriates conservatism to cover a radical ideology and policy agenda. For example, Calleo's multiculturalism is a far cry from the liberalist atomistic view of cultural wars and individuals, and his conservatism will never agree with the "neo" conservative agenda of imposing an ideology through the power of coercion, both at home and abroad. As he pointed out, "If conservatives were to preserve what was best in the traditional order, they had to find some means to capture the lost allegiance of the disaffected elements of society . . . force alone could not create consensus."[17]

The visions and methods of Coleridge and Calleo could undermine the prevailing view on modern Chinese politics in the West, which is essentially sustained by the Enlightenment ideology and democratic theories of politics, state, and economy. The chief contribution of the Romantics to political theory is to remove the mechanical psychology of Hobbes and Locke and develop an adequate psychology of consensus and hence a richer view of the State. Hence, if we jettison the predominant Enlightenment prejudice on politics, new horizons could be opened for understanding modern and contemporary China.

We may start with the question "What was the Enlightenment for China?" The European Enlightenment was a crucial historical moment of delegitimizing the unique Chinese vision of the state, the Mandate of Heaven. The Mandate of Heaven is a dynamic "deeds-based" rather than static "procedure-based" argument. The Enlightenment had suppressed it with a mechanical constitutional arrangement of divisions of power, which is considered the superior form of human society. But any emphasis on superiority would reflect a teleological view of linear history. The Chinese view of history is cyclical, not linear, and hence does not aim toward a predestined end. According to the cyclical view, dealing with legitimacy questions at home is a never-ending process of moral self-adjustment.

There were three images of China created by the Enlightenment scholars: first, the Jesuit image of a pagan but essentially benign China whose value system, including monotheism, was fundamentally akin to the ethics of Christianity. The Jesuits were the true heirs to the Italian Renaissance. This image was also taken by philosophers such as Leibniz and Christian Wolff at the time, and later Voltaire, Rousseau, and many others; second, the Rococo image of an exotic China, reflected mainly in arts and architecture by a method known as *chinoiserie*. The tendency of many contemporary "China Hands" to idealize China derives from this tradition of superficial treatment of the culture; and the third, the later *Philosophe* image of a nasty and primitive despotism, presented especially by Baron Montesquieu. It is this image that is most enduring and still prevailing.

Of course, the shifting images of China were determined above all by political expediency in Europe. The early Enlightenment thinkers still considered China to be a crucial debating asset in their own ideological battles, for they needed China as a sharp weapon against their own feudal societies, a kind of corrupt political system that had long been eliminated in China. But as the new bourgeois ideology was winning the day in Europe after the French Revolution, the later Enlightenment intellectuals began to see China as a rhetorical liability, for it challenged their ultimate objective of inventing a new set of ideological concepts taken to be uniquely European but must have universal applications at the same time; hence the birth of "Gothic" theory of modern democracy.

If the French man Montesquieu de-legitimated the entire Chinese internal system for lacking "scientific" designs, from Britain came a crushing condemnation of the Chinese culture itself by the so-called "utilitarians," led by Jeremy Bentham. The economic interests thrust themselves almost exclusively to the foreground. Continental Europe lagged behind the British Industrial Revolution. The British influence led to the imaginary conception of China as a first-rate world market, and *nothing else*, and this became the sole preoccupation of the much-vulgarized public opinion in Europe. Serious studies of the Chinese philosophy, language, and history gave way to "encyclopedic" manuals about natural resources, population, climate, agriculture, and husbandry in that country.

As a relatively brief but most effective counter-Enlightenment movement, Romanticism could be well positioned to challenge the prevailing methodology in the West in China studies by returning to a multi-cultural and interdisciplinary tradition. The Chinese tradition of understanding truth in human affairs matches the Romantic perspectives: truth can only be *accessed* as much as possible, but human beings can never obtain the absolute truth. Ancient Chinese philosopher Lao Zi once stated, "He who knows does not speak, he who speaks does not know." Romantic poets Coleridge and Wordsworth would surely agree with the Chinese nature poets of the Tang Dynasty (618–907 AD) that it is always futile to strive for a verbal exposition of the deeper meaning residing in the interplay between the poet and the natural scene.[18] The untamable, inscrutable nature of reality, however, proves fatal to the Enlightenment and to its dream of controlling the world. The assumption that the world was clear, or could be made crystal clear, by compartmentalized, empirical investigation, and the assumption that human reason, being the same everywhere, could be trusted to bring about harmony and agreement among people, are both fatally flawed. The Confucian tradition always stresses moral adjustment to the world, but never rational domination of the world.

The Chinese view of the state is also akin to the Romantic view that political power can never be truly separated in a mechanical sense. In the West, the original meaning of politics came from the metaphor of *polis*, a small city-state, hence the subsequent western metaphors of politics are metonymically anchored to space. Politics has been seen as "area," "domain," "field," "sector," "sphere," "arena," "stage," even a "scene," etc. Since the French Revolution, even political attitude acquired a sense of spatial direction, *la gauche, le droit*, etc. The separation of powers derived above all from this conception of politics. The Chinese, however, prefer to anchor politics to morality and virtue, hence the dynamic context of "justification," "legitimating," "action," "process," "way," "relationship," "tendency," etc. The contemporary communist Chinese language retains this Confucian trace and is not just banal Leninist propaganda.

In sum, every political system acquires its own legitimacy only through a constant legitimating process based on moral adjustment to society and nature. The existence of one type of political legitimacy does not need to depend upon the act of de-legitimating another political system. What is beyond dispute, and what the Enlightenment did not bargain for, was that not everyone would agree with the ideals of rationality, universality, and national autonomy. The result would be the most violent disagreements in history, no longer caused by pride, avarice, or religious competition, but by *ideology* buttressed by the confidence in "self-evident" truths about the nature of "human nature." Thus, without a return to Romantic vision, it is almost impossible for anyone to find a ground for compromise between the Chinese vision of politics and that of the contemporary West. As Henry Kissinger pointed out long ago, "If a society legitimizes itself by a principle which claims both universality and exclusiveness, if its concept of 'justice,' in short, does not include the existence of different principles of legitimacy, relations between it and other societies will come to be based on force." (Kissinger, *The World Restored*, p. 328, 1957)

MONEY AND POLITICS

Firmly grounded in Coleridgean tradition, David Calleo has been especially insightful on the international monetary system, treating it not just as an economic but political inquiry. Calleo sees monetary politics as an engine for the rise and decline of great powers. Economists often misunderstand economy and monetary issues. As he pointed out, "Abstracting the manifold phenomena of economic life out of full stream of human affairs inevitably distorts the significance of these phenomena. Economic theory, when heedless of the political dimension, tends to be either irrelevant or else a self-serving ideology of power."[19]

Coleridge's fights with Adam Smith, Thomas Malthus, and other "political economists" on monetary matters are well known.[20] The work that is usually regarded as the summation of Coleridge's social and political thought, *On the Constitution of Church and State*, made him a pre-eminent Romantic critic of economic modernity and its intellectual products. Economic liberalism was a product of the Enlightenment in its emphasis on universal laws governing economy and affirmation of self-interest. The Romantics were disgusted with the mechanical, "scientific" and "utilitarian" discussions of money, but much taken with the symbolic meaning of money, reflected by the imagery of water. Money circulates constantly, acquires a fluid character, is often affected by unexpected interruptive movement but is never cut off from its origins. Towards the end of 1797, Coleridge was obsessed with the image of the river and it was used in multiple poems including *Kubla Khan* and *The Brook*. In his *Biographia Literaria* (1817), he explained that:

> I sought for a subject, that should give equal room and freedom for description, incident, and impassioned reflections on men, nature, and society, yet supply in itself a natural connection to the parts and unity to the whole. Such a subject I conceived myself to have found in a stream, traced from its source in the hills among the yellow-red moss and conical glass-shaped tufts of bent, to

the first break or fall, where its drops become audible, and it begins to form a channel.[21]

Monetary issues were fascinating for the Romantics, not so much for money's "natural" role in economy, as for its sudden interruptive movements, like a stone thrown into the river or some unexpected visitor, a "person on business" (named Porlock) to interrupt Coleridge's dream about the "dome of pleasure" of *Kubla Khan*. No matter whether you call such sudden interruption a "risk" or "uncertainty" (to paraphrase Keynes), it is all the same from the Romantic point of view, for it turns an otherwise coherent thought and vision into a "fragment." After all, to be "Romantic" is to know how to live this uncertainty, or with uncertainty.

The Chinese, like the Romantics, considered money a fluid commodity that can never be cut off from its origins (no matter what they are called, gold, silver, or "real economy"). A "bank" in Chinese language is a "Silver Shop"(*Yin Hang*), stressing the character of a particular species for commercial transaction, but never the "*banca*" in its original Italian sense denoting a place, hence a spatial conception, for transaction. The Chinese are credited with the original idea of establishing the basic principles of specie standard in the tenth century and the invention of *Gresham's Law* (*bad money drives out good if the exchange rate is set by law*) before Thomas Gresham himself did.

Although an international monetary "system" is a new topic for the modern Chinese, it is China that had contributed a great deal to the creation of the British-led Gold Standard system, which was born in the Romantic period of the 1790s. The reason is simple: the modern gold standard was a reaction to China's silver standard and its strong trading position which was considered responsible for "global economic imbalance" at that time and a major cause for the crisis of silver currency and bank notes (1750–1870) in Britain. In the late eighteenth century, wars within Europe as well as an ongoing trade deficit with China (which sold goods to Europe but had little use for European goods) drained silver from the economies of Western Europe and the United States.

But international trade was never a crucial element in the Chinese economy until the twenty first century. Thus the traditional Chinese monetary system was essentially rooted on domestic economy, and its long-standing silver standard was also an internal system. The large-scale opium smuggling operation led by Britain brought out for the first time a huge outflow of silver in China, and thus China was forced to enter the "international" monetary system. "Monetary nationalism" in Friedrich von Hayek's conception is as alien to the Chinese today as was in the past. But since the Opium War, China had been forced to cope with, for the first time, an international dimension of its monetary policy, hence the need for creating modern banking. But after the Opium War defeat, the Chinese economy declined rapidly and occupied an insignificant portion of global GDP, which was 32.9 percent before the Opium War and down to less than 5 percent in 1949.[22] Thus China's monetary policy did not matter much for the international monetary system. Today the reverse is true. Even if the Chinese currency is not yet convertible, China's monetary moves cause concerns and disturbances all over the world. Hence we are hearing the same outcry against Chinese economy as if in 1820s and history is coming full circle.

Coleridge once bantered that abstract and unfeeling science reduced all human behavior, into "debtor and creditor accounts on the ledgers of self-love."[23] Like the Romantics, however, modern Chinese have never fully come to terms with symbolism of money. Because the modern Chinese policy elite have had little practical experience in international banking, they are always puzzled by the question of how currencies and central banks relate to the concept of national identity? Surely western countries have already provided us with a ready interpretation of monetary institutions with a variety of banal concepts of nationalism. Through the natural permeation of everyday-life, currency as a national symbol reinforces a collective feeling of national identity. The importance of cultural and symbolic components of communities has been stressed by Anthony D. Smith's ethno-symbolic approach to nationalism. According to Smith, ethnic myths and symbols of community are particularly important elements in the construction of nations. These symbols, which include flags, totems, hymns, anthems—and most notably coins and money bills—are potentially invested with meaning and significance, and they serve as powerful motifs of nationalism that sustain a national community.[24]

Thus in the West, state and national elites are often obsessed with monopolizing the use of such powerful symbols in an effort to dictate how they are used. Gertrude Stein once half-jokingly urged people to make up their minds; if money is money or money isn't money?[25] Sometimes money is actually "just" money in the traditional quantifiable economic sense—a means of payment, a unit of account or a technology for storing wealth. Other times, money is a symbolic sign that stands for something unrelated to economic value. It is a "signified" (in Ferdinand de Saussure's language), which denotes an arbitrary relationship between the real-world and the sign (signifier). Money as symbol of national power, as in the case of the U.S. dollar, is not always related to its true economic value.

For decades, China's banking community and the central bank elite had failed to grasp this power symbolism of money, which was very much in operation as a political action in the West before the current financial crisis. Above all, such symbols have historically been politicized as nation-building instruments, while in China there has simply been no need for such cultural symbols to help in creating a collective identity that has existed continuously on solid cultural foundations for at least two millennia. Moreover, the Chinese had little historical experience in paper-money dominated economies, for they never really trusted paper money and did not abandon a specie standard (silver and gold) until the Communists came to power in 1949. Previous regimes, however clever or wicked, had never succeeded in replacing the specie standard with paper money without causing serious inflation and political turmoil. In fact, Chiang Kai-shek's regime was, to a large extent, destroyed by the hyperinflation triggered by the "Gold Yuan" policy in 1948, which was its last attempt at printing large quantity of paper money in order to raise funds for his civil war efforts, but no one believed that Chiang could honor the official guarantee of this new currency with gold.

After the communist takeover, the Chinese economy was transformed into a Stalinist economic autarchy and the central bank of China from 1949 to 1985 was nothing but a "super-cashier" for the state; there is no real banking, not to mention international banking, businesses. Therefore, up until the reform started in the early 1980s, the Chinese banking system had experienced little exposure to the disturbances of the international monetary system as was reflected by tumultuous events related to the rise and fall of the Bretton Woods system.

Worse still, most members of the new banking elite during Deng Xiaoping's reform were trained by the "Chicago School" and are self-claimed believers in the Washington Consensus and the "nation-state in retreat" fantasy, so they often refuse to accept that currencies and banks can serve as power symbols that demarcate national boundaries and often help the wealth accumulation to the original owner of a most convincing currency. And they never consider that Chinese monetary policy should serve its geopolitical and foreign policy purposes.

The learning process for China about the post-Bretton Woods international monetary system is painful and full of setbacks. During the 1997 Asian Financial Crisis, for example, the Chinese began to feel the turbulent effect of international money movements. But its currency (RMB) was not convertible and induced little panicky capital outflow. The lesson China learnt from this crisis was to accumulate as much hard currency as possible in its central bank reserves, as a firewall against future capital outflow. But such view proved mistaken during the current world economic crisis, for holding another nation's currency on a large scale could create a hostage situation in which no firewall can isolate the one from the other. As Keynes once observed, "When I owe my bank a thousand dollars, I have reason to fear my banker; if I owe it a million, he fears me."

Nevertheless, a central bank as a key government institution did not come into existence until 1995. Its lack of global experience can be an excuse that somehow shields it away from the popular criticism of incompetence. When the world financial crisis broke out in 2008, I was the first to launch attacks on our banking elite through a series of columns at the Chinese popular paper *The Global Times*, criticizing our central bank for its ignorance of international political economy and its mistake of accumulating excessive amount of U.S. debts, coining the expression "the Chinese people's sweat and blood money" could be wasted. Later, the official media was forced to initiate a heated debate over whether the central bank's foreign exchange holdings are in fact Chinese people's "sweat and blood money." The launching of this debate is, of course, a panic reaction to the surprising level of criticism in China. The central bank invited several "authoritative" central bankers and their intellectual cohorts to explain why the foreign exchange reserves are not "sweat and blood money" and more shockingly argued that they do not even belong to the population at large due to the prior "ownership transfer" from the people to the government. But it has backfired badly. This is in fact the first public debate on international monetary policy in China since 1949.

It is thus not surprising that most people in China have increasingly come to the belief that the central bank's obsession with the U.S. dollar assets must have been motivated by reasons beyond national interests. Official corruption is the first thing coming to mind. Are there kickbacks involved for purchasing foreign bonds? In fact, the historical trajectory of official corruption is revealing, for it shifts over time from one sector to another. In the 1980s when reforms just started, selling government import licenses was the key means of becoming overnight parvenus; in the 1990s during the so-called company "marketization" process, acquiring stock shares of the state enterprises proved a most effective way of accumulating a quick fortune. Now, we have reached a stage where huge windfalls can be more easily, quickly, and secretly collected through the least transparent sector, the banking system. It is no surprise that the elite and their family members have flocked to the financial sector in recent years.

It seems that China's monetary elite are scurrying for ways to avoid a political crisis, but this poorly organized collective denial of their errors in managing the "sweat and blood money" shows their political vulnerability rather than strength. Hence the Chinese international monetary policy, for the first time after 1949, has become a most sensitive political issue, potentially undermining the regime's Mandate of Heaven.

In this delicate political context, China's participation in Euro rescue operations is surprisingly free of domestic opposition, because China's EU policy does not have a major negative impact on internal stability. First of all, the government can advertise this move as its willingness to start correcting its previous mistakes in excessive dollar purchases. Secondly, such pro-EU policy is publicly interpreted as being driven by geopolitical factors. Since 2003 China has recognized the long-term importance of European economic and political integration. The most effective way to delink Chinese economy from dollar dependency is to encourage the Euro's rise to challenge the

"indispensable position" of the dollar. Therefore, supporting the EU economy is a win-win policy for the leadership in cushioning against future reserve
losses as well as reducing the dominant power of the current monetary hegemon.

But such long-term objective of reducing dollar's hegemonic power must
be matched with short and medium term strategies to help keeping the Euro
afloat as a leading international currency. Even in the short-run, Beijing's EU
policy has strong domestic sympathy. From a moral perspective, the Chinese
leaders and the population at large agree on at least one thing: the overspend-
ing habit can only be cured by cutting expenses. The term "debt" (*Zhai*) in
Chinese language means "when you owe someone's money, you deserve
moral rebuke." That is to say, "debt" has no positive connotation under any
circumstances. Thus the Eurozone austerity policy is welcomed as a courageous but morally correct move, and in sharp contrast, the United States,
where the government is continuously expanding money supply, is losing
moral ground and international respect.

In the policy arena, the Chinese policy-makers traditionally do not trust
the effectiveness of monetary policy. Our understanding of the limitations of
monetary policy has been enhanced further during the current crisis. For
instance, even if central banks succeed in getting treasury bill rates close to
zero, the interest rates at which banks lend can remain high; and it is now
recognized that availability of credit matters as much as interest rates, especially for small and medium-sized businesses that depend on the ability and
willingness of banks to lend. This is one of the reasons for government
obsession with the recapitalization of banks. The achievement of the central
banks has been modest: having brought the global economy to the disaster,
they succeeded in avoiding a complete collapse by throwing enough money
at the financial system to keep banks afloat.

In the second place, Chinese policy-makers traditionally take the role of
fiscal policy far more seriously. But during the current financial crisis, as
indicated by the western policy practice, fiscal policy does not function well
either, for it has worked, not in preventing a Great Recession, but in preventing the Great Recession from turning into Great Depression. Therefore, the
distrust about western governments' macroeconomic policies in general has
been important in China's decision toward the Euro crisis. But China is
encouraged by the conservative fiscal response to the Euro crisis in the
Eurozone. The Chinese understand that the very actions that rescued the
economies of the world have presented a new problem for the effectiveness
of fiscal policy, as questions about governments' ability to finance their
deficits arise. Since many EU countries find themselves caught between a
rock and a hard place, the pre-Keynesian policies according to which down-
turns were met with austerity returned with a vengeance. As long as the EU is
firmly grounded on this path, there should be no alarm, for the EU economy

is under *real* adjustment, as the U.S. economy is not, at least from the Chinese perspective. The Chinese have little sympathy with the contemporary Keynesians, who, having enjoyed their moment of glory for a couple of years before, seem to be wrong again and unhappily in retreat.

But the most important motivation for China to support the Euro remains geostrategic: the need for a spiritual, if not material, western ally to formulate a multilateral challenge to the American hegemony both in political and economic terms. The large indebtedness of the United States makes it vulnerable to threats to move holdings out of dollars on the part of foreign governments. But in a floating exchange rate world, the effect of such a shift would be dollar depreciation. In any event, there is a countervailing factor that helps the American government overcome the fear of the creditor. In the case of the United States, it owes several trillion dollars to China, and there is nowhere else with financial markets that are large enough to give China a realistic possibility of moving more than a small fraction of its holdings. Any Chinese threat to move the bulk of these balances would certainly result in dollar depreciation. But to make such a threat credible, China has to find new and promising outlets.

The Euro represents a "fair" western monetary model based on multilateralism. The recent attempt by Beijing at diversification of China's reserve holdings, indicates the belated realization that monetary symbolism, that is, the relationship between the *signifier* and the *signified* in the international monetary system today remains in fact a most important power relationship. Moreover, if Beijing were to seriously help the Eurozone, it would prefer, until recently, to lend to the Eurozone through the IMF rather than lending to it directly. For China, contributions to the global organization to help ease the crisis may give it the political leverage to demand a larger role in the IMF. On February 14, 2014, China's Central Bank pledged that it would increase its holdings of euro-denominated assets (such as European government bonds) in an effort to diversify its investments away from the U.S. dollar, but maintained that its interest was in less-risky European assets, such as EFSF bonds.

Has the European Sovereign Debt crisis reduced Chinese exports and caused China to re-evaluate the structure of its economy? The answer is yes. China's economy, monetary policy, and fiscal policy have all been affected by the crisis in Europe. Moreover, China sends 20 percent of its exports to the EU, but demand from Europe has fallen as European economies have entered recessions. Realizing its vulnerability to changes in foreign demand, which was made evident by the onset of the European sovereign debt crisis, China is now determined to make its economy fundamentally domestically driven. To do this, China plans to increase its minimum wage, government support for consumer credit, and pension and healthcare assistance in an attempt to encourage Chinese citizens to spend more money. China also attempts to make its economy more domestically driven by allowing its currency to appreciate, which would give Chinese citizens more purchasing power and thereby increase domestic demand for Chinese products. The IMF has warned that the worsening debt crisis in the Eurozone poses a "key risk" to China's growth. But it also admitted that China had ample room and the fiscal tools "to respond forcefully" to any such developments.

In conclusion, economic arguments for explaining China's policy toward the Eurozone crisis are often off the mark. One needs a "Romantic" or an interdisciplinary approach to observe this issue. Using analytical tools from history, economics, sociology, and politics, one may be able to come to a far more precise understanding of critical issues for world economy and international politics.

NOTES

1. David S. Landes, *The Wealth and Poverty of Nations: Why Some Are So Rich and Some So Poor?* (New York, New York: W. W. Norton & Company, 1998).

2. John M. Hobson, *The Eastern Origins of Western Civilization* (New York, New York: Cambridge University Press, 2004).

3. Mark Elvin, "The high-level equilibrium trap: the causes of the decline of invention in the traditional Chinese textile industries," in *Economic Organization in Chinese Society* (Stanford, California: Stanford University Press, 1972).

4. Max Weber, *The Religion of China* (New York: Free Press; Collier-Macmillan, 1951), 149–150.

5. Angus Maddison, Chinese Economic Performance in the Long Run, 960–2030 AD (OECD: OECD Publishing, 2007), 44. Available online at: http://browse.oecdbookshop.org/oecd/pdfs/product/4107091e.pdf/.

6. Seymour M. Lipset, *Political Man: The Social Bases of Politics* (Baltimore, Maryland: The Johns Hopkins University Press, [1963] 1988), 28.

7. Murray Rothbard, *Economic Thought Before Adam Smith* (Northampton, Massachusetts: Edward Elgar Publishing, 1995), 386.

8. David S. Landes, *The Unbound Prometheus: Technological Change and Industrial Development in Western Europe from 1750 to the Present* (New York, New York: Cambridge University Press, 1969).

9. Walt W. Rostow, *The Stages of Economic Growth: A Non-Communist Manifesto* (New York, New York: Cambridge University Press, 1960).

10. A.F. K. Organski, *The Stages of Political Development* (New York, New York: Alfred A. Knopf Publishing, 1965).

11. Immanuel Wallenstein, *World Systems Analysis* (Durham, North Carolina: Duke University Press, 2004).

12. Francis Fukuyama, *The End of History and the Last Man* (New York, New York: Avon Books, 1992). Also see: Thomas L. Friedman, *The World is Flat: A Brief History of the Twenty-First Century* (New York, New York: Farrar, Straus and Giroux, 2005).

13. G.W.F. Hegel, *Lectures on the Philosophy of World History* (New York, New York: Cambridge University Press, 1975), 54.

14. For a brilliant recent study on White Man's Burden, please see: Michael Keevak, *Becoming Yellow: A Short History of Racial Thinking* (Princeton, New Jersey: Princeton University Press, 2011).

15. David P. Calleo, *Coleridge and the Idea of Modern State* (New Haven, Connecticut: Yale University Press, 1966), 51.

16. David P. Calleo, *Coleridge and the Idea of Modern State*, 45.

17. David P. Calleo, *Coleridge and the Idea of Modern State*, 74.

18. James Miller, "English Romanticism and Chinese Nature Poetry," *Comparative Literature* 24, no. 3 (1972): 223–224.

19. David P. Calleo and Ben Rowland, *America and World Political Economy* (Bloomington, Indiana: Indiana University Press, 1973).

20. Alexander Dick, *Romanticism and the Gold Standard: Money, Literature, and Economic Debate in Britain 1790–1830* (New York, New York: Palgrave Macmillan, 2013).

21. David P. Calleo, *Coleridge and the Idea of Modern State*, 76.

22. Angus Maddison, *Chinese Economic Performance in the Long Run, 960–2030 AD* (OECD: OECD Publishing, 2007), 44. Available online at: http://browse.oecdbookshop.org/oecd/pdfs/product/4107091e.pdf/.

23. Samuel T. Coleridge, *The Statesman's Manual* (London, England: Published in 1816). Available online at: http://books.google.com/books?id=40ISAAAAIAAJ&printsec=frontcover&source=gbs_ge_summary_r&cad=0#v=onepage&q&f=false/.

24. Anthony D. Smith, *Theories of Nationalism* (New York, New York: Harper & Row, [1972] 2005), 28.

25. Gertrude Stein, *Writings and Lectures 1911–1945*, edited by P. Meyerowitz (London, England: Peter Owen, 1967), 333–334.

BIBLIOGRAPHY

Calleo, David P. *Coleridge and the Idea of Modern State.* New Haven, Connecticut: Yale University Press, 1966.

Calleo, David P. and Ben Rowland. *America and World Political Economy.* Bloomington, Indiana: Indiana University Press, 1973.

Coleridge, Samuel T. *The Statesman's Manual.* London, England: Published in 1816.

Dick, Alexander. *Romanticism and the Gold Standard: Money, Literature, and Economic Debate in Britain 1790-1830.* New York, New York: Palgrave Macmillan, 2013.

Elvin, Mark. "The high-level equilibrium trap: the causes of the decline of invention in the traditional Chinese textile industries." In *Economic Organization in Chinese Society* (Stanford, California: Stanford University Press, 1972.

Fukuyama, Francis. *The End of History and the Last Man.* New York, New York: Avon Books, 1992.

Friedman, Thomas L. *The World is Flat: A Brief History of the Twenty-first Century.* New York, New York: Farrar, Straus and Giroux, 2005.

Hegel, G.W.F. *Lectures on the Philosophy of World History.* New York, New York: Cambridge University Press, 1975.

Hobson, John M. *The Eastern Origins of Western Civilization.* New York, New York: Cambridge University Press, 2004.

Keevak, Michael. *Becoming Yellow: A Short History of Racial Thinking.* Princeton, New Jersey: Princeton University Press, 2011.

Landes, David. S. *The Unbound Prometheus: Technological Change and Industrial Development in Western Europe from 1750 to the Present.* New York, New York: Cambridge University Press, 1969.

Landes, David S. *The Wealth and Poverty of Nations: Why Some Are So Rich and Some So Poor?* New York, New York: W. W. Norton & Company, 1998.

Lipset, Seymour M. *Political Man: The Social Bases of Politics.* Baltimore, Maryland: The Johns Hopkins University Press, [1963] 1988.

Organski, A.F. K. *The Stages of Political Development.* New York, New York: Alfred A. Knopf Publishing, 1965.

Rothbard, Murray. *Economic Thought Before Adam Smith.* Northampton, Massachusetts: Edward Elgar Publishing, 1995.

Rostow, Walt W. *The Stages of Economic Growth: A Non-Communist Manifesto.* New York, New York: Cambridge University Press, 1960.

Stein, Gertrude. *Writings and Lectures 1911-1945*. Edited by P. Meyerowitz. London, England: Peter Owen, 1967.

Smith, Anthony D. *Theories of Nationalism*. New York, New York: Harper & Row, [1972] 2005.

Maddison, Angus. *Chinese Economic Performance in the Long Run, 960-2030 AD*. OECD: OECD Publishing, 2007.

Miller, James. "English Romanticism and Chinese Nature Poetry." *Comparative Literature* 24, no. 3 (1972): 223–224

Wallenstein, Immanuel. *World Systems Analysis*. Durham, North Carolina: Duke University Press, 2004.

Weber, Max. *The Religion of China*. New York: Free Press; Collier-Macmillan, 1951.

Chapter Four

Habsburg Decline Revisited

The Virtues of Cosmopolitan Empire

Thomas Row

DOOMED TO DECLINE?

What if Gavrilo Princip had missed? A century after the outbreak of the First World War, it is not amiss to wonder.[1] Richard Ned Lebow in "Archduke Franz Ferdinand Lives! A World without World War I" has imagined a whole counterfactual series of scenarios for subsequent historical develop- ment—both positive and negative. And this is appropriate: for in its own time, the Habsburg Monarchy was seen in both positive and negative lights. Even before the dissolution of the Habsburg Monarchy in 1918 a fierce debate had raged between its enemies and defenders over its viability. To its many critics, the Monarchy was the oppressor of the nations, a decaying anachronism, and a pathetic troublesome player in the international state system. To its defenders—who would find their clearest voice most fully only after the Monarchy had vanished—it was "the world of security" as depicted in Stefan Zweig's "The World of Yesterday." As Simon Winder puts it in his own rumination "If Franz Ferdinand had Lived," "The Habsburg rulers might have been shortsighted, cynical, and incompetent, but they ruled over a paradise compared to the horrors that followed."[2]

The arguments between the critics and the nostalgic have ebbed and flowed now for over a century. Waves of nostalgia have crested around the time of the end of the Cold War (with the great revival of the idea of Central Europe) and they are quite prominent today. At the heart of the matter lies one basic issue: could a super-national dynastic empire be reconciled with the rise of virulent ethno-nationalism? Could a cosmopolitan political struc- ture embrace a multitude of nationalities and cultures? Could an empire based on tradition (and invented traditions) survive in a world increasingly shaped by the rampant liberal capitalism pushed by the Anglo-Saxon liberal empires?

A.J.P. Taylor thought not. "The conflict between a super-national dynastic state and the national principle had to be fought to the finish; and so, too, had the conflict between the master and the subject nations. Inevitably, any concession came too late and was too little; and equally inevitably every concession produced more violent discontent. The national principle, once launched, had to work itself out to its conclusion."[3]

Henry Wickham Steed, on the other hand, and certainly no friend to Austria, drew the opposite conclusion: "Errors, weakness, or prejudice on the part of the Monarch, of statesmen, or of races may, it is true, bring the Monarchy again to the verge of ruin; disaster may seem to portend the fulfillment of prophecies of disintegration; but I have been unable to perceive during ten years of constant observation and experience—years, moreover, filled with struggle and crisis—any sufficient reason why, with moderate foresight on the part of the Dynasty, the Habsburg Monarchy should not retain its rightful place in the European community." [4]

Two facts, however, are important to keep in mind. First, the Monarchy proved remarkably resilient in the nineteenth century. It survived the Revolutions of 1848, it made a deal with the Hungarians in 1867, it became a constitutional monarchy at the end of the century, and it could very well have continued to change and reform subsequently. Second, it was the fact of the war that brought the Monarchy down. And this was no more predictable than the fall of the German and Russian empires.

Ultimately the real issue at hand is not "Was the Habsburg Monarchy doomed to decline?" But rather, the issue is "What does the Habsburg Monarchy represent in the history of international relations?" The idea of the Habsburg Monarchy was what I would call that of a great "cosmopolitan" empire. That idea has continued to resonate. The rest of this chapter is an attempt to sketch out a broad picture of the evolution of the Habsburg Monarchy in the broader international state system. And to do so, I will include a consideration of its mirror image—the other cosmopolitan empire: the Ottoman Empire.

COSMOPOLITAN EMPIRES IN THE INTERNATIONAL STATE SYSTEM

Historically, the Habsburg Monarchy and the Ottoman Empire were the two great cosmopolitan empires that together were the organizing principle of the state system in its Eurasian heartland. Both were old empires, with roots in the Middle Ages. Both were dynastic and the standard bearers of the great religions. While the Habsburgs famously expanded through marriage, the Turks did so through force of arms. They were arch rivals—and twice in 1529 and 1683 the Ottomans came close to taking Vienna. The Habsburgs' systemic role was to contain the Turkish advance—a role that became complicated with the rise of France and the Atlantic and protestant powers. The Monarchy though stalemated in the West by the outcome of the Thirty Years War managed to begin its "roll back" advance in the East against the Ottomans after 1683.

How might we characterize these two old empires? They were arch-rivals, but they also had much in common (strengths and also weaknesses). They were dynastic and faith-based, but also slow, inefficient, and burdened with layers of antiquated social and political structures. Both rested on traditional agrarian political economies hardly penetrated by an emerging capitalism. Both were subject to the predations of rising neighbors and both faced periodic revolts from below. But above all, they were cosmopolitan—tolerating various minorities as long as obeisance and correct form were maintained. In both empires reform was difficult and usually stunted. Nevertheless, both empires embraced a wide variety of peoples, languages, cultures, and religions within their boundaries. This toleration by our contemporary standards was limited and conditioned; but by the standards of other empires and other times was relatively remarkable before the nineteenth century. To be sure, as it entered severe decline in the second half of the nineteenth century, Ottoman repression intensified in its violence. The Bulgarian massacres, for example, where Gladstone was a kind of forerunner of Samantha Power, shocked opinion. In the first two Balkans Wars, though, the new Slavic nationalists demonstrated a savagery to each other worthy of the Turks. Nothing similar happened in the Habsburg Monarchy—though the treatment of the Hungarian rebels after 1849 was deeply criticized.

"Cosmopolitan empires" might be contrasted with what Daniel McCarthy has recently called "Liberal Empires." By these he means free-trading empires with both liberal and democratic systems. "What in fact triumphed," McCarthy writes, "over the last 250 years—not since the battle of Jena but since the end of the Seven Years' War in 1763—is not an idea but an institution: empire. Successive British and American empires created and upheld the world order in which liberalism could flourish." Fukuyama's "liberal democracy" turns out to be a synonym for "the attitude and institutions of a world in which Anglo-American power is dominant."[5] The Anglo-American concept of Liberal Imperialism is deeply antithetical to the concept of cosmopolitan empire represented by the Habsburg Monarchy and the Ottoman Empire. Liberal Imperialists saw these old empires as decadent, decayed, and declining. As the liberal imperialists imagined "new world orders" there was no room for them. And as we shall see, when the old empires were swept away, the master plans for the order that would replace them were mainly crafted by the Anglo-American liberal imperialists.

By the end of the eighteenth century one can indeed see a process of relative decline in the position of the Habsburg Monarchy and the Ottoman Empire within the international state system. Both the Ottomans and the Habsburgs were pressed by the consolidation and expansion of Russia. The emergence of a dynamic Prussia on the other hand began a mortal duel with Austria which would lead eventually to her total defeat in the Germanies in 1866. Systemically, the center of gravity in the world was shifting to the Atlantic powers and the projection of power moving out to the rest of the world. Neither the Ottomans nor the Habsburgs would become world empires in the age of the new imperialism. (Despite Franz Josef Land; the Emperor Maximilian in Mexico; and the Empress of Brazil.)

Napoleon in Egypt (1798) and Napoleon in Vienna (1805, 1809) are emblematic of the challenges the old empires faced. Here was the modern nation state literally at the gates and the shock was profound. The relative decline of the cosmopolitan empires was not only systemic, but also internal. Here the process of relative decline was due to the birth of modern nationalism and to socio-economic backwardness as industrial capitalism started to develop. It is thus no wonder that for Metternich both liberalism and nationalism were anathema and that the Congress of Vienna both systemically and internally aimed to set up a conservative world order.

As I have mentioned above, the Habsburg Monarchy proved to be remarkably resilient in the century following the Congress of Vienna in 1815—the Ottoman Empire much less so. But if the Habsburg Monarchy could both survive and transform its state structures, it could not prevent massive defeats within the international system. The unification of Italy in 1860 eliminated Austrian hegemony in the peninsula; Bismarck completely won the duel with the Habsburgs over Germany by 1871. As a great power, the Habsburg Monarchy could now but look to the southeast. Austria-Hungary may have been in better shape than the Ottomans, but was considered by many too, to be a "sick man of Europe."

In the Ottoman Empire, nationalist revolt first showed its face in Serbia already during the time of Napoleon. But it was the intervention of the great powers (Algeria, Greece) and internal struggle (Mehmet Ali, Egypt) that proved decisive. Throughout the nineteenth century the Ottoman Empire degenerated, losing battles, losing control of finances, losing sovereignty. The first Armenian massacres are at the end of the century. The Ottoman Empire was clearly the sick man of Europe. Only by the eve (1908) of the First World War could the Young Turk Revolt offer the promise of renewal in the Ottoman world.

THE BLOODLANDS OF CENTRAL EUROPE

The systemic crisis of the First World War destroyed both the Habsburg Monarchy and the Ottoman Empire. Perhaps it was not by chance that the crisis began in Sarajevo on the border between the two. By 1914 both the Habsburgs and the Ottomans were seen as backward and in dire need of impossible reform. Systemically they both remained the organizing principles for international order in their parts of the world. To be sure, the Turks had lost control of large swathes of territory (even more after Italy's Libyan war in 1911) and the great powers were in de facto control in many areas. In Central Europe, though, the Habsburg Monarchy remained very much the basic organizing principle of order, however challenged from within and without. A solution, as A.J.P. Taylor suggested, for this part of the world that would neither be German nor Russian. If the challenge to the Ottomans was largely external, from the great powers, that to the Habsburgs was largely internal, from the nationalities.

The outcome of the destruction of these two cosmopolitan empires has not been a happy one. In Central and Eastern Europe, both a great tragedy and the eventual establishment of systemic stability (with the exception of the unfinished business of Ukraine) took place between 1918 and the early 1950s. In the lands of the former Ottoman Empire, a great tragedy is now unfolding and there is no systemic stability in sight.

In Central and Eastern Europe all the old multinational empires were swept away after the First World War. In the case of the Habsburg Monarchy a great Common Market was shattered and broken into pieces. As is well known, the successor states faced enormous problems during the interwar years in setting up essentially new nation-states from scratch. The political, economic, and social problems were severe. In no case could a nation-state be constituted purely on the basis of national self-determination. Each one: Czechoslovakia, Poland, Hungary, etc., was a bundle of contradictions and resentments. The architects of the new world order in Central Europe were liberal imperialists. Perhaps next to Hitler, the greatest opponent of the Habsburg Monarchy was Thomas Woodrow Wilson. The 14 points were to be the basis of the peace and the experts in Paris redrew the borders in Europe accordingly. There was no chance for a continuation of the Monarchy: many of the new national committees had already been formed in the United States.

Systemically, with the disappearance of the Habsburg Monarchy, the "third way" of a regional order that was neither German nor Russian vanished. The new states found themselves in a zone of insecurity: they were safe only so long as the Russians (now Soviets) were kept out and the Germans (under Versailles) were kept down. These conditions changed in the 1930s. Now it was the Russia of Stalin and the Germany of Hitler (to which the rump Austrian part of the Monarchy cheerfully joined in 1938) which stood on either side. The basic formula of what Timothy Snyder has called the "Bloodlands" was already in place and in action well before Nazi Germany and the Soviet Union invaded Poland in September 1939.

The outcome was one of the great tragedies of the twentieth century, and indeed, the epicenter of this human tragedy was right in the heart of Central Europe. As we now see, the interwar period as a whole was a time of mass-murder, genocide, ethnic cleansing and forced expulsions of populations. Though these were concentrated in the Second World War, they began before and continued immediately after.

Systemic stability, however, was achieved—achieved at an enormous human cost. Borders were rearranged (Poland for example was picked up and dropped to the West); some populations had been murdered and driven out (the Jews and Roma); master nation populations (mainly the Germans) were expelled as were minority populations almost everywhere. The result was the reconstitution of nation-states in Central and Eastern Europe to the greatest extent possible on ethno-nationalistic lines. (Though of course this was an incomplete process). The outcome has meant that the ethnic conflicts that have historically plagued Central Europe have largely disappeared. But the cost was great: one cannot imagine a Kafka in Prague today.

Systemic stability was, ironically, further reinforced by the division of Europe and the Cold War. The Soviet Union reversed Brest-Litovsk and the Central and Eastern European states found themselves now behind the iron curtain in the Russian sphere. (Austria, as Hitler's first victim escaped this fate.) Periodic revolts within the Eastern bloc (Hungary, Czechoslovakia, Poland, etc.) now were nationalist in character and repressed as in days of old. Even when the Cold War ended, stability persisted—the structures of the European Union and the transformation of Germany have created (as I will argue shortly) a benevolent cosmopolitan imperial framework for the new member states.

Ukraine is the great exception to the general systemic stability in the east and the reasons for that lie in the complex and convoluted evolution of Ukrainian history and nationalism. The Ukrainians never managed after the First World War to secure a viable state. The territory was divided between Poland and the USSR. By the end of the Second World War the country was united under the Soviet Union and large-scale ethnic cleansing had taken place. The heartland of Ukrainian nationalism is in the west—and particularly in the former Habsburg lands of Galicia. Lviv, which was once an Austrian city populated by Poles and Jews is now entirely Ukrainian. It remains to be seen how the contest between Kiev—which looks to the benevolent empire of the EU—and the rebels—who look to the Kremlin—will be resolved.

BLOODLANDS: THE FORMER OTTOMAN EMPIRE

The new international order which followed the First World War in the Ottoman Empire took a different path from that of Central Europe. Systemic and internal stability were never fully realized and conflict exploded particularly in the latter part of the twentieth century continuing to this day. The case of Yugoslavia (European Turkey) will be analyzed separately. Anatolia, or Modern Turkey carried out a full-fledged nationalist revolution under Ataturk, a process accompanied by one of the earliest ethnic cleansings in contemporary history as Greek and Turkish populations were expelled from ancient lands. This followed the earlier genocide of the Armenians, carried out by the old regime during the war.

Elsewhere, a generalized systemic stability has been postponed (and even Turkey's former Kemalist consensus has been diminished, while the Balkans remain a potential tinderbox). The fate of the Ottoman Empire was determined by the "lines in the sand" drawn by the British Liberal imperialists together with the French. Sykes-Picot (1916) is the emblem of this process. The European imperialist framework received a liberal gloss once Wilson and the Americans got involved (with the formula of mandates under the League of Nations). In 1917 the British even promised a Jewish homeland in Palestine with the Balfour Declaration, a project realized with the establishment of Israel in 1948.

For the most part, the imperial system in the Middle East lasted until well after the Second World War. Following Suez, in 1956 the Liberal American Empire moved to the fore as the Europeans powers retreated. And, if the British Empire devolved power, the French were more tenacious. The Algerian War against France was incredibly bloody as was the civil war there at the end of the last century.

During the long period of the Cold War, the state system in the Middle East was bounded externally by the super powers and their respective allies. Internally, for the most part a series of strong men held power within the boundaries of the lines in the sand drawn up after the First World War. With the end of the Cold War, however, things began to change. Regional state rivalry got out of control (Iraq's invasion of Kuwait). And the subsequent international intervention led by the sole—at this point—remaining superpower failed to achieve a durable equilibrium. Internally a series of movements arose that accepted neither the traditional internal arrangements in the Middle East, nor the systemic position of the great powers in the region, the chief expression of which was Al-Qaeda. Israel, seen by the people in the region as a colonial settler state was a perpetual source of tension.

Thus, systemic and internal stability throughout the Middle East has proved elusive. Now the system seems to be unraveling and it seems as if the lines-in-the-sand will be redrawn. The Arab Spring, like the Revolutions of

1848, has not led to the springtime of the peoples. According to Andrew Bacevich's count, the United States has been engaged in fourteen wars in the Middle East since 1980.[6] It is by no means clear that liberal interventionism is capable of bringing either peace or stability to the region (see Libya).

Instead, a process of mass-murder, genocide, war, ethnic cleansing, and forced expulsions of populations seems to be under way now throughout many of the lands of the former Ottoman Empire. Moreover, a series of religious wars akin to Europe's own Reformation-Counter-Reformation struggles in the sixteenth and seventeenth centuries is spreading across the region and this adds an additional layer of conflict to the pre-existing ones.

THE LESSONS OF THE BALKANS

In his famous book on the Habsburg Monarchy, A.J.P. Taylor argued that, "Marshal Tito was the last of the Habsburgs: ruling over eight different nations, he offered them 'cultural autonomy' and reined in their nationalist hostility." "More fortunate than the Habsburgs," he writes, "Marshal Tito found an "idea." Only time will show whether social revolution and economic betterment can appease national conflicts and whether Marxism can do better than Counter-Revolution dynasticism in supplying central Europe with a common loyalty."[7]

Alas, time did show that Tito had ultimately failed. The Balkans wars in the 1990s were the bloodiest and most terrible in Europe since World War II. It was here that systemic and internal instability, genocide, ethnic cleansing, and war returned with a vengeance to contemporary Europe. (The ethnic cleansing of the Italian populations in Istria and Dalmatia was a forerunner and took place in the 1950s.)

Tito's Yugoslavia did not long outlast Tito. But a familiar pattern emerged: unchecked ethno-nationalism in a multinational society led to chaos. The supra-national idea did not hold, but importantly, there was no super-national power to hold things in check. A survey of Bosnian history is instructive: Bosnia has tended to do well in periods of peace and stability when there is imperial rule. This was true when Bosnia belonged to the Ottoman Empire. It was true when Bosnia belonged to the Habsburg Monarchy (now remembered with great nostalgia in Sarajevo). It was also true under Tito's Yugoslavia. It was not true during the Kingdom, nor at any time when a super-national power was not present.

This is not to say that Bosnians were necessarily happy with their imperial overlords. But except in times of transition, there was stability. It was external intervention that brought a truce to the recent wars in the Balkans. The Liberal American Empire brought in force to create a truce. It is the European Union, however, which has brought order, and the EU might now be seen as the new cosmopolitan imperial overlord not only of Bosnia, but of the whole western Balkans. It is Europe's softpower and the promise of accession which keeps a still difficult situation under control. If the EU is the new Tito, we might also argue that the EU is the new Habsburg Monarchy.

CONCLUSIONS: THE EUROPEAN UNION AND THE HOLY ROMAN EMPIRE

In our still-Westphalian world we are still obsessed with nation states. Other forms of political order such as Empires are feared or frowned upon. The American empire pretends not to be one despite perpetual imperial war and a global military presence. And the United States is usually joined by "post-imperial" Britain, ensuring the 250-year tradition of liberal imperialism. The old empires, which I have called cosmopolitan, have long been consigned to the dustbin of history. When, however, we start to look at their history and the consequences following their demise, certain positive features emerge.

In contemporary history, one of the greatest problems is unchecked eth-no-nationalism, a force which often, and particularly in multi-ethnic contexts leads to one group savaging another. Within a national community the task of Leviathan can go to the national state. But even so-called national states are complex. Ask the Scots. Ask the Catalans. Imperial structures developed historically to encompass broad and diverse populations. Both the Habsburg Monarchy and the Ottoman Empire, despite their ups and downs, were ex-traordinarily successful for a very long time. At their best, like Marshal Tito, they were able to deliver: a). an idea, b). cultural autonomy; c). economic betterment; d). security.

These cosmopolitan empires were very different from the liberal empires in philosophy and world-view. They were empires of civilization rather than commerce. They were based on subjects rather than economic men. They were rooted in tradition rather than expediency. They also, having reached a certain territorial extent, came to represent regional stability and order. The contemporary liberal empires, in contrast, driven by an ideology of neo-conservatism, are endlessly restless and on the move, constantly pushing through force and commerce to impose an abstract order all over the globe.

Were the old empires doomed? In the case of the Habsburg Monarchy, I would argue that they were not necessarily doomed. It was the war that brought the crisis—as it did to Russia and Germany. The Monarchy was capable of change—had Franz Ferdinand come to power, sacked Conrad, and forced through a tri-partite solution, things might have been different. The case of the Ottoman Empire is more complicated. The empire had already been so gravely compromised by the predations of the great powers. Within the empire, the stirrings of nationalism and internal revolt were brewing, too.

In the absence of the war, one can only speculate whether or not a reformist regime in Istanbul might have achieved something along the lines of Ataturk: a renewed nation-state based on Anatolia.

But regardless of whether or not they were doomed, the human costs of systemic and internal disorder in the lands that they once ruled are enormous. The Bloodlands of Central Europe still haunt us. The Bloodlands of the Middle East are still very much with us and unresolved. Given this cost, a revisionist interpretation of the cosmopolitan empires seems to have a certain appeal. One need not fall into the trap of blind nostalgia to see the positive features of large political structures that, when successful, provide a framework for multi-national and multi-ethnic communities to live together. To be sure, such empires may experience periods of corruption and decay. And there is, as in any nation-state, a tension between central power and the periphery, between carrots and sticks.

Perhaps the European Union is the contemporary institution that best embodies today many of the positive features of the cosmopolitan empires of old. This was precisely the argument of Robert Cooper in his 2012 article, "The European Union and the Habsburg Monarchy." (Though he also emphasizes the role of NATO in providing a basis of collective security.) "Like the Habsburg Monarchy," he writes, "the EU is not a nation state but a complex confection of states, nations, centralized bureaucracy and local autonomy. Both have grown by voluntary accession (in the old days it was called dynastic marriage) rather than by conquest. The EU is partly bound together, as the Habsburg Monarchy was, by transnational elites." "Above all," he continues, "both the Habsburg Monarchy and the EU have provided a home for the small nations of Europe who would have difficulty surviving alone . . . In the twentieth (century), belonging to a larger framework has brought both political and economic security."[8]

There has always been a certain "Habsburgian" strain or current within the movement toward European union. Perhaps Richard Coudenhove-Kalergi's Pan Europa movement is the most familiar. But to me the most stimulating recent analysis is that offered by Jan Zielonka in his "Europe as Empire: The Nature of the Enlarged European Union." Zielonka contrasts the idea of the EU as a Westphalian superstate with a neo-medieval paradigm. In Zielonka's view, it is the model of the EU as a neo-medieval empire that offers the best solutions for Europe. "It is time," he writes "to recognize the neo-medieval reality and make it work."[9]

The greatest of the medieval empires, of course, was the Holy Roman Empire which was for so long dominated by the Habsburgs. The Empire was long dismissed famously as being neither holy nor Roman, nor an Empire. Recent interpretations see it in a more positive light. The Holy Roman Empire managed, within its limits, to achieve a large amount of coordination and cooperation amongst a multitude of states and societies.

The European Union today is in considerable difficulty and disarray. If compared to the ideal of a Westphalian super state it is surely to be found greatly wanting. If we compare it though, to a neo-medieval empire, to the Holy Roman Empire, we should expect to evolve and to survive and maybe even flourish. "The Habsburg Monarchy lasted five centuries" writes Robert Cooper, "It was both solid and flexible; it aroused genuine affection among its citizens. But it vanished in a puff of smoke. Should we expect the European Union, shallow in history and unloved by those it serves to do better?"[10] I think we can, for as I have suggested, the Habsburg Monarchy was by no means doomed to decline and even though it is long gone, many of its positive virtues are still remembered.

NOTES

1. The author would like to thank Philip Van Engeldorp Gastellars in Vienna and Andrew Whitworth in Bologna for their comments and suggestions.

2. Simon Winder, "If Franz Ferdinand had Lived," *The New York Times*, June 27, 2014.

3. A.J.P. Taylor, *The Habsburg Monarchy 1809-1918: A History of the Austrian Empire and Austria-Hungary* (London: Hamish Hamilton, 1948), 7.

4. Henry Wickham Steed, *The Habsburg Monarchy* (New York, New York: Howard Fertig [1914] 1969), xiii.

5. Daniel McCarthy, "Why Liberalism Means Empire," *The American Conservative*, July 16, 2014.

6. Andrew Bacevich, "Even if we defeat the Islamic State, we'll still lose the bigger war," *The Washington Post*, October 3, 2014.

7. A.J.P. Taylor, *The Habsburg Monarchy 1809-1918*, 260–61.

8. Robert Cooper, "The European Union and the Habsburg Monarchy," *Eurozine*, December 10, 2012.

9. Jan Zielonka, *Europe as Empire: The Nature of the Enlarged European Union* (Oxford: Oxford University Press, 2006).

10. Robert Cooper, "The European Union and the Habsburg Monarchy," *Eurozine*, December 10, 2012.

BIBLIOGRAPHY

Bacevich, Andrew. "Even if we defeat the Islamic State, we'll still lose the bigger war," *The Washington Post*. October 3, 2014.

Cooper, Robert. "The European Union and the Habsburg Monarchy." *Eurozine*. December 10, 2012.

Fromkin, David. *A Peace to End all Peace: The Fall of the Ottoman Empire and the Creation of the Modern Middle East*. New York: Henry Holt, 1989.

Kozuchowski, Adam. *The Afterlife of Austria-Hungary: The Image of the Habsburg Monarchy in Interwar Europe*. Pittsburgh: University of Pittsburgh Press 2013.

Lebow, Richard Ned. *Archduke Franz Ferdinand Lives! A World Without World War I*. London: Palgrave MacMillan, 2014.

Macfie, A.L. *The Eastern Question, 1774-1923*. London: Longman, 1996.

Macfie, A.L. *The End of the Ottoman Empire, 1908-1923*. London: Longman, 1998.

McCarthy, Daniel. "Why Liberalism Means Empire." *The American Conservative*. July 16, 2014.

Okey, Robin. *Taming Balkan Nationalism: The Habsburg "Civilizing Mission" in Bosnia, 1878-1914.* Oxford: Oxford University Press, 2007.

Remak, Joachim. "The Healthy Invalid: How Doomed the Habsburg Empire?" *The Journal of Modern History* 41, no. 2 (1969): 127-143.

Rodogno, Davide. *Against Massacre: Humanitarian Interventions in the Ottoman Empire 1815-1914.* Princeton: Princeton University Press, 2012.

Taylor, A.J.P. *The Habsburg Monarchy 1809-1918: A History of the Austrian Empire and Austria-Hungary.* London: Hamish Hamilton, 1948.

Wickham Steed, Henry. *The Habsburg Monarchy.* New York: Howard Fertig [1914] 1969.

Wank, Solomon. "The Nationalities Question in the Habsburg Monarchy: Reflections on the Historical Record." *Center for Austrian Studies Working Paper* 93, no. 3 (1993).

Wawro, Geoffrey. *Quicksand: America's Pursuit of Power in the Middle East.* New York: Penguin, 2010.

Winder, Simon. *Danubia: A Personal History of Habsburg Europe.* London: Picador, 2013.

Winder, Simon. "The House of Habsburg Revisited." *Foreign Policy.* May 27, 2014.

Winder, Simon. "If Franz Ferdinand had Lived." *The New York Times.* June 27, 2014.

Yapp, M.E. *The Making of the Modern Near East, 1792-1923.* London: Longman, 1987.

Zielonka, Jan. *Europe as Empire: The Nature of the Enlarged European Union.* Oxford: Oxford University Press, 2006.

Chapter Five

Europe after the Crisis

A Case of Temporary or Morbid Decline?

Gabriel Goodliffe

Any discussion of Europe's presumptive decline must perforce begin by introducing certain ontological and analytical concepts. First of all, what do we mean by decline and how do we define and measure it? Is it an absolute concept, whose most salient trait is the diminishing of Europe's influence and capacities in comparison to some earlier measure? Or is it a relative concept, whereby the attributes that are ascribed to Europe are diminishing in relation to the influence and capacities of other national and/or supranational actors? Secondly, are we to view decline as something that is temporary or irreversible? Drawing on the language of organic processes as these would pertain, say, to a diseased body, is the latter resilient enough to throw off the illness and regain its former vitality, or is it on the contrary the victim of a pathological syndrome that ultimately condemns it to die, that is, to "morbid" decline.[1] Thirdly, to what forms of influence or power is the concept of decline to be applied and how are these to be empirically measured? Do we restrict ourselves solely to the concrete indicators of what Joseph Nye Jr. has termed "hard, command power" or does such power also have a "soft," ideational dimension?[2]

This last question is particularly salient when it comes to "Europe"—or more properly European integration—since the latter, in contrast to its constituent states the ontological definition and empirical attributes of which are broadly agreed upon, has given rise to a sustained debate regarding its essential character, qualities, and evolution. Indeed, two competing ideas of Europe have emerged since the inception of the European project in 1952, which have divided statesmen, politicians, and scholars regarding the nature of European integration and the methods and institutions required to advance it. The first of these ideas, that of federal Europe, denotes the transfer of sovereignty on the part of individual states to a higher central authority, with the goal of reducing conflict between them by ultimately subsuming these sovereign states into a larger whole. The second idea, that of an intergovernmental or confederal Europe, rejects this possibility. Instead, it posits that European integration is only possible through the cooperation of the continent's nation states, and that accordingly it will always be subject to and constrained by the national interests of the latter. In short, a fundamental disagreement between federalists and confederalists hinges around their divergent interpretations of the strength and durability of national sovereignty and their contrary assessment of the possibility for Europe's diverse peoples to permanently identify with and transfer their allegiance to a higher, supranational authority.

Fourth and finally, how is one to assess Europe's influence and capacities with respect to its constituent peoples and the states to which they are bound? Here we are in effect talking about the "legitimacy" of Europe in the eyes of both the national publics and the elites who ostensibly serve them, that is, the capacity of a political regime to impose measures that may be deemed unpopular by its citizens, but which are nevertheless accepted as necessary by them.[3] Needless to say, such legitimacy becomes particularly important during periods of economic and political crisis facing a regime.

Legitimacy can be broken down into three types. The first is "input" or democratic legitimacy, that is, the legitimacy of European institutions and by extension, of the policies they enact, conceived in terms of their representativeness and accountability vis-à-vis the people they are meant to serve.[4] The second type is their "output" or technocratic legitimacy, that is, Europe's legitimacy as measured by the efficacy of the policies it enacts in terms of securing outcomes that are judged to maximize the well-being of the greatest number of Europeans, regardless of their political preferences.[5] The third and final type of legitimacy is "telos" or ideational legitimacy, that is, the projection of Europe as an ideal that legitimizes in the eyes of its peoples the fact of integration and its impacts—both positive and negative—upon them. As Joseph Weiler has put it, according to this form of legitimacy, "the justification for action and its mobilizing force derive not from process, as in classical democracy, or from result and success, but from the ideal pursued, the destiny to be achieved, the 'Promised Land' waiting at the end of the road."[6]

Armed with this conceptual framework, this chapter seeks to evaluate the process of European integration and then to relate it to the broader question of decline. It proposes to do this in three stages. First, it looks to historically identify and situate the various modes of integration that have animated the European project, as well as the policy regimes and national influences these reflected, over the course of its history. Correlatively, we will examine the shifts that have occurred in this process and attempt to account for why they occurred. Secondly, the paper assesses the power and standing of Europe in the eyes of its citizens according to the types of legitimacy introduced above. In particular, these should prove useful in gauging the consequences and implications of the European sovereign debt crisis, as well as of the policies adopted by Europe's national and supranational elites in order to resolve it. Third and finally, building on this assessment the paper concludes by characterizing the nature and extent of Europe's decline as a result of the Eurozone crisis. In turn, it tries to specify the avenues for future integration, as well as the associated policy regimes, that are suggested by the foregoing analysis. Before we proceed, however, it is necessary to say a bit more about the historical evolution of Europe's nation states and the two forms of integration—federalism and confederalism—that were envisioned for them in the postwar era.

OF NATIONAL, FEDERAL, AND CONFEDERAL EUROPE

At base, Europe is a collection of nation states: participatory political communities subtended by a collective national identity that is defined by a common history, culture, and language. In their external political aspect, following from the Treaty of Westphalia these states came to affirm their sovereign national identities in contradistinction to one another whether through war, diplomacy, or their economic and cultural interactions. In domestic political terms, in the wake of the French Revolution this sense of national identity and the sovereignty to which it gave rise evolved in either an "open," inclusionary and democratic guise, or a "closed," exclusionary and authoritarian one.[7] Whichever form it assumed, however, the nation state became the principal locus of collective identification and mutual obligation for Europeans.

The advent of Europe's states in turn raised the question of how the collective identities underpinning them were to be sustained. This was particularly the case in the face of the social dislocations attending economic modernization as well as the political institutionalization of social conflicts, particularly along class lines, due to the extension of the franchise and the ensuing democratization of European states. By the same token, international economic competition, particularly with the establishment in the mid-nineteenth century of a free trade regime undergirded by the classical gold standard in replacement of the mercantilist system that had previously held sway between Europe's states, also had disruptive economic and social impacts on European societies.

Since the mid-nineteenth century, European history has essentially been about how to manage this contradiction between political and economic liberalism and its implications for the nation state. Domestically, the imperative of collective obligation and solidarity underpinning the democratic nation state inevitably conflicted with the affirmation of individual self-interest and competition affirmed by classical economic liberals. Internationally, it was reflected in the contest between the defenders of free trade and of the gold standard who saw them as necessary agents of national development and growth, and the advocates of protectionism and state economic intervention in order to dampen the impact of foreign competition on domestic industries and workers. This conflict came to a head during the 1920s and 1930s when the disruptive social impacts of the operation of the free market, compounded by the deflationary effects of the interwar gold standard, served to obliterate the communitarian foundations of the democratic polity. In the most extreme cases, these fueled an anti-liberal communitarian backlash in which the nation state reconstituted itself in totalitarian guise such as in Italy and Germany.[8]

In order to preserve the collective national basis of the democratic state, this experience suggested the need for a commensurate collective form of national economy. Hence, as early as the mid-nineteenth century when liberal capitalism and free trade gained intellectual and institutional primacy, dissenting communitarian nationalists began to argue for state intervention in economic affairs—that is, capitalist regulation—on the grounds that economic, social, and political life could not be assessed and arbitrated exclusively by reference to the market.[9]

These debates led to two principal forms of capitalist regulation that would set the template for future European national development and regional integration. At the interstate level, such regulation meant employing a combination of protectionist and interventionist policies in order to build up the nation state's comparative advantages vis-à-vis more technologically advanced and economically productive competitors while safeguarding social cohesion from the divisive impacts of trade competition.[10] At the domestic level, capitalist regulation was embodied in communitarian policies such as statism or corporatism on the one hand, and welfarism on the other. By statism or corporatism was meant the coordination of investment and production by the state or by state-sanctioned collective economic actors in order to promote modernization while improving the living standards and enhancing the consumption possibilities of the citizenry. For its part, welfarism implied the establishment and underwriting by the state of a system of social security to dampen the potential material and social impacts of economic modernization. In both instances, key sectoral and class actors were enlisted in the framing of economic and social policies in order to ensure that these enjoyed the legitimacy flowing from societal consensus while squaring with the imperatives of modernization and growth.

Such consensus-building mechanisms served to reinforce the democratic basis of economic as well as political life in Europe's nation states, giving rise to models of regulated capitalism that underpinned the thirty-year boom that followed World War II. Though they came in various guises, these models shared a common commitment to fashioning economic and social policy with the goal of strengthening the communitarian bases of the national democratic state. This was not simply a matter of tempering the socioeconomic inequities and class divisions that were exacerbated by the free operation of the market for the utilitarian purpose of preserving social stability. More importantly, such policies were also geared toward strengthening the bonds of trust that bound the members of the national community and underpinned the social contract that defined democratic citizenship and participation within it. [11] By the end of the postwar boom, the welfare state and other forms of capitalist regulation had established themselves not only as the central leitmotivs of economic theorizing and policymaking, but also as the functional and normative lynchpins underlying the democratic nation state and securing citizens' allegiance to it.

This regulated capitalist dispensation underlying postwar (Western) European democracy in turn set the conceptual and functional stage for the process of European integration that was to take shape during this period. The latter would successively reflect two distinctive and competing conceptions of state cooperation. The first, more ambitious and far-reaching conception was federalism. Espoused by such political luminaries of the immediate postwar era as Altiero Spinelli, Alcide de Gasperi, Paul-Henri Spaak, and Robert Schuman, federalism as noted above implied the constitutional transfer of sovereignty on the part of Europe's individual nation states to a central European authority. At base, such a constitutionally defined government would ensure that, by subsuming the sovereignty of the nation states into a higher locus of political identification and policy making, the forces of national rivalry and exclusion that had culminated in the horrors of World War II would be definitively put to rest, thereby paving the way for permanent European peace and comity.

In terms of its constitutional definition and institutional functioning, such an arrangement would reflect the following traits. First of all, it implied a division of powers between two or more levels of government, leading to a partition of functions between a federal core and its constituent units. Secondly, by virtue of the competencies that would be invested in it, the central authority would be able to act directly upon its citizens, thereby bypassing the member states as a focus of policy action. Thirdly, the central government could only come into being as a result of the voluntary, democratically approved transfer of political power on the part of the constituent members. In short, federalism sought to reconcile the imperatives of freedom and unity within pluralistic societies or multinational arrangements by allowing distinct territorial and cultural communities to govern themselves while at the same time surrendering their sovereignty to a central government equipped to solve common problems.

Given Europe's make-up of historically ancient and often conflicting national states, however, such a federal government could obviously not be created from one day to the next. Instead, establishing federal Europe would follow from a "Community method" that, first spelled out by Jean Monnet, forged "special functional links between states in a manner that d[id] not directly challenge [their] national sovereignty."[12] As a result of the implications of cooperation in one area for developments in other related areas, federalists predicted that such cooperation would naturally "spill over" into the latter. This would produce a "gradual [and] reciprocal adaptation of national institutions" that would ultimately yield a European federal government that superseded the nation states.[13] In short, the advocates of federalism saw the latter as a functionally endogenous and self-sustaining outcome resulting from the natural cooperation of states in order to overcome their common problems. In the words of Ernst Haas, through this "process whereby political actors in several distinct national settings [we]re persuaded to shift their loyalties, expectations and political activities towards a new center . . . a new political community, superimposed over the pre-existing ones," would be created.[14]

Institutionally and ideologically, this federal conception of Europe would be increasingly associated with a "German" view of Europe. Not only did the Federal Republic of Germany (FRG) represent the most prominent national exemplar of federalism among the original members of the European Coal and Steel Community (ECSC) and Common Market, but federalism was very much in keeping with the Christian Democratic ideals of the FRG's founding leaders, such as Konrad Adenauer and Walter Hallstein. As we shall see, as European integration advanced and Germany's economic power increased through the postwar era, this conception of European integration would gather force and come to be married with distinctly German ideas of economic and by extension, political, governance that would ultimately shape Europe in its current guise.

The second principal model of integration that emerged in postwar Europe was intergovernmentalism or confederalism. It explicitly rejected the federalist assumption that once integration was under way, the alternatives available to the state would progressively be limited by the fact that withdrawal would result in the loss of the advantages of functional integration. Instead, intergovernmentalists affirmed the continued predominance of nation states and national interests as the constitutive basis for international cooperation, rather than supranational actors and institutions. At one level, this implied that states remained the sole arbiters of their foreign policies—and thus themselves defined the character and limits of their cooperation with other states. In turn, this led them to reject the conception of functionalist spillover advanced by European federalists as posing an unacceptable challenge to the sovereign autonomy of the nation state.

The main reason that intergovernmentalists rejected the federal conception of the transference of national sovereignty and the functionalist process by which it was to occur was that, particularly in the case of Europe, its constituent states were at the same time too culturally, politically and economically diverse, too differentially endowed in terms of power, and hence too variegated in terms of their respective national interests to be able to federate into a superior supranational whole.[15] This was especially the case in the realm of "high" politics or "zero-sum" economic and social policy areas where the state's autonomy, conceived in terms of the capacity to maximize its freedom of action, is valued over the attainment of short-term gains.[16] Where states might envision cooperating in areas of "low" politics in which positive sum gains are possible and which are not perceived to conflict with the national interest, this could be pursued through lesser modes of integration that would not conflict with the state's fundamental autonomy and capacity. Instead, intergovernmentalists argued, cooperation could be achieved through states "pooling" their sovereignty within a confederal arrangement or international regime in order to achieve their common aims, whilst preserving the freedom to abandon this arrangement if they saw it in their interests to do so.[17]

Since France emerged from the war as the most politically powerful Western European continental power, it is no accident that this confederal view of Europe came to be associated with a French—and specifically Gaullist—view of Europe. This conviction that subordinated European cooperation to the dictates of the national interest would account for France's refusal to approve the entry of the UK into the European Economic Community (EEC) in 1963 or its decision to boycott Europe's central institutions in 1965. Such a conviction also underlay the conditional approach developed by de Gaulle in respect to the EEC, viewing it as essentially a free trade agreement that was perhaps in France's economic and political interests in the short term, but also regarding it as a potential threat to French national autonomy in the long term.[18] By the same token, concerns about preserving French freedom of action would grow increasingly pressing as Germany's economic power in Europe came to exceed that of France and its other European partners. For de Gaulle, this would inevitably translate into an expansion of German political power at the expense of France, which would end up condemning the latter to a subordinate status within a German-dominated federal Europe.[19] Given the recent turn of events, it must be said that he was remarkably prescient in this prediction.

In short, then, accompanying the process of European integration has been a dialectical debate opposing a federal-German view of Europe to a confederal-French view. From the early 1950s until the mid-1980s, reflecting the relative differential in political credibility between France and Germany during the initial decades of the postwar era as well as the hawkishly inter-governmental approach to Europe adopted by de Gaulle and his successors, confederalism was the predominant mode of European integration. Advancing according to the conception of a "Europe of states" pooling their sovereignty across a growing array of functions and competencies, this approach was grounded in the conviction that Europe's nation states "would and should remain the continent's centers of democratic legitimacy" as a function of the historical and cultural bonds that held their peoples together. [20]

Reflecting the postwar interventionist and welfarist consensus, a key rationale for Europe's model of intergovernmentalism was that it enabled the continent's nation states to safeguard the material and institutional requisites of their communitarian compacts and social cohesion in an era of growing international economic competition and rapid technological change. This implied extending nation states' communitarian mercantilism to the confederal level. Accordingly, under the guise of the EEC, Europe's western states set up an external customs union in order to minimize the dislocations of international economic integration on their societies while opening their economies to one another so as to reap the efficiency gains of a larger internal market. At the same time, Europe's confederal form of mercantilism was essential to sustaining the collective identities of the continent's nation states through the postwar period. By coordinating the actions of states which, due to their geographic proximity and political and cultural diversity, had always impinged upon one another, the EEC in practice expanded the freedom of action of its members. Thus, it served to enrich their real sovereignty within the European and global systems as well as to enhance their legitimacy in the eyes of both their citizens and state partners. [21] In short, the European confederation that grew up through the postwar period simultaneously fed off and helped sustain Europe's democratic nation states.

By the late 1970s and early 1980s, however, international economic competition, abetted by the growing magnitude and fluidity of global capital flows, underlined the limitations of the nation-based-model of European intergovernmental cooperation. The collapse of the Bretton-Woods system triggered a cycle of competitive, beggar-thy-neighbor protectionist policies and devaluations that effectively nullified the efficiency gains of the EEC. Likewise, uncoordinated macroeconomic policies within the member states—fiscal reflation in France and Italy, austerity in Germany and the Benelux—in order to counter the effects of the oil shocks ushered in a protracted period of Eurosclerosis which, for many of Europe's leaders, highlighted the weaknesses of confederalism. Hence, starting with the launch of the European Monetary System (EMS) in 1979, which marked the attempt to restore currency stability within the EEC by effectively pinning the national currencies to the deutschmark, a new, more supranational approach to European economic and ultimately, political, governance came to the fore. Passing through the Single European Act (SEA) of 1986 that established a unitary market across the European Community and the Maastricht Treaty of 1992 that set out the conditions and institutions for creating a common European currency, this process culminated in 1999 with European Monetary Union (EMU)—marking in effect the advent of monetary federalism within the European Union.

This period, which heralded the passage from a confederal, French model of European integration to a (semi)federal, German model, reflected the conjunction of two phenomena. First, it translated the primacy of German economic power—particularly in relation to France. And secondly, particularly since the advent of Unification and the passing of Helmut Kohl, it signaled the increasing willingness of Germany's new postwar generation of leaders to press for the satisfaction of the country's national interests and, by extension, its political dominance, within Europe. This German domination of Europe assumed two forms. At an institutional level, it was reflected in the fashioning of European institutions, and particularly those charged with economic governance—the European Central Bank (ECB) and European Constitutional Court come most prominently to mind—along German federal lines. Secondly, at the level of policy, Germany's dominance could be seen in the imposition of its rule-bound, ordo-liberal principles for overseeing the single currency and enforcing Europe's economic liberalization.

As we shall see, one of the perverse effects of this shift from French confederalism to German-dominated federalism has been that European integration under a supranational guise came to undermine the social cohesion and political legitimacy of the democratic polities that it had been so instrumental in helping to consolidate during its intergovernmental period. Specifically, the abandonment of the regulated capitalisms that sustained the resurgence of the democratic nation state in Europe after World War II in favor of institutions and policies that increasingly sought to determine social outcomes according to the sole criteria of market rationality and efficiency, rolled back the European social model that had tied European publics to their democratic polities, fueling a growing disenchantment with Europe. The current Eurozone crisis represents both the culmination of and microcosm for this neoliberal shift in economic policy and its adverse sociopolitical impacts. In turn, the severity of this crisis—the worst that Europe has experienced since the 1930s and certainly the worst since the beginning of European integration—poses hard questions about the viability of this course of integration and indeed, the prospective survival of the European project.

In the remainder of the chapter, we consider how this fundamental economic and political crisis that threatens Europe came to pass. First we examine how the process of capitalist deregulation that was abetted and legitimized by European integration up to and through the 2010-2013 European debt crisis progressively served to delegitimize the latter in the eyes of its national publics. In turn, we consider whether this delegitimization might be reversed and accordingly, what the prospects are for Europe beyond the crisis.

FROM CONFEDERAL TO FEDERAL EUROPE AND THE CRISIS OF EUROPEAN LEGITIMACY

From the mid-1980s on, a process of substantive economic liberalization and welfare retrenchment was undertaken at both the national and European levels which effectively eviscerated Europe's social model by eroding the communitarian framework of mutual obligations and protections that characterized the postwar European nation state. Instead was advanced a supply-side oriented model of market liberalization that successively targeted product, capital, and labor markets, subtended by a reflationary monetarist or "ordo-liberal" macroeconomic paradigm of German inspiration, the principal purpose of which was to keep labor costs low—even at the risk of generating high unemployment—so as to restore the competitiveness of European firms in global markets and make them attractive to foreign investors. In view of achieving these supply-side monetarist objectives, the European social model was dismantled following a two-step process. In a first phase, markets were liberalized and structural and institutional impediments to their function were removed, particularly in respect to labor. In turn, in a second phase, the welfare state, which had grown rapidly as a result of the explosion of social spending in order to help cushion the pain of liberalization, was progressively cut back. [22]

The successive stages of economic integration that were undergone by the European Community and Union beginning in the early 1980s served as important practical levers and sources of political legitimation for this process of reform. First, the European Monetary System in the 1980s and 1990s followed by currency union in the 2000s constituted important constraining macroeconomic frameworks that impelled and sustained the structural reform and welfare retrenchment undergone by Europe's states. The imperative of price stability governing these frameworks implied severely restricting the money supply and corresponding interest rate rises that forced the latter to achieve competitiveness through "competitive disinflation," that is, internal adjustment by enhancing worker productivity and reducing wage costs. This imposed unprecedented labor market flexibility in member states. In turn, the Maastricht criteria—later replaced by the Stability and Growth Pact—that were set out as preconditions for European Monetary Union (EMU) acted as powerful constraints on fiscal policy. By limiting aggregate government debt levels and annual budget deficits to strict ceilings of 60 percent and 3 percent of GDP respectively, these constraints served as the bases for reducing welfare expenditures, introducing "workfare" laws, and enacting pension reform. By the same token, once state budgets were brought under control, these criteria justified lowering income and corporate tax rates on the grounds that this was necessary in order to promote domestic savings and investment, as well as to attract foreign investment. Finally, the Single Market Act of 1986 was the driver of widespread privatization and public sector retrenchment throughout the member countries, subjecting formerly public as well as any remaining state-run firms to the rigors of market competition while launching the Europe-wide liberalization of services, in particular finance.

Taken together, these reforms have dramatically eroded the postwar social models of the Western European democracies. They eliminated the skein of protections and benefits that had been secured by workers and their organizational representatives as part of the postwar communitarian social compact. They downgraded the corporatist mechanisms of social concertation and degraded the regulatory frameworks safeguarding the rights of workers and other sectoral actors in the economy. Finally, these reforms marked the abandonment of the stakeholder conception of the firm, in which investment and production decisions were made with longer-term, communitarian as well economic imperatives in mind, in favor of a shareholder model of corporate governance that privileges the maximization of short-term profits over any other consideration. In short, the process of economic integration engaged at the European level since the 1980s has surreptitiously but steadily moved the Western European political economies in a classical liberal—or American—direction that favored growth over security, enrichment over stability.[23]

The social costs of this process have been immense. First and most obviously, it has led to the rapid rise in unemployment and increasingly precarious forms of temporary and part-time employment throughout the EU. The privileging of price stability over reflation by the Bündesbank and then the ECB, large-scale privatizations, and the dismantling of the social and labor market protections afforded workers under the postwar welfare state led to massive layoffs and high unemployment rates which, particularly in Europe's Latin and Southern economies, have yet to abate.[24] Secondly, financial liberalization, the reduction of corporate and income tax rates, and the loosening of regulations on capital in order to encourage private investment and a fall in workers' real wages has presided over a noticeable increase in income and wealth inequality by enabling a rapid transfer of wealth to the EU's richest citizens.[25] Third, there has been a substantial rise of poverty in European states. This is due in part to the persistence of unemployment and the growth of low-paid and precarious employment, and to the evisceration of social safety nets as a result of EU-driven welfare retrenchment. Fourth and finally, this growth of poverty has been accompanied by a corresponding rise in the social pathologies that are linked to it as well as higher crime and incarceration rates.[26]

In turn, these negative indicators linked to the evisceration of the European social model have dramatically worsened since the onset of the European sovereign debt crisis, particularly in the worst-affected deficitary countries on the Eurozone's periphery—the so-called PIIGS.[27] The insistence of EU technocrats and leading member states such as Germany that these countries adopt draconian austerity programs in exchange for assistance effectively stripped their welfare states to the bone, thereby generating levels of unemployment, inequality, and poverty within them that have not been seen since the Great Depression.[28] Such levels of unemployment and impoverishment are clearly politically unsustainable. Unless something is quickly done to arrest the crisis and restore these countries to growth, it is only a matter of time before they experience severe social and political backlashes, revealing a fundamental crisis of democracy within the member states and a progressive delegitimization of the European project as a whole.

Returning to the empirical schema that was established at the outset, it is worthwhile to pause on this crisis of legitimacy that is afflicting Europe and to consider what it means for the future of the EU. As we saw, three types of sociopolitical legitimacy can be applied to a political regime: input, or democratic legitimacy, output or technocratic legitimacy, and ideational or "telos" legitimacy. How do these apply to the two broad stages of European integration—confederal Europe versus federal Europe—that we saw above?

In the case of confederal Europe, with its preservation of the locus of political action within the members states and the "pooling" of their sovereignty in areas deemed not to touch on their vital national interests, only output legitimacy effectively obtained at the European level. Indeed, input legitimacy continued to be situated at the level of the states themselves, while "ideational" legitimacy was bound up in member states' national perceptions of themselves (e.g., Germany reentering the fold of "civilized" democratic nations, France approximating de Gaulle's ideal of national *grandeur*, etc.)

However, as the European states progressively adopted a supranational mode of integration under the auspices of the Single Market and EMU, the categories of legitimacy that were applicable to the EU expanded to include legitimacy in its input and ideational dimensions, as well as output legitimacy. In the case of the former, it is worth noting that, because it lacked a "demos"—that is, a culturally and socially uniform and self-identifying electorate at a European level as existed in the member states—to approve its policies, Europe's federalizing project was stripped, at least in its initial phase, of input legitimacy. In particular, the two primordial norms of accountability and representation that are central to democratic governance were effectively absent from the structures and processes of the Union.[29]

This lack of input legitimacy thus put the onus on "output" and ideational legitimacy to justify the EU's political operation to its citizens. Let us consider each of these in turn.

As we saw, output legitimacy is based on the idea that European integration is 1.) effective (i.e., that it "works" in terms of generating optimally defined policy outcomes), and 2.) that it is politically neutral (i.e., that it is pareto optimal or maximizes the welfare of the greatest number of Europeans, regardless of social or sectoral background.) Accordingly, this conception presumes that both national political elites and EU technocrats know what is best for Europe's people and that, consequently, an alternative model of European integration to the supply-side, ordo-liberal economic federalism advanced under the auspices of the SEA and EMU would have been less economically and socially successful and hence undesirable.[30] For its part, ideational legitimacy derived from the idea that a federal Europe would not only deliver economic efficiency and prosperity, but safeguard the higher ideals of peace and comity within Europe. Thus, Jacques Delors speeches heralding the Single Market and the common currency were rife—much as the Schuman Declaration prior to the establishment of the ECSC—with evocations of the messianic or utopian world-historical character of the European project. Politically, the upshot was that the grandiose ideals driving the establishment of federal Europe rendered worthwhile the short and medium-term economic sacrifices and painful social adjustments it implied. In addition, they justified the foregoing of democratic accountability until a new supranational European political identity could be forged through the processes of functional spillover.[31]

For roughly the first decade and a half of this experiment in creeping European federalism (i.e., 1985 to 2000), this concatenation of output and ideational legitimacy outweighed Europe's lack of input legitimacy or "democratic deficit" in the eyes of both its publics and elites. For many academic observers during this period, Europe could not be judged in the same terms as a national democratic polity due to its unique institutional structure and functionalist progress.[32] However, by the mid-2000s, the pain of adjustment, combined with chronically high unemployment rates across the Eurozone (cushioned somewhat in the peripheral states by the inflationary investment boom that was triggered by the inflow of capital from the surplus countries as interest rates converged across the Eurozone) began to cast doubt on the EU's technocratic legitimacy. The prosperity and jobs promised by national and European leaders as a result of the euro's introduction were not only failing to materialize, but in some cases—Germany comes most notably to mind[33]—social and economic conditions were in fact worsening. Worse, it was increasingly clear that the euro was not an economically and politically neutral project, benefiting as it did employers and investors at the expense of workers and social benefit recipients. This fostered the impression that the

EU governing structures, as well as the political elites in the member states themselves, were the pawns of big business interests who had designed the Single Market and EMU to serve as levers for maximizing their enrichment and global reach at the expense of average workers and citizens.[34]

In turn and correlatively, there has been a progressive erosion of the EU's ideational legitimacy as European economic governance evolved in the 2000s. As unemployment and falling living standards spread across the Eurozone, it became increasingly more difficult to justify the socioeconomic costs of EMU by continuing to appeal to the ideals of intra-European peace and comity. This was especially the case as popular memories of World War II receded into the past and European publics and elites alike were increasingly composed of younger generations of voters and politicians for whom these ideals began to seem increasingly pious and wooly.[35]

By contrast, in these conditions of faltering output and ideational legitimacy the issue of Europe's democratic deficit—that is, lack of input legitimacy—grew increasingly salient among Europe's national electorates. Domestically, anti-EU populist parties emerged as increasingly popular electoral alternatives on both the Far Right and Far Left in a number of European countries. Likewise, there was a growing contestation of European monetary federalism in national referenda held in states across the continent. These included the rejection by Irish voters of the Treaty of Nice in 2001; Danish and Swedish voters' refusal to join the euro in 2000 and 2003; France and the Netherlands' rejection of the draft European Constitutional Treaty in 2005; and the Irish refusal of the Treaty of Lisbon in 2009. In turn, the EU's democratic deficit was further worsened by pro-European national elites' effective overturning of these popular rejections of further European integration either by restaging, as in Ireland with respect to the Nice and Lisbon Treaties, new referenda until these initiatives passed, or, as in the case of France and the Netherlands for the Lisbon Treaty, by pushing through constitutional amendments that rendered possible their approval by parliamentary means contra the *vox populi*. Thus, rather than address the causes of the democratic deficit by instituting more consultative mechanisms that would have given ordinary citizens a greater voice in shaping the course of European policies, these solutions in effect served to further insulate the European policy process from any real democratic input.

Last but not least, the European Parliament failed to live up to the hopes that it would emerge as an authentically representative agent of political and policy debate at the European level. On the contrary, it was held to be too distant from the national loci of political debate and its party groups too removed from domestic partisan competition to be democratically representative of Europe's peoples in any meaningful sense. By the same token, its lack of power in contrast to the Commission limited the Parliament's capacity to serve as a democratic counterweight to the Eurocracy in initiating and overseeing policy. Instead, its role was confined to rubberstamping laws that had been previously agreed by the Commission and the Council so as to give them a supercilious democratic imprimatur. Given this fact, it is not surprising that European elections continued to be run not on European issues, but instead effectively served as "second-order national contests" in which voters pronounced themselves on the performance and programs of the national parties.[36] Thus, combined with the EU's flagging technocratic and ideational legitimacy in the wake of monetary union, this further underscoring of (semi) federal Europe's democratic deficit threatened it with a generalized crisis of legitimacy that could only put its core principles and institutional advances at risk.

It was this generalized crisis of legitimacy that would erupt to the fore with such disastrous economic and political effect when the European sovereign debt crisis broke out in early 2010. The worsening unemployment, inequality and poverty that resulted from the crisis and the counterproductive austerity policies that were imposed by the so-called "Troika" (ECB, European Commission, and the IMF) on crisis-ridden states in order, resolve it critically—even perhaps irreparably—damaged the legitimacy of the European project in its respective technocratic, democratic, and ideational dimensions.

Starting first at the level of output legitimacy, the European sovereign debt crisis and its aftermath have served to highlight the economic imbalances and social costs of the Single Market and EMU. Internally, as we saw the run-up to EMU forced great sacrifices upon future Eurozone members in order to join the single currency, particularly the peripheral countries. These were forced to privatize state services and public firms in order to comply with the dictates of the Single Market while slashing social spending in order to meet the debt-to-deficit and GDP ratios stipulated by the Maastricht Treaty followed by the Stability Pact. In turn, in order to remain competitive under an overvalued euro, which was kept deliberately strong at German insistence, these states were forced to liberalize their product, capital and labor markets, and to adopt supply-side policies—in effect opting for a strategy of "competitive disinflation" or internal devaluation that came at a high cost in terms of unemployment and budgetary retrenchment.

In turn, externally, EMU resulted in serious macroeconomic imbalances within the Eurozone that directly led to the balance-of-payment asymmetries and ensuing asset bubbles in peripheral states that would trigger the European debt crisis in 2010. In the first place, following its establishment in January 1999, EMU provoked a rush of capital flows from core to peripheral countries in order to take advantage of higher yields that were possible in the latter until interest rates equalized across the Eurozone. In turn, this provoked an asset boom in the PIIGS which had an inflationary effect within them, ultimately increasing real wages and reducing these economies' cost competitiveness relative to the core countries, notably Germany. This resulted in growing balance-of-payments asymmetries between the Eurozone's core and periphery which, following the 2008 financial crash, raised financial risk premiums to unsustainable levels in the latter, thereby provoking massive capital flight and setting in motion the European financial crisis that started in Greece in early 2010.[37]

The ensuing economic downturn, itself following on the heels of the recession precipitated by global crisis of 2008, worsened the problem of unemployment in the deficitary countries of the Eurozone. However, what was to follow, that is, the policies that were imposed by the European authorities and the IMF on these countries to resolve the crisis, was arguably even worse. First of all, the draconian austerity programs that were drafted by the Troika under the influence of Germany in exchange for rescuing the most debt-ridden states—Greece, Portugal, Ireland, and Cyprus—further worsened unemployment and poverty within them. These went hand in hand, notably under the External Adjustment Procedure affixed to the Fiscal Compact agreed by the Eurozone's members in November 2011 in order to address external imbalances, with the adoption of supply-side structural reforms that sought to restore the PIIGS' competitiveness through wage and cost deflation.[38] This exacerbated layoffs and the fall in workers' living standards across these countries. In turn, the spending cuts that were imposed under the Fiscal Compact's Excessive Deficit Procedure so as to reduce the PIIGS' national debt and budget deficits—which in the case of Portugal, Ireland, and Spain had exploded as a result of governments assuming unsustainable private debts as a condition of receiving the Troika's financial assistance—eviscerated unemployment benefits and public pensions, thereby deepening poverty and inequality in the Eurozone's periphery.[39] As the PIIGS' economies continued to worsen and their debt to expand under the deflationary effects of these programs, the technocratic competence of Europe's key economic and political authorities—and by extension, of national leaders in the core countries who were pushing for these policies—were increasingly contested by the national publics in the peripheral countries, as well as among a growing number of academic observers and policy experts both within and beyond the Eurozone. Accordingly the EU's output legitimacy found itself seriously impaired.

In turn, the unequal adjustment costs implied by the rescue programs that were put in place by the Troika to either bail out or assist the PIIGS brought into question the EU's political neutrality, the second key condition of its "output" legitimacy. Indeed, it was clear that the costs of the budgetary austerity and structural reforms stipulated in these programs would not be evenly borne across and within the Eurozone member states. Banks and bond holders concentrated mainly in the core countries would be secured against loss, while the slashing of state budgets would hurt pensioners and social benefit recipients in the peripheral countries. Meanwhile, the deflationary impacts of these programs would disproportionately impact workers while benefiting employers in the peripheral states by enhancing their capacity to cut costs and enhance their export competitiveness. Thus, as Fritz Scharpf has observed, though these rescue programs were ostensibly designed to rescue the euro by reassuring the markets of the PIIGS' creditworthiness, their longer term objective was to in fact consummate the neoliberal "process of transforming the 'social market economies' of some EU member states into 'liberal market economies.'"[40] More broadly, both in terms of its differential sectoral and national impacts as well as its ideological motivations, the pretense of political neutrality that undergirded European market and monetary integration in the wake of the Eurozone crisis has grown increasingly untenable. This also severely eroded the output legitimacy that had been so vital to justifying this form of integration to Europe's publics in the 1990s and 2000s.

The profound crisis of output legitimacy affecting on the Eurozone's member states could not but spill over and reinforce the sense of input illegitimacy that has plagued European integration since the mid 1980s. Specifically, once Europe's governing instances resolved to "save the euro at any cost," any pretense of democratic input from Europe's citizens in framing the policies that would be imposed on them to address the crisis went out the window.[41] Citizens in debt ridden countries were given no say in approving the austerity programs that their governments had agreed to impose in exchange for financial assistance. And when their governments either balked at implementing these programs—the Papandreou government in Greece in November 2011—or were subsequently defeated at the ballot box—the Berlusconi government in Italy in October 2011—these were replaced by technocratic caretaker governments—the Papademos government in Greece, the Monti government in Italy—which diligently pursued the Troika's austerity and structural policies, but were never democratically elected.[42]

In turn, whereas in the past the EU's democratic deficit could be offset by the Commission and the Council's procedural efficiency and the promise of greater policymaking autonomy invested in the European Parliament, the experience of the past few years has shown the promise of greater EU-level democratization to be a sham. In fact, the rescue packages that have been enacted in order to save the euro have been resolutely anti-democratic. This has been the case both politically, in terms of denying European publics an effective say in shaping and approving these programs, as well as economically, in terms of disproportionately imposing the burden of adjustment of these programs on workers and on the poor, while largely sparing big business and the wealthy.

Last but not least, the collapse of the EU's input and output legitimacy has put paid to the source of its ideational legitimacy, that is, the idea that it is advancing the cause of European peace and solidarity. For a growing number of voters, this pronouncement is revealed to be increasingly untenable in the face of the draconian adjustment costs that are being imposed on the Eurozone's peripheral societies, not to mention the growing social inequalities that the ordo- and neoliberal policies underlying European economic governance since the 1980s have wrought across the EU as a whole. In turn, the grandiose evocation of Europe as the institutional *sine qua non* for peace is ringing increasingly hollow for ordinary Europeans as they face mounting unemployment, poverty, and inequality—especially as memories of World War II fade into the past. In fact, the ceaseless evocation of the EU's peacemaking vocation by European and national leaders in order to justify the imposition of austerity and structural reforms within the periphery is coming to be seen as an increasingly self-serving and vapid ploy by European voters, thus discrediting Europe's higher normative and symbolic appeal. [43]

This generalized crisis of legitimacy afflicting the EU as a function of the unsupportable economic and social costs of the supply-side and ordo-liberal model of monetary federalism that it has pursued since the 1980s has caused people to fall back on the form of communal organization that historically offered them the most security and protection: the state. In the wake of the Eurozone crisis, people are increasingly turning to the state for assistance as a final preserve against despair and want. Yet, this falling back of Europeans onto the state is taking increasingly disturbing form. At a first level, this communitarian reversion is increasingly occurring in the form of a restrictive, exclusionary nationalism that conflates growing distrust of the EU with a wholesale rejection of foreigners and immigrants. It is captured in the upsurge of radical right-wing parties across Europe who, in addition to the fight against immigration, have made the rejection of Europe their signature issue. [44] The latter has become particularly salient since the eruption of the Eurozone crisis in early 2010, both in the peripheral countries directly affected by the crisis—witness the entry of the neo-Nazi Golden Dawn party in the Greek parliament following the May and June 2012 national elections— as well as in Northern European states increasingly professing bailout fatigue. These notably include the Freedom Party in Austria and the True Finn party in Finland, which became the third largest and principal opposition parties in their countries' parliaments in the 2013 and 2011 elections respectively, as well Geert Wilder's Party of Freedom in the Netherlands, which also won the third highest number of seats in the national parliament in 2010.

In turn, this anti-European *repli identitaire*, fueled by the social and political costs of the austerity policies that were adopted by the EU in exchange for bailing out the peripheral states at the center of the debt crisis, reached a new peak and embraced new forms of populism during the May 2014 European parliamentary elections. Anti-immigrant and anti-EU parties came first in Britain, where the UK Independence Party won 27 percent of the vote, and

France, where the FN secured 25 percent, while in Greece nearly four in ten voters supported Euroskeptic parties, including the victorious far left Syriza party (27 percent) and neo-Nazi Golden Dawn (10 percent.) Meanwhile, in Denmark, the far right Danish People's Party topped the poll with 27 percent of the vote and doubled its representation to the European Parliament to four, while in Spain, the nascent Podemos Party, composed of representatives from the Indignado movement and the hard anti-globalization left, broke the two-party duopoly with 8 percent of the vote, thereby forcing the resignation of Socialist Party leader Alfredo Pérez Rubalcalba. Even Germany, historically the most pro-EU country, saw the anti-euro Alternative for Germany collect 7 percent of the vote while the neo-Nazi National Democratic Party managed to win European parliamentary representation.

In short, up to 30 percent of the seats in the European Parliament are now held by populist and anti-European parties. And though these reflect disparate ideological aims and policy orientations—often as a function of their respective countries' economic position within the EU and Eurozone—their electoral success testifies to the strength of national populist and sovereignist feelings expressed by ordinary Europeans as they are confronted with the neoliberal and monetarist consensus underlying European economic integration and the austerity policies adopted by the EU to salvage the latter in the wake of the debt crisis.[45]

At a second level, in part as a reflection of domestic political pressures but also suggesting the weakening of Europe's confederal structure, we are also witnessing the resurgence of nationalist competition and rivalry *between* states, a phenomenon that has grown more pronounced since the onset of the Eurozone crisis. Firstly, these divisions are evident in the split between northern European states, who profess to be tired of bankrolling the profligacy of their southern partners, and those southern countries who view themselves as victims of the unreasonable demands and antidemocratic dictates of Europe's north.[46] Secondly and of potentially greater concern has been the new particularistic nationalism displayed by Germany vis-à-vis the rest of Europe since the start of the crisis. This is not simply a question of the xenophobic tenor of the country's tabloid press in respect to the Greeks and other southern Europeans. It is also evident in the increasingly highhanded and dismissive character of Germany's European diplomacy. According to one seasoned EU observer, whereas in the past Germany fully embraced European integration and assumed the burdens of European solidarity so as "to reenter the good graces of neighbors, prove Germany civility and reliability, and overcome memories of the Nazi era," the country, particularly in reaction to the Eurozone crisis, has shed the postwar solicitude and restraint it formerly showed its European partners in favor of a far more assertive, even domineering great power politics.[47] For example, its forcing through of the adoption of the "Fiscal Compact"—a more intrusive and restrictive version of the Stability and Growth Pact—during the winter of 2011 despite widespread opposition from other EU members, including France, signaled for this observer "a fundamental shift in [the country's] European outlook . . . from a position that sought to defend German positions and ideas to one which sought to impose German approaches on others."[48]

Notwithstanding the economic spuriousness of its one-size-fits all deflationary prescriptions,[49] Germany's new assertiveness is disturbing because it is likely to disrupt the internal balance of power central to Europe's confederal system of governance. Exemplified in the Franco-German partnership that steered Europe from the beginnings of the EEC through EMU, the two countries had married the effective imperatives of hard command power as Europe's core continental powers with the political legitimacy—or "soft" power—they garnered as representative agents for their partners within the EU.[50] However, the delicate balance that underlay this relationship is threatening to become undone as Germany increasingly seeks a political role that is commensurate with its economic predominance.

Thus, roughly eighty years after they shattered the bases of political and economic liberalism in Europe, the forces of nationalism and populism are on the march in the continent once again. This time, however, they threaten to undo the system of European governance that ensured democratic moderation at home and collaborative restraint abroad, prompting the late Tony Judt to observe, "it is as if the twentieth century never happened."[51]

CONCLUSION

From the foregoing, it is hard to escape the conclusion that the European sovereign debt crisis and its aftermath represent not just an economic but a political tipping point in the history of European integration. The generalized crisis of legitimacy that has overtaken the latter, compounded by the resurgence of nationalism it has provoked both within and across its constituent states, begs the question of where the European project goes from here and, to return to the question posed at the outset, of the nature and extent of its decline. The EU's present institutional make-up, presenting a half-baked economic federalism, appears to have reached the limits of its utility and is no longer sustainable. EU integration is accordingly condemned to either press ahead or else to regress. As Stanley Hoffmann presciently observed as far back as 1966, "Between the cooperation of existing nations and the breaking in of a new one, there is no stable middle ground . . . half-way attempts like supranational functionalism must either snowball or roll back."[52]

In light of Europe's current predicament, three potential alternatives present themselves. These in turn square with the different conceptions of decline which we specified at the outset. The first alternative entails the advance toward full economic and, by extension, political federalism. Implying the establishment of a fiscal union in order to complete monetary union, thereby creating a single economy for the Eurozone, such an arrangement would require ever greater political federalism so as to define common economic policies and legitimate their distributive effects. Realistically, in order to work such an arrangement would have to adopt macroeconomic policies that reflect a balance between the interventionist, coordinated market economies of Europe's southern periphery and the supply-side, ordo-liberal economies of its northern core. [53] Yet, it is not at all clear that such a compromise on macroeconomic policy would be acceptable to Germany, which in exchange for disproportionately assuming the debt of the peripheral countries would doubtless demand its economic and political pound of flesh in return. In effect, what this means is that, should full European economic federalism with its attendant political spillovers come to pass, it will most likely take the form of Germany's own ordo- and neoliberal federal dispensation.

Needless to say, this would pose serious legitimacy problems of its own. At the level of output legitimacy, such a dispensation would perpetuate and aggravate within a federal Europe the macroeconomic imbalances between core and periphery that currently obtain between the Eurozone's northern and southern states. In effect, not everyone could become like Germany and the periphery would be relegated to a secondary economic and political status within a federal Europe, much like Eastern Germany today within the Federal Republic. In turn, at the level of input legitimacy, the continuing lack of a European demos and persistence of atavistic political and cultural differences between Europe's constituent states means that such a federal structure would lack the requisite democratic legitimacy to sustain it. [54] Finally, it is not clear where this tight-fisted, ordo-liberal federalism of German inspiration would get its ideational legitimacy from. Indeed, what universal ideal could be derived from this highly technocratic German vision of Europe, and would it be sufficient to unite such a culturally and temperamentally diverse assemblage of peoples as those comprising the contemporary EU? One is entitled to be skeptical.

In short, due to its own legitimacy shortcomings, a federal Europe constructed along German lines would most likely be economically, politically, and ideologically unsustainable over the long term. Should it come to pass, such a model, at least in this supply-side, ordo-liberal incarnation, would herald the continued decline of European integration, in both absolute and relative terms. Furthermore, it is not clear that once begun, this decline could be staunched and reversed, thereby possibly portending an inexorable—or morbid—process of collapse.

The second alternative facing Europe is the diametrical opposite of federal consolidation: Europe's breakup or dissolution. More likely than not to result from a catastrophic collapse (perhaps as a result of an unsuccessful attempt to federate Europe under either an ordo-liberal or Keynesian guise), such an outcome would effectively deal a death blow to European integration, leaving the European project in ruins. Such an outcome would represent not so much an instance of morbid as of catastrophic decline—the medical equivalent of sudden and generalized organ failure producing the immediate death of the subject, rather than of a long, debilitating, and ultimately fatal illness.

Finally, between these less than felicitous outcomes, a third intermediary alternative might be available to Europe—the return to the looser form of intergovernmental economic and political cooperation that characterized Europe during its opening decades and most recently, in the EMS. Such an arrangement could provide greater flexibility and hence, output effectiveness in absorbing asymmetric shocks and resorbing the macroeconomic imbalances that gave rise to the latter as evidenced in the European sovereign debt crisis.[55] By the same token, since responsibility for overseeing economic policy would revert back to the states, the input legitimacy lacking under Europe's current monetary federalism or a presumptive full economic federalism could be restored.

In short, compared to the two outcomes outlined above, such an alternative presents the "least worst" option. In terms of decline, it might signal a period of absolute and relative decline compared to other large economic regions of the world but, compared to the other alternatives, it would be technically and politically more sustainable over the long run. In addition, contrary to the prospects of morbid or catastrophic decline attending the first two outcomes, a reversion to intergovernmentalism would also offer the eventual promise of recovery and hence of reversing Europe's current trajectory of economic and political decline. Given the economic and political dysfunction into which the continent has fallen, and the generalized crisis of legitimacy it has suffered as a result, this would be no mean achievement.

The problem, however, is that the EU's present institutional configuration makes the reversion to a previous, lesser state of integration extremely difficult to effect in practice. The Lisbon Treaty contains no prescriptions for how to "de-integrate" the Union and step back from the monetary federalism of today to recreate the confederal Europe of yesterday. Indeed, it does not even outline the procedure by which a current Eurozone member might opt out of the euro. More realistically, then, what might be called for is replacing the Lisbon Treaty with a less federalizing, more intergovernmental blueprint for European cooperation. Such a step would require a unanimous vote on the part of the Union's members, however, an outcome that would be far from guaranteed in a Europe of 28 states.

Notwithstanding these institutional and procedural obstacles, this alternative and the limited and temporary decline it presents are surely preferable to the morbid decline of Europe that continued ordo-liberal federalism implies or the catastrophic decline suggested by the Union's sudden breakup. On the contrary, given the national political constraints and economic divergences currently presented by Europe's states, perhaps this more modest but also more durable basis for resuming European integration, with its attendant benefits, is the best outcome one could reasonably hope for.

More broadly, whether the federal or confederal vision triumphs, or indeed if Europe should precipitatedly collapse, the debate over these outcomes serves to illustrate the logical and normative primacy of politics over economics rather than vice-versa. As David Calleo once observed, the economic and political dynamics of the European sovereign debt crisis "help to remind us that economies exist to serve societies, not the other way around."[56] Society and politics must be restored once again to their rightful dominion over economics. Accordingly, the bonds of mutual obligation and protection that had defined the postwar democratic European nation state must be redefined and Europe's governance refurbished to reflect a fundamental reordering of economic and political priorities.

NOTES

1. Joseph S. Nye, "The Changing Nature of World Power," *Political Science Quarterly* 105, no. 2 (1990): 177–192.
2. Joseph Weiler, "In the Face of the Crisis: Input Legitimacy, Output Legitimacy and the Political Messianism of European Integration," *Journal of European Integration* 34, no. 7 (2012): 827.
3. Joseph Weiler, "In the Face of the Crisis," 829–830. Please also see: Fritz Scharpf, *Governing in Europe: Effective and Democratic?* (Oxford: Oxford University Press, 1999).
4. Giandomenico Majone, "The Rise of the Regulatory State in Europe," *West European Politics* 17, no. 3 (1994): 77–101.
5. Joseph Weiler, "In the Face of the Crisis," 832.
6. Michel Winock, *Nationalism, Anti-Semitism and Fascism in France* (Stanford, California: Stanford University Press, 1998).
7. Karl Polanyi, *The Great Transformation* (Boston: Beacon Hill, 1957.)
8. David Calleo, *Rethinking Europe's Future* (Princeton: Century Foundation, 2011), 60–61, 69–72.
9. Friedrich List, *The National System of Political Economy* (New York: Kelley, 1966.)
10. Tony Judt, *Ill Fares the Land* (New York: Penguin: 2010), 52–65.
11. Mette Elstrup-Sangiovanni, "Introduction: Pre-Theories of International Integration," in *Debates on European Integration: A Reader* (New York: Palgrave Macmillan, 2006).
12. Mette Elstrup-Sangiovanni, "Introduction: Pre-Theories of International Integration," in *Debates on European Integration: A Reader* (New York: Palgrave Macmillan, 2006).
13. Ernst B. Haas, *The Uniting of Europe: Political, Social and Economic Forces 1950–1957* (London: Stevens and Sons, 1958), 16.
14. Expressing this point in a press conference from September 1960 devoted to the question of European integration, Charles de Gaulle, the foremost exemplar of the intergovernmentalist position among Europe's postwar political leaders, remarked: "What are the realities of Europe? Where are the pillars on which it can be built? The truth is that those pillars are the states of Europe . . . states each of which, indeed, has its own genius, history and language, its own sorrows, stories and ambitions; but states that are the only entities with the right to give orders and the power to be obeyed." Charles De Gaulle, "A Concert of European States," in

The European Union: Readings on the Theory and Practice of European Integration. eds. B. Nelsen and A. Stubb (Boulder, CO: Lynne Rienner, 1994), 41.

15. Stanley Hoffmann, "Reflections on the Nation-State in Western Europe Today," *Journal of Common Market Studies* 21, no. 1 (1982): 29–30.

16. Once again, to quote de Gaulle from his September 1960 press conference on the matter: "Although it is perfectly natural for the states of Europe to have specialist bodies available to prepare and whenever necessary to follow up their decisions, those decisions must be their own." Charles De Gaulle, "A Concert of European States," 41.

17. Reflecting this conditional approach to European integration, in June 1958, Olivier Wormser, the head of the Directorate of Economic and Financial Affairs at the Quai d'Orsay, sought to convince de Gaulle of the wisdom of France joining the EEC in the short to medium term, but argued that a point would inevitably come when their interests "bifurcated," at which point France should exit the EEC and abandon the Treaty of Rome. See Laurent Warlouzet, *Le choix de la CEE par la France: L'Europe économique en débat de Mendès France à de Gaulle (1955–1969)* (Paris: Comité pour l'Histoire Economique et Financière de la France, 2011), 262.

18. Critiquing the federal vision of Europe that was advocated by Walter Hallstein, the first—German—president of the European Commission, in the early 1960s, de Gaulle averred in his memoirs: "[A]fter meeting him more than once and observing his activities, I felt that although Walter Hallstein was in his way a sincere European, he was first and foremost a German who was ambitious for his own country. For in the Europe that he sought lay the framework in which his country could first of all regain, free of charge, the respectability and equality of rights which the frenzy and defeat of Hitler had cost it, then acquire the preponder-ant influence which its economic strength would no doubt earn it, and finally ensure that the cause of its frontiers and its unity was backed by a powerful coalition . . . These factors did not alter my esteem and regard for Walter Halstein, but the goals I was pursuing on behalf of France were incompatible with such projects." Charles De Gaulle, "A Concert of European States," 36.

19. Calleo, *Rethinking Europe's Future*, 139.

20. Calleo, *Rethinking Europe's Future*, 141.

21. Jonah Levy, "Redeploying the State: Liberalization and Social Policy in France," in *Beyond Continuity: Institutional Change in Advanced Political Economies*, ed. W. Streeck and K. Thelen (New York: Oxford University Press, 2005), pp. 103–126. Although Levy limits his analysis to the French case, his argument broadly applies to the other continental European coordinated market economies as well.

22. Objections to this argument often note that the persistence of some of the specific institutional attributes of the European social model across European countries disprove its implication of a convergence between the continental European and American/Anglo-Saxon political economies. However, it can be shown that though they continue to give European economies their specificity in a formal sense, these institutions—such as co-determination in Germany, or branch-level collective contracts in France—have seen their protective or regula-tive function either bypassed or diminished by the adoption of new, often *ad hoc* measures with the unstated but clear goal of removing impediments to market efficiency. Likewise, the similar impacts of the 2008-2009 financial crash in Europe and the United States and the common systemic risk it posed on both sides of the Atlantic underscore the extent to which the European political economies reformed themselves along Anglo-Saxon lines, in this instance in the area of corporate governance and financing, with many of their own banks having internalized the risky, profit-seeking culture of Wall Street in their lending and leveraging practices. Chris Howell, "The Dilemmas of Post-Fordism: Socialists, Flexibility, and Labor Market Deregula-tion in France." *Politics and Society* 20(1) (1992), 71–99; Anke Hassel, "The Erosion of the German System of Industrial Relations," *British Journal of Industrial Relations* 37, no. 3 (2009): 493–495, and Michael Lewis, "It's the Economy Dumpkopf!" *Vanity Fair*. September 2011. Available from http://www.vanityfair.com/business/features/2011/09/europe-201109.

23. Unemployment for the 9 EEC members, which was under 5 percent in 1980, increased to 8.1 percent in 1990 (EU15) and peaked at 10.5 percent in 1994, before falling to a new low of 7.4 percent in 2001. Since then, the Eurozone's unemployment rate rose to a new high of 12.0 percent in March 2013 before declining to 11.5 percent in July 2014. Even in countries

such as Germany in which unemployment has substantially fallen since undertaking pro-market reforms, this has been accompanied by a substantial transfer of value-added away from labor toward capital so that, despite the country registering robust economic growth since the mid-2000s and successfully weathering the shock of the 2008-2009 financial crisis, German workers have seen their real wages stagnate or even fall. See: 1) U.S. Department of Labor, "Unemployment rates in the European Union and Selected Member Countries Civilian Labor Force Basis (1), Seasonally Adjusted, 1990-2004." October 9, 2004. Online at: http://digitalcommons.ilr.cornell.edu/key_workplace/.

24. Unemployment for the 9 EEC members, which was under 5 percent in 1980, increased to 8.1 percent in 1990 (EU15), and peaked at 10.5 percent in 1994, before falling to a new low of 7.4 percent in 2001. Since then the Eurozone's unemployment rate rose to a new high of 12.0 percent in March 2013 before declining to 11.5 percent in July 2014. Even in countries such as Germany in which unemployment has substantially fallen since undertaking pro-market reforms this has been accompanied by a substantial transfer of value-added away from labor towards capital so that, despite the country registering robust economic growth since the mid-2000s. See U.S. Department of Labor, "Unemployment Rates in their European Union and Selected Member Countries Basis (1), Seasonally Adjusted1980–2004" October 9 2004. Available from http://digitalcommons.ilr.cornell.edu/key.workplace/67 and Eurostat, "Unemployment Statistics." August 28, 2014. Available online at: http://epp.eurostat.ec.europa.eu/statistics_explained/index.php/ Unemployment_statistics; Markus Grabka *Entwicklung der Einkommens und Vermögensverteilung in Deutschland.* (Berlin: Friedrich Ebert Stiftung 2008.) Available from: http://www.fes.de/wiso/pdf/ verbraucher/2008/190608/grabka.pdf, and Markus Dettmer and Dietmar Hawranek, "Letter from Berlin: Despite Boom, Little Hope of Big Pay Hikes in Germany," *Der Spiegel* [online]. September 8, 2010. Available from: http://www.spiegel.de/international/business/letter-from-berlin-despite-boom-little-hope-of-big-pay-hikes-in-germany-a-716376.html.

25. For the EEC/EU15 as a whole, the Gini coefficient, the standard measure of inequality, has increased from 28.8 in 1985–1990 to 30.5 in 2010 (compared to 30.1 to 38.6 for the U.S.) However, this broader trend masks significantly greater increases in certain countries, which can be attributed in part to the unequal impact of European economic integration. Thus, the three countries which saw the biggest jumps in inequality were Sweden (from 19.7 to 24.1), the UK (from 27.0 to 32.9), and, perhaps most surprisingly, Germany (from 24.4 to 29.3). See A.B. Atkinson, "Income Distribution in Europe and the United States," *Oxford Review of Economic Policy* 12, no.1 (1996), 20. Please also see: Eurostat, "Tables, Graphs and Maps: Gini coefficient (Source: SLC.)" September 20, 2012. http://epp.eurostat.ec.europa.eu/tgm/table.do?tab=table&init=1&plugin=1&language=en&pcode=tessi190, and Francesca Bastagli et al., "Income Inequality and Fiscal Policy," *IMF Staff Discussion Note.* June 28, 2012, p. 20. Available from http://www.imf.org/ external/pubs/ft/sdn/2012/sdn1208.pdf.

26. In this last respect, continental European societies, though not yet exhibiting the levels of inequality, crime, and incarceration of the United States and UK, have displayed a worsening secular trend in regard to these indicators which in turn tracks fairly closely with the liberalizing course engaged by these states from the 1980's on. Thus, from 1990 to 2007 Austria saw its prison population increase from 82 to 108 per 100,000 people, Belgium from 66 to 101, France from 82 to 100, Germany from 82 to 90, the Netherlands from 44 to 115, and Sweden from 58 to 75. This compares to a jump of 90 to 148 per 100,000 people for the UK (England and Wales) and 297 to 506 for the U.S., which presents the highest incarceration rate in the world. Council of Europe, "Detention rate per 100,000 population on 1 September: 1990–1997," *European Sourcebook of Crime and Criminal Justice Statistics—1999* (Strasbourg: Council of Europe, 1999). Available from: http://www. europeansourcebook.org/chapter_4/4b1.pdf; and in *European Sourcebook of Crime and Criminal Justice Statistics—2010* (Strasbourg: Council of Europe, 2010), 295, and Department of Justice: Bureau of Justice Statistics, "Incarceration rate, 1980–2009." December 21, 2010. Available from http://bjs.ojp.usdoj.gov/content/glance/tables/incrttab.cfm.

27. This unfortunate—and one suspects, not accidental—acronym stands for Portugal, Ireland, Italy, Greece, and Spain.

28. In Greece and Spain, the two worst-hit Eurozone economies, the unemployment rate reached 26.7 percent and 25.3 percent in January 2014. Meanwhile, youth unemployment in both countries hit catastrophic levels of 56.8 percent for Greece and 53.9 percent for Spain. Eurostat, "March 2014 Euro area unemployment rate at 11.8 percent." Available from: http://csdle.lex.unict.it/Archive/LW/Press percent20releases/EUROSTAT percent20press percent20releases/20140506-092807_2014_70pdf.pdf.

29. Weiler, "In the Face of Crisis," 829–30.

30. Fritz Scharpf, *Governing in Europe: Effective and Democratic?* (Oxford: Oxford University Press, 1999).

31. Jacques Delors, "A Necessary Union," in *The European Union*, 51–64; Weiler, "Crisis," 833–37.

32. Andrew Moravcsik and Andrea Sangiovanni, "On Democracy and the 'Public Interest' in the European Union," *Center for European Studies Working Paper* No. 93 (2003). Available from: http://aei.pitt.edu/9135/1/MoravcsikSangiovanni93.pdf. It is important not to overstate this point, however. Quite early on, the issue of Europe's democratic deficit became a subject of contestation and debate in national politics. For example, as the slender passage of the Maastricht Referendum in France in September 1992 suggested, the EU's technocratic supremacy was not universally taken for granted and the monetarist and supply-side template for integration it pursued was not universally approved. Broadly speaking, however, the technocratic argument that the EU's publics would be ultimately better off with the Single Market and EMU than without them and that, following the initial sacrifices, particularly in the peripheral countries that had to make "heroic" efforts in order to meet the monetary and budgetary criteria of EMU, those sacrifices were worth it, was generally accepted. See: Fritz Scharpf, "Monetary Union, Fiscal Crisis and the Preemption of Democracy," *MPIfG Discussion Paper* 11, no. 11 (2011): 6–13.

33. Aggregate German unemployment peaked at 12.1 percent in February 2005, surging in the formerly Communist East to 20.5 percent. Luke Harding, "German jobless rate soars to 70-year high," *Guardian* [online.] February 3, 2005. Available from: http://www.theguardian.com/world/2005/feb/03/germany.lukeharding.

34. In this connection, despite arguments that Europe's coordinated market economies had managed to safeguard stakeholder values by preserving their corporatist systems of interest intermediation, a number of studies have shown that a U.S.-style, "winner-take-all" pluralist model of interest intermediation has effectively emerged at the European level by which the most economically powerful corporate actors are able to play an increasingly preponderant role in shaping public policy. According to a study carried out by the European Commission, in 1985 there were 583 business and employer associations operating at the European level versus 112 representing the interests of workers, artisans, professionals, and consumers combined. By October 31, 2013, these respective shares had grown to 2,668 in the case of the former versus 304 in the case of the latter—underscoring the massive disproportion in the lobbying clout of business versus employee associations within the EU. See: Philippe Schmitter and Wolfgang Streeck, "Organized Interests and the Europe of 1992," in *The European Union*, 176 and Joint Transparency Register Secretariat of the European Parliament and European Commission. *Annual Report on the Operations of the Transparency Register 2013.* (Brussels: European Union, 2013), 14.

35. Weiler, "Crisis," 836–7.

36. Simon Hix, "The Study of the European Union II: The 'New Governance' Agenda and its Rival," in *Debates on European Integration*, 353.

37. Erik Jones and Gregory Fuller, "Europe and the Global Economic Crisis," *Europe Today: A Twenty-First Century Introduction*. 5th ed. ed. R. Tiersky and E. Jones (New York: Rowman and Littlefield, 2014), 346–9, and Fritz Scharpf, "Political Legitimacy in a Nonoptimal Currency Area," *MPIfG Discussion Paper* 13, no. 15 (2013): 3–6.

38. Scharpf, "Political Union," 11–12.

39. Scharpf, "Monetary Union" 32.

40. Scharpf, "Monetary Union," 36.

41. Fritz Scharpf, "Political Legitimacy," 7.

42. Matthias Matthijs, "Mediterranean Blues: The Crisis in Southern Europe," *Journal of Democracy* 25, no. 1 (2014): 110–11.

43. Citing various iterations of this argument as it was advanced by its defenders at different stages of the European integration process, Marine Le Pen, leader of the Europhobe Front National in France, conveyed this point in the following terms: "Let us remember the manner in which the European project was sold to us as a force for modernization, for comity among [Europe's] peoples and of prosperity. . . . We were told that only stubborn nationalists and primitive populists could be stupid enough not to see that these European advances constituted 'the three keys of the future: the single currency, which would mean less unemployment and more prosperity; the common foreign policy, which would mean less dependence and more security; and [European] citizenship, which would mean less bureaucracy and more democracy!'. . . By contemplating voting no to the euro, did not French voters see that they would be 'giving a wonderful present if not to Hitler, then at least to Bismarck,' that they could possibly 'rekindle war in the Balkans,' or that they would be responsible 'for the worst catastrophe since the disasters occasioned by Hitler's arrival to power?' . . . The victory of the no would imply 'a general disaster and an epidemic of populism that would sweep away everything in its path, the European project, enlargement, the elites, capitalist regulation, reformism, internationalism, even generosity itself.'" *Pour que vive la France* (Paris: Grancher, 2012), 12–14.

44. The Front National is a case in point. Presenting the FN as the principal bulwark against EU-led globalization as well as against immigration, party leader Marine Le Pen garnered a record 18 percent of the vote in the first round of the 2012 presidential election. When this result is combined with the 11 percent polled by the far left *Parti de gauche*, we surmise nearly one Frenchmen out of three cast their vote in favor of explicitly anti-EU parties in the first round of the presidential election.

45. For a recap of the 2014 European election results and their political implications, see *The Economist*, 411(8889) (May 31 2014), 12–47.

46. Perhaps the most strident expression of this sentiment was the comparison of Chancellor Angela Merkel to Hitler and of present-day Germany to its Nazi precursor in the Greek media following her insistence that Greece adopt a draconian austerity program in exchange for EU assistance in meeting its debt payments.

47. George Ross, *The European Union and its Crises: Through the Eyes of the Brussels Elite* (New York: Palgrave, 2011), 155.

48. George Ross, *The European Union and its Crises: Through the Eyes of the Brussels Elite* (New York: Palgrave, 2011).

49. See Matthias Matthijs and Mark Blyth, "The World Waits for Germany," *Foreign Affairs* [online], June 8 2012. Available from: http://www.foreignaffairs.com/articles/137697/mark-blyth-and-matthias-matthijs/the-world-waits-for Germany, accessed June 20, 2012, and Adam Tooze, "Germany's Unsustainable Growth," *Foreign Affairs* 91 (5) (2012), pp. 23–30.

50. Calleo, *Rethinking Europe's Future*, 141.

51. Tony Judt, *Ill Fares the Land*, 193.

52. Stanley Hoffman, "Obstinate or Obsolete? The Fate of the Nation-State and the Case of Western Europe," in *Debates on European Integration: A Reader* (New York: Palgrave Macmillan, 2006), 157.

53. It is such a dispensation, with a decidedly stronger emphasis placed on the former type of policy regime, that currently animates European federalists on the Left for example. Jürgen Habermas, *The Crisis of the European Union: A Response* (London: Polity Press, 2011).

54. A particularly fashionable prescription according to which a EU-level federal democracy was envisioned was in the form of a "consociational regime" that would seek to defuse national-cultural cleavages by institutionally empowering competing minorities within the political system in ways that would force their consensual entente and rule. However, as Fritz Scharpf has noted, the linking of the fallout from the European sovereign debt crisis and the policies designed to address it with the vital economic and political interests of the various national players would be likely to impede the kind of elite consensus necessary for such a consociational arrangement to function. This makes the emergence of a Europe-level federal democracy increasingly unlikely and conversely, the backsliding of European integration increasingly probable. "Political Legitimacy," 27–28.

108   *Gabriel Goodliffe*

55. See Scharpf, "Monetary Union," 34.
56. David P. Calleo, "American Decline Revisited," *Survival* 52, no. 4 (2010): 215. "Reflections on the Idea of the Nation State," in *Nationalism and Nationalities in the New Europe*. ed. C. Kupchan. (Ithaca NY: Cornell University Press, 1995), 36.

BIBLIOGRAPHY

Atkinson, A.B. "Income Distribution in Europe and the United States." *Oxford Review of Economic Policy* 12, no.1 (1996).
Bastagli, Francesca. "Income Inequality and Fiscal Policy." *IMF Staff Discussion Note*. June 28, 2012. Available from: http://www.imf.org/ external/pubs/ft/sdn/2012/sdn1208.pdf.
Calleo, David P. "American Decline Revisited." *Survival* 52, no. 4 (2010): 215-227.
Calleo, David P. *Rethinking Europe's Future*. Princeton: Century Foundation, 2011.
De Gaulle, Charles. "A Concert of European States," in *The European Union: Readings on the Theory and Practice of European Integration*. Boulder, CO: Lynne Rienner, 1994.
Dettmer, Markus and Dietmar Hawranek. "Letter from Berlin: Despite Boom, Little Hope of Big Pay Hikes in Germany." *Der Spiegel* [online]. September 8, 2010.
Elstrup-Sangiovanni, Mette. "Introduction: Pre-Theories of International Integration." In *Debates on European Integration: A Reader*. New York: Palgrave Macmillan, 2006.
Haas, Ernst B. *The Uniting of Europe: Political, Social and Economic Forces 1950-1957*. London: Stevens and Sons, 1958.
Habermas, Jürgen. *The Crisis of the European Union: A Response*. London: Polity Press, 2011.
Hassel, Anke. "The Erosion of the German System of Industrial Relations." *British Journal of Industrial Relations* 37, no. 3 (2009): 493-495.
Hoffmann, Stanley. "Reflections on the Nation-State in Western Europe Today." *Journal of Common Market Studies* 21, no. 1 (1982): 29-30.
Hoffman, Stanley. "Obstinate or Obsolete? The Fate of the Nation-State and the Case of Western Europe." In *Debates on European Integration: A Reader*. New York: Palgrave Macmillan, 2006.
Howell, Chris. "The Dilemmas of Post-Fordism: Socialists, Flexibility, and Labor Market Deregulation in France." *Politics and Society* 20, no. 1 (1992): 71-99
Jones, Erik and Gregory Fuller. "Europe and the Global Economic Crisis." *Europe Today: A Twenty-First Century Introduction*. New York: Rowman and Littlefield, 2014.
Judt, Tony. *Ill Fares the Land*. New York: Penguin: 2010.
Levy, Jonah. "Redeploying the State: Liberalization and Social Policy in France," in *Beyond Continuity: Institutional Change in Advanced Political Economies*, ed. W. Streeck and K. Thelen (New York: Oxford University Press, 2005).
List, Friedrich. *The National System of Political Economy*. New York: Kelley, 1966.
Majone, Giandomenico. "The Rise of the Regulatory State in Europe." *West European Politics* 17, no. 3 (1994): 77-101.
Matthijs, Matthias and Mark Blyth. "The World Waits for Germany." *Foreign Affairs*, June 8 2012. Available from: http://www.foreignaffairs.com/articles/137697/mark-blyth-and-matthias-matthijs/the-world-waits-for Germany.
Matthijs, Matthias. "Mediterranean Blues: The Crisis in Southern Europe." *Journal of Democracy* 25, no. 1 (2014): 110-111.
Moravcsik, Andrew and Andrea Sangiovanni, "On Democracy and the 'Public Interest' in the European Union." *Center for European Studies Working Paper* No. 93 (2003).
Nye, Joseph S. "The Changing Nature of World Power." *Political Science Quarterly* 105, no.2 (1990): 177-192.
Polanyi, Karl. *The Great Transformation* (Boston: Beacon Hill, 1957.)
Ross, George. *The European Union and its Crises: Through the Eyes of the Brussels Elite*. New York: Palgrave, 2011.
Scharpf, Fritz. "Monetary Union, Fiscal Crisis and the Preemption of Democracy." *MPIFG Discussion Paper* 11, no. 11 (2011): 6-13.

Scharpf, Fritz. *Governing in Europe: Effective and Democratic?* Oxford: Oxford University Press, 1999.

Scharpf, Fritz. "Political Legitimacy in a Non-optimal Currency Area" *MPIFG Discussion Paper* 13, no. 15 (2013): 3-6.

Tooze, Adam. "Germany's Unsustainable Growth." *Foreign Affairs* 91, no. 5 (2012): 23–30.

Warlouzet, Laurent. *Le choix de la CEE par la France: L'Europe économique en débat de Mendès France à de Gaulle (1955-1969).* Paris: Comité pour l'Histoire Economique et Financière de la France, 2011.

Weiler, Joseph. "In the Face of the Crisis: Input Legitimacy, Output Legitimacy and the Political Messianism of European Integration." *Journal of European Integration* 34, no. 7 (2012).

Winock, Michel. *Nationalism, Anti-Semitism and Fascism in France.* Stanford, California: Stanford University Press, 1998.

II

National Studies of Decline

Chapter Six

Obama's America and the Question of Decline

Dana H. Allin

Ronald Reagan was a lucky president. He entered the White House in an era of American turmoil, exhaustion, and palpable malaise. The country had been humiliated by Iranian revolutionaries who held American diplomats hostage in their own embassy for 444 days. The economy had a suffered a new demoralizing mix of high inflation and high unemployment, at least in part a legacy of the Vietnam war's deficit financing and consecutive oil-price shocks. After a period of détente, U.S.-Soviet confrontation had entered a very serious "second Cold War."

Reagan was lucky because, in the course of his administration, all of these problems corrected themselves for reasons only partly related to his policies. The hostage crisis was resolved through negotiations between the Carter administration and the Islamic Republic of Iran, facilitated by the government of Algeria (though, in a final insult to Carter, the Iranians delayed the hostages' release until the precise moment of Reagan's inauguration). Inflation was defeated because Paul Volker, a Carter appointee as chairman of the Fed, engineered a painful recession that lasted into the second year of Reagan's presidency. The subsequent recovery was perhaps boosted by the Keynesian effects of Reagan's increased defense spending (which also started under Carter) and tax cuts. The supply-side theory that the tax cuts would pay for themselves by encouraging investment proved as ridiculous as it sounds—when Reagan left office he bequeathed the country large structural budget deficits. However, the underlying economy was strong enough that when Presidents George H. W. Bush and Bill Clinton reversed Reagan's fiscal policies, cutting defense and raising taxes, there were large budget surpluses by the end of Clinton's second term. Finally, the Cold War rapidly unwound when a new Soviet General Secretary, Mikhail Gorbachev, launched radical reform at home and conciliatory diplomacy abroad. Reagan reacted with wisdom and skill when he embraced Gorbachev's radicalism, rather than distrusting it as many in his administration advised. The notion that Reagan's early hardline policies actually produced the Gorbachev moment does not withstand historical scrutiny.[1] The rapid dismantlement of Soviet state and empire was an historic surprise of such magnitude as to render moot the question of whether America's increased war footing would be sustainable. The end of the Soviet Union made Clinton's surpluses possible.

In any event, good things happened on Reagan's watch and soon thereafter, and he was able to take credit for them in ways that set the parameters of American political debate for the next generation. A generation—exactly 20 years—after Reagan left office, Barack Obama entered the White House hoping to move those political parameters to the left precisely as Reagan had moved them to the right. Obama was quite explicit about this: before becoming president he spoke and wrote admiringly about Reagan's achievement.[2]

To emulate that achievement, Obama needed some of Reagan's luck. Instead, he was inaugurated in the vortex of financial and economic catastrophe, and the extreme radicalization of the Republican opposition created conditions of political paralysis for much of his presidency.[3] Nonetheless, after six wearying years of economic and political crisis, Obama in his 2015 State of the Union address to Congress looked and sounded like he had finally gotten lucky. "We are 15 years into this new century," the President began.

> Fifteen years that dawned with terror touching our shores; that unfolded with a new generation fighting two long and costly wars; that saw a vicious recession spread across our nation and the world. It has been, and still is, a hard time for many. But tonight, we turn the page. Tonight, after a breakthrough year for America, our economy is growing and creating jobs at the fastest pace since 1999. Our unemployment rate is now lower than it was before the financial crisis.[4]

As Obama spoke, that unemployment was 5.6 percent. Mitt Romney, when he ran for president in 2012, promised that if elected he would bring the unemployment down to 6 percent by the end of his first term—that is, two years from now. And he almost certainly would have succeeded. Had he done so, he would have vindicated conservative policies on spending, taxation, and regulation that, in truth, had little or nothing to do with causing economic recovery.

This is not to imply that Obama deserves no credit for America's recovery. The huge stimulus package that he marshalled through a Congress that was controlled by Democrats in his first two years, government rescue packages for financial institutions and auto makers, financial regulation to curb the excesses that led to the crash, the extension of some middle-class tax cuts that he was able to get through a Republican House of Representatives without extending Bush era cuts for the very rich—these and other measures were sensible policies that, together with very aggressive monetary loosening from the Fed, have quite possibly saved America from the deflationary conditions that have produced a lost decade in Europe.[5] But Obama's main achievement was in not thwarting a recovery that was overdue anyway. Budget deficits have gone way down, but reducing them faster would have had that bad effect. In the long run, in order to be as lucky as Reagan, and to leave a legacy of confidence and growth, it would seem that Obama and his successor need the gift of a relatively benign international environment, such as Reagan and his successor suddenly were handed at the end of the 1980s. To understand Obama's America and the question of decline, we must assess that environment.

OVERSTRETCHED?

At a September 2014 IISS conference in Oslo, Chinese businessman Eric Li cast Chinese claims for a revised Asia-Pacific order in terms that seemed both reasonable and inevitable. The world order set up after the Second World War, in large part through the exertions of the United States, was not a bad one, but it was set up without the participation of China, and now that China has arrived at a stage of much greater wealth and considerably greater power, its demand for a larger share of the pie was simply in the nature of things. The only real question was whether China has the clout to achieve this larger share, and Li's answer was yes:

> The United States is, of course, much more powerful than China in all respects, but it is not when considering the sizes of their respective objects at the moment. China's objectives in Asia are modest, relative to its national capabilities. It is punching below its weight. America's objectives in the world are enormous, compared to its national capabilities and the internal problems it faces. It is punching above its weight.[6]

Li's performance was impressive, not least because he was articulating nationalist, unsettling, and potentially dangerous claims in the most reasonable tones. But his core analysis of America's intrinsic over-extension—and the opportunities this presents to rising powers like China—was persuasive. Whether the United States is in a condition of resurgence or decline at any given moment, it seems undeniable that its responsibilities, ambitions, and pretensions in the global order make it difficult for the U.S. leadership to set priorities and adequately attend to the domestic sources of American strength.

There is no reason to doubt the sincerity of President Barack Obama's repeated assertions that American decline is a "myth," or that the United States is an "exceptional" nation with exceptional global responsibilities. Still, the past six years have amply demonstrated that the president's core strategic instincts favor restraint (if not retrenchment), and that these instincts derive from a keen understanding of the chronic overstretch that Li expressed so succinctly. From his December 2009 West Point speech to his policies in Syria, Obama has shown in words and action his belief that the central mistake of the past decade consisted in strategic over-commitment and military entanglement.

"Don't do stupid stuff" (if "stuff" is the word he used) may not inspire, but it still seems a sensible prescription for avoiding more self-inflicted wounds after the reckless wars of the George W. Bush era. And yet—Obama becomes the fourth president in succession to order military action in Iraq, and he has now extended that action to Syria. Is it simply impossible to orchestrate a managed retrenchment from what was rightly seen as debilitating overextension? Grappling with this question requires attention to three considerations. Firstly, what is the reasonable balance of domestic and foreign responsibility? In insisting that the latter should not crowd out the former, Obama has been attentive to what John F. Kennedy called "the substance" rather than "the shadow" of power.[7] But working on the substance has been difficult, to put it mildly, in an American political context where the conservative minority rejects the very legitimacy of his presidency.

Secondly, how have Obama's efforts at retrenchment and restraint fit with previous efforts to avoid being drawn into military commitments? Dwight Eisenhower in regard to Suez and Hungary; Kennedy's Bay of Pigs and Cuban Missile Crisis (and, arguably, his determination to avoid a ground war in Vietnam); even Ronald Reagan after the Marine barracks bombings in Lebanon—these and other examples show that Obama's restraint can only be considered radical in the context of the George W. Bush wars of the preceding decade.

Third, and most problematic: prior efforts at restraint did not, in the end, work out very well. Kennedy, whatever his own instincts, did lay the basis for escalation in Vietnam (not to mention a counterproductive 60-year embargo of Cuba). The Reagan administration's hyper-realist, if not cynical, strategy of supporting Ba'athist Iraq against revolutionary Iran did not preserve the United States from grave moral compromise, nor did it provide a stability that saved Reagan's successors from the commitment of air power, collective economic punishment, ground wars, and disastrous occupation in Iraq. Over recent months, Obama has genuinely confronted the choice between allowing genocide or deploying military force. His decision for using but also circumscribing air power seems necessary but also fraught with future problems. The strategic and moral commitments of American power remain extensive and, arguably, debilitating.

The lines between domestic vitality and foreign exhaustion are complex and disputed. It seems evident, however, that chronic over-commitment must, over time, degrade the domestic political economy.[8] Osama bin Laden certainly thought so, seeing 9/11 as part of a plan to exhaust and bankrupt the United States. His formative experience had been organizing support for and fighting in the anti-Soviet resistance in Afghanistan. "We, alongside the mujahedin, bled Russia for ten years, until it went bankrupt," he would claim in a 2004 video. "So we are continuing this policy in bleeding America to the point of bankruptcy."[9]

He did not succeed: America was not bankrupt and was able in the end to kill its tormentor and degrade his terrorist organization. So bin Laden's strategy was based on a highly exaggerated view of American weaknesses. One must concede, however, that he was shrewd about the national psychology that would compel the United States to expend vast treasure and blood in reaction to the attacks on New York and Washington. The American reaction to September 11 also destroyed or blighted hundreds of thousands of lives in Iraq and Afghanistan while degrading America's moral reputation at Abu Ghraib and Guantanamo. In broader strategic terms, the United States was weakened as it was drawn into land wars in the Middle East and South-Central Asia.[10]

The economic costs were also immense. The Iraq war and the Afghanistan war, together with upgrades to general counter-terrorism and homeland security, have cost trillions over the past decade and a half.[11] There arguably were also huge indirect costs stemming, as Ezra Klein has written, from the Federal Reserve's decision to cut interest rates to counter both a possible "fear-induced recession" as well as high oil prices after the Iraq invasion. "That decade of loose monetary policy may well have contributed to the credit bubble that crashed the economy in 2007 and 2008."[12]

It is worth dwelling on this for a moment, precisely because further U.S. wars in the Middle East would almost certainly rely on deficit financing, like the Bush wars. Robert Skidelsky, drawing on the work of David Calleo, is among the economic writers who have drawn a connection between the financial crash of 2008 and foreign-financed chronic deficits that have "enabled the US government to live beyond its means, by getting other countries to finance its imperial pretensions."[13] The link to America's strategic role is convincing, according to Skidelsky, if one is "clear about the causal mechanisms by which "surplus Chinese saving" became "excessive American spending." Evidently, the Americans didn't directly spend Chinese savings. Instead, the dollars paid to Chinese exporters were lent to and used by the

Chinese central bank to purchase U.S. treasury bills. This operation had the dual effect of "sterilizing" China's dollar inflow—thus keeping the renmin-bi's exchange-rate low—and allowing the U.S. government to borrow vast sums without "crowding out" lending and spending at home. So it was that "Chinese savings made it possible for the U.S. consumer to go on a spending spree. This explanation brings out the role of the U.S. fiscal deficit in precipi-tating the financial meltdown." [14]

It could be argued, of course, that these systemic imbalances were better than any alternative. One such argument held that, in the face of a massive East Asian propensity to save, American spending staved off global defla-tion: the United States served in this period as "borrower and spender of last resort," as Martin Wolf has put it. [15] But, for the imbalances to be sustainable, the system somehow needed to recycle Chinese savings into productive U.S. investments, rather than a manic bidding up of house prices. A second argu-ment, as expressed by Klein above, would posit expansive credit as prefer-able to letting the 9/11 attacks cause a "fear-induced recession."

More was financed, however, than just a recovery from panic. Skidelsky has suggested that American conservatives ignored the fiscal side of Bush-era easy money "no doubt because they believed the deficits were incurred in the worthy cause of the 'war on terror.'" [16] Bill Emmott, the former Editor of *The Economist*, has gone further. Like Skidelsky, Emmott believes that the wars bin Laden provoked were a direct cause of the 2008 crash—both in the direct costs they incurred and in the wider mind-set they inspired. "Think of the psychology," Emmott writes:

> If Mr. Greenspan was so ideologically determined to keep his hands off the markets, why did he raise rates six times to burst the dotcom bubble in 1999? Why after 2001, by contrast, did he keep pumping in credit to housing and banks, even as another bubble formed? Why did fiscal policy under the presi-dency of George W. Bush, a supposed conservative (compassionate or other-wise) also turn expansionary, with spending soaring and taxes cut? Why, in the run-up to the 2005 election did Tony Blair and Mr. Brown keep up their spending splurge on health and education? The answer is simple. There was a war on, or rather two wars, not even counting the vague one on terror. At such times the inclination to risk an economic slowdown or new recession dimin-ishes: after 9/11, President Bush said that Americans should do the patriotic thing and go out spending again. [17]

This argument relies on some hypothetical assumptions. Yet Emmott is clearly onto an important insight regarding the psychology of the American political class in relation to America's world role. That class is unlikely to concede that the role of world policeman requires an explicit trade-off against Americans' living standards. The Johnson administration was not willing to propose such a trade-off to pay for the Vietnam War, and the

George W. Bush administration was unwilling to do so regarding Iraq. Future presidents are unlikely to propose taxing Americans adequately for such adventures as a major intervention in Syria's civil war.

Barack Obama entered office articulating a clear understanding that domestic economic stability required an acceptance of limits on strategic commitments abroad. Since the possibility of another great depression was the primary threat of his early months in office, Obama took many opportunities to draw this connection. One of the most specific came at the end of his first year, in December 2009, when he spoke to U.S. military cadets at West Point. "Over the past few years," said the president in clear reference to his predecessor, "[we've] failed to appreciate the connection between our national security and our economy." Obama was announcing an escalation—a "surge"—of 30,000 more troops to fight the war in Afghanistan. But he was at the same time taking great care to delineate the limits of America's commitment to that country, dictated by competing interests and limited resources.

> As President, I refuse to set goals that go beyond our responsibility, our means, or our interests. And I must weigh all of the challenges that our nation faces. I don't have the luxury of committing to just one. Indeed, I'm mindful of the words of President Eisenhower, who—in discussing our national security—said, "Each proposal must be weighed in the light of a broader consideration: the need to maintain balance in and among national programs."[18]

Obviously, if the administration has failed to make any progress on the problems that have ailed America's domestic political economy, then foreign-policy restraint will have served limited purpose. But the administration has not failed domestically. In June 2014, *New York Magazine* writer Jonathan Chait posted on his blog a piece with the following headline: "Obama Promised to Do 4 Big Things as President. Now He's Done Them All."[19] In the piece, Chait supplied the following quote from the president's first inaugural address: "Homes have been lost, jobs shed, business shuttered. Our health care is too costly, our schools fail too many, and each day brings further evidence that the ways we use energy strengthen our adversaries and threaten our planet." Those two sentences encapsulated the list of problems to fix: economic meltdown, failed education, healthcare, and climate change. The striking thing to which Chait points is that the administration has now made serious progress on all of them. Against the financial and economic meltdown there was an $800 billion stimulus package, passed while Democrats still had control of both houses of Congress. The amount was insufficient, but it seemed unimaginably huge at the time, and probably averted a catastrophic depression. At the time of writing the U.S. economy is growing faster than the economy of any other major industrial economy.

Healthcare and insurance reform was the big domestic fight of Obama's first term. He won it also thanks to Democratic control of both Houses; and while the result was complicated and messy, it has withstood Supreme Court challenge, and so far its positive results have exceeded predictions. [20]

Just as expanding healthcare was the great fight of Obama's first term, the battle over carbon regulation is likely to dominate the final two years of his second. What is interesting here is that, on arguably the most important threat and challenge both foreign and domestic, the current administration has given a text-book demonstration of what "leadership" can mean in concrete rather than magical terms. In spring 2014 the administration unveiled new Environmental Protection Agency regulations for limiting carbon emissions by coal-fueled power plants. This executive action was necessary because there is precisely zero chance of legislation from a Republican-controlled House of Representatives. It was possible because the U.S. Supreme Court ruled in June that the EPA under current law has not only the authority but also the obligation to regulate greenhouse gasses as pollutants. [21] And it could very possibly be effective in keeping U.S. carbon emissions to a level consistent with the commitments that successive U.S. administrations have undertaken in international negotiations.

It is undeniably the case that the United States cannot by its own actions do anything significant to affect climate change. But it is also the case that the necessary international policies are unimaginable if America refuses to take part. If the new regulations stand—and they will certainly be challenged in court—then America will at least be in a position of "leadership" for the necessary, and excruciatingly difficult, negotiations with China and other large polluters. Indeed, in November 2014, Obama reached an agreement with Chinese President Xi Jinping matching a U.S. commitment to cut emissions by 26-28 percent from 2005 levels by 2025 with China's intention that its emissions should peak in 2030, by which point it aims to have increased the share of non-fossil fuels in primary energy consumption to 20 percent. Together, the two countries account for more than four-tenths of global carbon emissions, so their agreed restraint would be important in itself. But it should also have a political and technological cascade effect on economic powers such as India, which is reluctant to commit itself to reducing emissions, and the European Union, which is already fully committed. Aside from diplomatic pressure, having the world's two largest economies and biggest polluters seriously regulating greenhouse gases will have economic and technological feedback effects that should encourage innovation and make low-carbon energy more feasible on a global basis.

The state of its economy, the health and education of its citizens, the nurturing of its human and natural resources—these are, in Kennedy's terms—elements of the "substance" rather than "shadow" of America's power. In similar terms, the future prospects for global security will be determined in a big way by whether this generation finds effective measures to avert irreversible and catastrophic climate change, and only negligibly, if at all, by ephemeral concepts like "credibility."[22]

SUSTAINING LIMITS

The administration's position in mid-2014, before the rapid advance of the Islamic State of Iraq and al-Sham (ISIS) in June, was underpinned by the idea that that the Bush administration had devoted too much blood, treasure, and attention to the Middle East, with counterproductive, not to say catastrophic, results. The "pivot" to Asia, an arguably botched strategic-rebranding exercise, together with a general retrenchment to focus on domestic demands, flowed from this premise. Peter Beinart was among the many analysts who identified a recognizable administration strategy of "off-shore balancing," which was to say, "the idea that America can best contain our adversaries not by confronting them on land, but by maintaining our naval and air power and strengthening those smaller nations that see us as a natural counterweight to their larger neighbors."[23] Thus America might be able to balance its continued responsibilities against limited resources and capabilities.

These residual responsibilities included, to be sure, substantial, continuing exposure and commitment in the Middle East. The number one commitment was to somehow stop Iran's nuclear program from leading to a weapon. There was considerable skepticism about what Israeli or American military action against Iran's nuclear facilities could achieve. Yet, if negotiations were to fail, such action remained a real possibility.

The Iran nuclear problem is in fact an excellent case for considering the ambiguities and difficulties of trying to maintain a more restrained military posture in the Middle East. In the run-up to the 2012 election, President Obama stated unambiguously that the United States would not permit Iran to develop nuclear weapons.[24] This statement came in the midst of months of acrimonious debate and pressure—from the Israeli government, from the Saudis and other Gulf allies, and from Republican critics at home, all of whom argued that the administration was fecklessly permitting Iran to continue developing its nuclear capabilities. In making such a clear statement about Iranian nuclear *weapons*, Obama probably believed he was acting with restraint; his critics generally want the United States somehow to prevent Iran from developing even a latent nuclear capability, a capability that could be said to exist well before actual weaponization. Obama, by contrast, was drawing a line quite a few steps back, and one that Tehran might be shrewd enough not to cross even as it endowed itself with most of the attributes of a "virtual" nuclear power.

But, of course, nobody knows for sure. The president had made a commitment that he or his successor might very well be required to fulfill. The administration in any event believed that weaponization would be an irrevocable step change in the strategic environment. And there were obvious limits to what the United States could do about it. The Obama administration was, in fact, hugely successful in organizing international sanctions—the unity and steadfastness of the Europeans had been perhaps a pleasant surprise—and the White House took some justifiable pride in keeping that alliance together. Direct negotiations between the United States and Iran were considered another achievement, but the two sides remained far apart. Obviously, there was serious disagreement between the United States, on the one hand, and Israelis, Saudis and other states in this region on the other hand, about what could be achieved. The United States simply did not buy the view that zero enrichment was a viable negotiating position.

Measured on the basis of diplomatic investment, the second priority had been the Israeli–Palestine peace effort. (This was a particular enthusiasm of Secretary of State John Kerry, but it still reflected an enormous expenditure of energy and time from the administration.) At the outset of Kerry's effort, critics questioned whether this was a justifiable use of the secretary's time. Those critics would now have the extra advantage of being able to say that the peace effort has, once again and fairly predictably, failed. So will the United States now face reality? Probably not. To begin with, as intractable as Israel–Palestine may appear, it is logically false to argue that the United States has less traction there than in nearby disaster areas such as Syria and Iraq. Secondly, Israel–Palestine is not a normal foreign-policy problem—it is a crucial and visceral American domestic issue. It goes to the heart of America's view of itself as a democracy at the hub of an alliance system of other democracies. The relationship with Israel is America's real "special relationship"—special in good ways and bad. (Whereas the British relationship is mainly a good one, and therefore not so special.) Israel is becoming a polarizing issue in American domestic politics, in a way that it never was before. So, even though hard-headed realism might suggest that we should walk away from the problem, it is not clear that we can.

The civil war in Syria came lower on the list of Middle East problems for which U.S. military or diplomatic engagement could provide a plausible answer: this at least seemed to be the administration's judgment by late spring 2014. America had been engaged in the Syrian civil war from the beginning, but not effectively and not to the satisfaction of those who, in anguish, called for us to do more. Though there was considerable dissent within the administration, the president seemed determined to avoid an open-ended commitment to bringing down the Assad regime. For various reasons, Syria was considered different from Bosnia, different from Libya and, in the opposite sense, different from our overarching confrontation with Iran, though obviously it is also a part of that confrontation.

RESTRAINT AND ITS CRITICS

On the eve of Obama's commitment to an air war against ISIS, prevailing assessments of his foreign policies were trending negative.[25] It was alleged that he did not channel enough support to "moderate" rebels against Syria's Bashar al-Assad regime at a time when such support (it is argued) might have tipped the balance in the rebellion away from extreme jihadists. He set a rhetorical red line against the regime's use of chemical weapons, but then opted for a Russian-brokered deal to remove those weapons from Syria instead of launching retaliatory air-strikes. His administration, according to critics, did not work hard enough with Iraq's government to negotiate a Status of Forces Agreement for keeping a residual U.S. military force in the country, and hence was unable to shape the country's political terrain to prevent the emergence of a Sunni extremist force that went on to capture much of the country. All of this reluctance, and especially the choice of diplomacy over military action against Syrian chemical-weapons use, was said to have nourished in Russian President Vladimir Putin a justified contempt for American resolve, emboldening Moscow to annex Crimea and stir civil conflict in the rest of Ukraine.

The overall picture was of a president and administration averse to the necessary use of American leadership and military power, watching passively as the world unraveled on his watch. But there were a few problems with this picture. Firstly, it required a lot of faith in the directed application of military force to satisfying political ends. The notion that early and more robust military support for the Syrian opposition would have shaped a different, more humane civil war is impossible to disprove but also a bit hard to believe. Calls for a deeper American engagement often relied on strategic arguments, but at bottom their appeal was a moral one. The moral problem that is Syria and Iraq is huge, but the strategic judgement of the administration—and this appears to come down to the president himself—is that the United States should not be dragged into an asymmetrical engagement where its interests are insufficient to justify a prolonged commitment. There was also a debate to be had about whether intervention really would serve the moral imperative. It would only do so if it led to a speedier end to the war or, in any event, to a just and lasting stability. Since this could not really be achieved in Iraq with a vastly greater commitment of resources and lives— Iraqi in greater numbers than American—it was at least uncertain that it could be achieved in Syria.

Secondly, the notion that American abdication has precipitated a general unravelling of world order required greatly overstating, if not completely inventing, both the abdication and the unravelling. Robert Kagan, one of the more thoughtful critics of this administration's instincts for foreign-policy restraint, has long argued that when America tires of its world role, increasing chaos will follow. At the outset of the first George W. Bush administration, Kagan in my journal criticized the outgoing Clinton administration for having failed to appreciate the enduring American responsibility.

> It is too easily forgotten that the plans for world order devised by American policy-makers in the early 1940s were not aimed at containing the Soviet Union, which many of them still viewed as a potential partner. Rather, those policy-makers were looking backward to the circumstances that had led to the catastrophe of global war. Their purpose was to construct a more stable international order than the one that collapsed in the 1930s: an economic system that furthered the aim of international stability by promoting growth and free trade; and a framework for international security that, although it placed some faith in the ability of the great powers to work together, rested ultimately on the keystone of American power. [26]

Kagan has repeated this basic theme over the ensuing 13 years, conceding along the way that the Bush administration made some mistakes, but always warning against overlearning the lessons of those mistakes. In a recent *New Republic* article, he continued the argument, observing that "signs of the global order breaking down are all around us." He attributes the breakdown not to American incapacity to shape events, but to "an intellectual problem, a question of identity and purpose."[27] But Boston University professor Andrew Bacevic objects that Kagan is conjuring a halcyon post-war order that didn't remotely exist:

> Disruptions to a "world order" ostensibly founded on the principle of American "global responsibility" included the 1947 partition of India (estimated 500,000 to one million dead); the 1948 displacement of Palestinians (700,000 refugees); the exodus of Vietnamese from north to south in 1954 (between 600,000 and one million fled); the flight of the pied noir from Algeria (800,000 exiled); the deaths resulting directly from Mao Tse Tung's quest for utopia (between 2 million and 5 million); the mass murder of Indonesians during the anti-Communist purges of the mid-1960s (500,000 slaughtered); the partition of Pakistan in 1971 (up to 3 million killed; millions more displaced); genocide in Cambodia (1.7 million dead); and war between Iran and Iraq (at least more 400,00 killed [*sic*]). Did I mention civil wars in Nigeria, Uganda, Burundi, Ethiopia, Mozambique, Sudan, Congo, Liberia, and Sierra Leone that killed millions? The list goes on. [28]

This post-war world was in fact a "disorderly conglomeration," and if it contained any kind of order, its main achievement "was to avoid a cataclysmic third world war." Here, to the extent America deserves some credit, it should be more for its restraint than its assertiveness. For evidence, Bacevic returns to Kennedy and Cuba, where, in October 1962, "Khrushchev's rashness handed John F. Kennedy the chance to liberate Cuba from communism." But Kennedy abjured. "Rather than confrontation," Bacevic notes, "he opted for negotiation, offering the Soviets an unearned concession—in exchange for their missiles out of Cuba, ours would come out of Turkey. Cubans remained unliberated."[29]

There is a third category of criticism against the Obama administration that can hardly be taken as seriously as the previous two. But, since it is ubiquitous in the general commentary, it requires some attention. This is the accusation that Obama has fallen disastrously short in some ineffable element of "leadership," such that he has proved unable to shape events through the power of his personality. Commentator Matthew Yglesias has parodied the idea brilliantly as the "Green Lantern Theory of Geopolitics" (he was referring to a comic-book hero whose boundless willpower is channeled and unleashed through a transformative ring).[30]

The critique of failed leadership relies in part on a fuzzy notion of "credibility." Obama's critics argue that because he didn't bomb Syria after saying he would, credibility was lost: Iran no longer takes the United States seriously, and even Putin was emboldened in Ukraine. Yet credibility doesn't really work that way. There is plenty of research to support the very different notion that credibility is a function of one's putative adversary's understanding of one's capabilities and interest in any particular face-off.[31] Moreover, taking military action for the purpose of bolstering credibility ignores the very significant opportunity costs of such action. Invading Iraq, and watching it go horribly wrong, didn't give the United States extra credibility and deterrent power in that region; quite the opposite. Each intervention has an opportunity cost that makes the next intervention more, rather than less, difficult, and less, rather than more, likely. Hence Libya made it harder, not easier, to intervene in Syria. Intervening in Syria would make it harder, not easier, for the United States to enforce its red line regarding Iranian nuclear weaponization.

RESTRAINT AS THE HISTORICAL NORM

A fourth problem with this critique of Obama's restraint is the assumption that it is at odds with the behavior of most past administrations. This is simply false. Yet the trope is so embedded in the collective imagination that the *Washington Post* can write in an editorial that Obama is the first U.S. administration since the 1970s to fail to "contest the Iranian bid for regional hegemony."[32] This astonishing claim ignores, among other things, how the

Reagan administration precipitously withdrew U.S. marines from Lebanon after hundreds of their comrades were killed in Iran-instigated bombings; how the same administration traded arms to Tehran in a forlorn effort to secure the release of American hostages from Lebanon; how the Clinton administration overlooked the Khobar bombing in an effort to accommodate the newly elected Khatami government; how the second Bush administration not only did nothing to retard the growth of Iran's nuclear program, but also empowered the country by destroying its only regional adversary. Against this history, Obama, who orchestrated multilateral sanctions and directed cyber sabotage to physically disable thousands of centrifuges, stands out as especially tough on Iran.

In truth, the United States became a major power in the Middle East after 1945 more or less by default. Though its power was considerable—at times and in certain respects even hegemonic—it was exercised for the most part indirectly. Indeed, American policy-makers recognized that strategies of in-direction and restraint were necessary to sustain the U.S. presence and pre-serve U.S. interests in the region.

After September 11, 2001, that recognition was lost. America for the first time took it upon itself to invade, occupy, and remake two states and frac-tured societies in the greater Middle East. It should never be forgotten what a departure this was from the normal course of American strategic and diplo-matic behavior. Although Washington was used to throwing its weight around, during the post-World War II era it was only in Vietnam that it attempted a comparably ambitious project—and with comparably disastrous results.

The Vietnam example is instructive in another way: it was a disastrous intervention conducted by three presidents who understood that it portended disaster, yet were, in varying degrees, helpless to abstain from it. The first of those three, John F. Kennedy, deserves some special attention, because, not-withstanding some soaring Cold War rhetoric, he came very close to articu-lating a doctrine of restraint similar to Obama's. The dilemmas of restraint confronted him in the first three months of his presidency, because of an inherited Eisenhower administration plan for deploying a proxy force of exile Cubans to overthrow the Castro regime.

When those 1,300 Cuban exiles landed at the Bay of Pigs on 17 April 1961, their CIA handlers believed two things. First, the mission to secure that beachhead and use it to launch a popular uprising could not succeed without direct U.S. military intervention. And second, it was unimaginable that the new U.S. president would allow American-trained Cuban guerrillas to be wiped out on that beach without lifting a finger to help them.

The CIA was correct in its first assumption, and spectacularly wrong on the second. The president had tried to make himself clear: the mission was approved, but there would be no deployment of air power to cover it, and no other direct U.S. military intervention. "They couldn't believe that a new president like me wouldn't panic and try to save his own face," Kennedy said later. "Well they had me figured all wrong."[33] Historian Gordon M. Goldstein describes the late-night scene at the White House after a harrowing day for rebels fighting with their backs to the ocean and 20,000 Cuban troops on surrounding land. The president had emerged from a reception in white tie—with his vice president, secretary of state, and secretary of defense—to meet with CIA Deputy Director Richard Bissell, Joint Chiefs Chairman General Lyman Lemnitzer, and chief of naval operations Admiral Arleigh Burke.

> "Let me take two jets and shoot down the enemy aircraft" [Bissell] implored the president. Kennedy refused, reminding Bissell and Burke that he had consistently insisted that no American military forces would be deployed to salvage the invasion. A heated exchange ensued. Burke grew angry. He pressed the president for just one destroyer, which would be sufficient to "knock the hell out of Castro's tanks." "What if Castro's forces return the fire and hit the destroyer?" Kennedy asked. "Then we'll knock the hell out of them!" the admiral promised. "Burke, I don't want the United States involved in this," admonished Kennedy. "Hell, Mr. President," retorted Burke, "but we are involved!"[34]

Castro's forces killed 114 of the fighters and captured another 1,189. General Lemnitzer would later describe the president's steadfast inaction as "absolutely reprehensible, almost criminal."[35] The Lemnitzer reaction was to be echoed famously 18 months later, during the Cuban missile crisis, when General Curtis LeMay, the Air Force chief, told Kennedy that his reluctance to invade the island was "almost as bad as the appeasement at Munich."[36] It is well documented that such contempt from some of Kennedy's generals was richly reciprocated. Kennedy believed that his military and, indeed, many civilian advisers were simply too casual about taking the United States to war, and he left many recorded explanations as to why this would be a bad idea. In respect to the Bay of Pigs, he promised Arthur Schlesinger Jr. that he would never again be "overawed by professional military advice." He told his friend and new assistant secretary of the navy Red Fay, "Nobody is going to force me to do anything I don't think is in the best interests of the country. . . . We're not going to plunge into an irresponsible action just because a fanatical fringe in this country puts so-called national pride above national reason." And, to Schlesinger again, he had more to say about the whole concept of credibility and prestige:

> What is 'prestige?' Is it the shadow of power or the substance of power? We are going to work on the substance of power. No doubt we will be kicked in the ass for the next couple of weeks, but that won't affect the main business.[37]

JFK's truncated presidency has been mined often for large lessons about leadership and power. Kennedy's articulation of his own lessons from that early Cuba debacle provide context for the claims, among which Goldstein's is an important contribution, that the president, had he lived, would not have expanded America's Vietnam intervention into a major ground war. The countervailing case has always rested on the fact that when LBJ did expand the war, he was listening to the advisers he had inherited from his slain predecessor. But one of Goldstein's important contributions is to document the five occasions in 1961 alone when Kennedy resisted the urgent counsel of those same advisers: they said the introduction of American ground troops into Vietnam was necessary to avert disaster there, but Kennedy refused.[38]

Counterfactual history has its limits, of course, but in a certain sense it is also unavoidable. It is the implicit comparative basis for any assessment of the actual history. In this case, it is useful to imagine what the consequences might have been had JFK lived and kept us out of Vietnam. Georgetown historian Michael Kazin did so in a 2013 article in *The New Republic*. Writing for the 50th anniversary of Kennedy's assassination, Kazin argued that the consequences of such restraint would hardly have been trouble-free. "[T]he Vietcong and North Vietnamese would probably have triumphed under his watch; hawks in both parties would never have forgiven him."[39] Kazin's broader point is that John F. Kennedy's imagined and mythologized second term has set a pernicious standard among American liberals for heroic presidential leadership, one that bears little comparison to the frustrating realities of actual governing. But there is also a very specific lesson regarding many decision points of military intervention. Even in the case of Vietnam, where hindsight strongly suggests that strategic restraint would have been the far wiser and far less costly policy, some political and moral consequences of such restraint would have been ugly. Which is not to say that restraint would have been wrong. It would almost certainly have been right, with fewer Vietnamese and Americans killed, less treasure exhausted, and U.S. morale and credibility sooner recovered. Still, the Kennedy presidency would have been tarnished, in his own time and thereafter, by the chaotic loss of Vietnam.

BETWEEN WEST POINT AND OSLO

A policy of realistic restraint in foreign military policy, as part of an effort to set priorities and to concentrate on domestic needs, was always going to be held hostage to ideals and events. Both have now intervened to frustrate the president's hopes for turning the page on the wars of the Bush era.

Obama has admitted that he underestimated the capabilities of ISIS, and it is also clear that there was a general overestimation of the state of Iraqi military forces. As ISIS overran much of Iraq, it also perhaps undermined Obama's assumptions about how weary Americans were of war. Videos depicting the grisly beheadings of two Americans were enough to shift U.S. public opinion dramatically on whether it was an American interest and responsibility to seek out more war with the Sunni extremists. As Beinart observed, channeling Walter Russell Mead's famous categories, these heinous acts revived America's "Jacksonian" instincts—"the peculiar combination of jingoism and isolationism forged on the American frontier."[40] All of a sudden, Vice President Joe Biden, not the most jingoistic among America's current crop of politicians, was vowing to follow the perpetrators "to the gates of hell."[41]

Beinart was warning that the American mood had changed abruptly, even though little had changed in the assessment of how direct a threat ISIS posed to American security or even America's broader interests, and so the new jingoism was a fertile field for more policy blunder. He was not, however, arguing that the proper American course would be to stand passive against ISIS's advances and atrocities. These jihadists' record of beheadings, crucifixions, burning alive, rape, enslavement, and genocidal determination against religious minorities posed a challenge to American identity and purpose that could not be discounted simply by more rigorous accounting of American interests.

Every American president, at least since World War II, has had to balance realistic against idealistic traditions, and the current one is no exception. Indeed, Obama, being especially articulate, has fully presented both traditions in what might be called his West Point Declaration and his Oslo Declaration.

The West Point Declaration of December 2009 has been discussed above. This speech was a classic expression of Obama's small-c conservatism, concerned with restoring a balance between international commitments on the one hand, and American capabilities and resources on the other. He delivered it at a tricky moment in his relationship with senior military commanders, whom he felt were trying to box him into a more open-ended escalation.[42]

The Oslo Declaration was crafted in response to a rather different political problem: the fact that so many considered his Nobel Peace Prize in the early months of his presidency to be some kind of bad joke. Obama signaled that he got the joke, but rather than decline the award he decided to confound the prize-givers by accepting it with a statement on why American exceptionalism is intrinsically tied up with the sometimes greater American understanding of the need for organized violence:

> Make no mistake: Evil does exist in the world. A non-violent movement could not have halted Hitler's armies. Negotiations cannot convince al Qaeda's leaders to lay down their arms. . . . The world must remember that it was not

simply international institutions—not just treaties and declarations—that brought stability to a post-World War II world. Whatever mistakes we have made, the plain fact is this: The United States of America has helped underwrite global security for more than six decades with the blood of our citizens and the strength of our arms. [43]

In respect to ISIS, the Obama administration is now trying to balance between the calculated caution of the West Point Declaration and the grim but noble imperative of the Oslo Declaration. In seeking this balance, the administration has indeed pursued a strategy that looks a lot like off-shore balancing. It has local allies to fight on the ground, and supports them with training, intelligence, and air power. The strategy makes sense, insofar as this author at least has not heard anyone propound a better one. But its flaws are nonetheless obvious. Two of ISIS's most potent enemies, Iran and the Assad regime in Syria, are, for different but related reasons, unfit for the coalition. Even America's preferred partners, such as Saudi Arabia and Turkey, have different and sometimes conflicting goals. Ankara, for example, has stated that it will fully join battle against ISIS only when Washington commits itself to also toppling Assad. Yet, while there is truth to the Turkish view that the Syrian regime's mass murders have fueled and will continue to fuel unending jihadism, there is as much truth to the American view that fighting two contending sides in a vicious civil war is a recipe for strategic incoherence.

And yet—strategic coherence will be difficult to maintain. Former White House official Steven Simon poses a key question:

> What happens if one of the non-jihadist opposition groups that the United States is aiding in the fight against ISIS requests urgent assistance against the Assad regime? If the United States fails to come to the group's aid, the support the United States enjoys among these groups by virtue of its airpower and train-and-equip efforts would swiftly fade. But if the United States accedes to the request, then it unequivocally becomes a combatant in the civil war. And if the United States consents to Turkey's proposal for a safe haven within Syria for refugees and possibly as a base for an opposition army—essentially a tethered goat stratagem designed to trigger regime attacks that American planes would then have to repel—Washington would become even more deeply engaged in the conflict. [44]

In his 2015 State of the Union speech, Obama made the case for a doctrine and an attitude of "strategic patience" (the actual phrase came in a rewrite of the U.S. National Security Strategy that the administration released some days later). [45]

> When we make rash decisions, reacting to the headlines instead of using our heads; when the first response to a challenge is to send in our military—then

we risk getting drawn into unnecessary conflicts, and neglect the broader strategy we need for a safer, more prosperous world. That's what our enemies want us to do.[46]

Like the war against ISIS itself, the president's balancing between the principles of the West Point and Oslo declarations is an act that his successor will almost certainly have to continue. And that successor, like Obama, will find this a very difficult task.

NOTES

1. For an extended historical critique of the "Reagan won the Cold War" argument, see: Dana H. Allin, *Cold War Illusions: America, Europe and Soviet Power, 1969–1989* (New York: St. Martin's Press, 1994).

2. Barack Obama, *The Audacity of Hope* (New York: Canongate, 2008), 32, 181, 289. See also: "Obama on Reagan," http://www.nytimes.com/ref/us/politics/21seelye-text.html.

3. On the extremism and obstructionism of Obama-era Republicans, see: Thomas E. Mann and Norman J. Ornstein, *It's Even Worse than It Looks: How the American Constitutional System Collided with the New Politics of Extremism* (New York: Basic Books, 2012).

4. "Remarks by the President in State of the Union Address," Jan. 20, 2015. Available online at: http://www.whitehouse.gov/the-press-office/2015/01/20/remarks-president-state-union-address-january-20-2015/.

5. Thomas Wright, "Europe's Lost Decade," *Survival: Global Politics and Strategy* 55, no. 6 (2014): 7–28.

6. Eric Lee, remarks, "A New Cold War in Asia?" Plenary Session, International Institute for Strategic Studies Global Strategic Review, Oslo Norway, 21 September 2014. Available online at: http://www.iiss.org/en/events/gsr/sections/global-strategic-review-2014-281a/plenary-4-9b37/discussion-38a2.

7. Kennedy to Arthur Schlesinger, Jr, quoted in: Gordon M. Goldstein, *Lessons in Disaster: McGeorge Bundy and the Path to War in Vietnam* (New York: Henry Holt and Company, 2008), 41.

8. David P. Calleo and Paul Kennedy are among those who made this strong case in the midst of the Reagan-era defense build-up of the 1980s. See, for example, David P. Calleo, *Beyond American Hegemony: The Future of the Western Alliance* (New York: Basic Books, 1987). See also Paul Kennedy, *The Rise and Fall of the Great Powers: Economic Change and Military Conflict from 1500 to 2000* (London: Fontana, 1989).

9. Brian Whitaker, "Al Qaeda is Bleeding US to Bankruptcy, Bin Laden Claims," *The Guardian* 3 November 2004, http://www.theguardian.com/world/2004/nov/03/usa.alqaida.

10. See: http://www.dlc.org/documents/RebuildingReserves111407.pdf.

11. Joseph P. Stiglitz, "The True Cost of 9/11," *Slate Magazine*, September 2011. Available: http://www.slate.com/articles/business/project_syndicate/2011/09/the_true_cost_of_911.single.html/.

12. Ezra Klein, "Osama Bin Laden Didn't Win, but he Was 'Enormously Successful,'" *Washington Post*, 3 May 2011, http://www.washingtonpost.com/business/economy/osama-bin-laden-didnt-win-but-he-was-enormously-successful/2011/05/02/AFexZjbF_story.html.

13. Robert Skidelsky, "The Economic Crisis and the International Order," Plenary Speech, the IISS Global Strategic Review, 13 September 2009, Geneva, http://www.iiss.org/conferences/global-strategic-review/global-strategic-review-2009/plenary-sessions-and-speeches-2009/lord-robert-skidelsky/. Skidelsky acknowledges his debt to Calleo for this line of argument in Robert Skidelsky, *Keynes: The Return of the Master* (London: Allen Lane, 2009), 191.

14. Robert Skidelsky, *Keynes: The Return of the Master* (London: Allen Lane, 2009), 191.

15. Wolf, *Fixing Global Finance*, 58–59.

16. Robert Skidelsky, "Notes on The Economic Crisis and the International Order," IISS Global Strategic Review, Geneva, 14 September, 2009.

17. Bill Emmott, "The world economy is Osama's biggest victim," *The Times*, 5 September 2011, http://www.billemmott.com/article.php?id=333.

18. Barack Obama, "Remarks by the President in Address to the Nation on the Way Forward in Afghanistan and Pakistan," West Point, NY, 1 December 2009. Available online at: http://www.whitehouse.gov/the-press-office/remarks-president-address-nation-way-forward-afghanistan-and-pakistan.

19. Jonathan Chait, "Obama Promised to Do 4 Big Things As President. Now He's Done Them All," 8 June 2014, *New York Magazine*. Available online at: http://nymag.com/daily/intelligencer/2014/06/obama-has-now-fulfilled-his-4-big-promises.html.

20. "Is the Affordable Care Act Working?" *New York Times*, 26 October 2014. Available online at http://www.nytimes.com/interactive/2014/10/27/us/is-the-affordable-care-act-working.html?_r=0#/.

21. Robert Barnes, "Supreme Court: EPA Can Regulate Greenhouse Gas Emissions, with Some Limits," *Washington Post*, 23 June 2014.

22. Dana H. Allin and Steven Simon, "Ukraine and Obama's 'Credibility,' Politics and Strategy," 6 March 2014. Available online at: http://www.iiss.org/en/politics%20and%20strategy/blogsections/2014-d2de/march-1ef8/ukraine-and-obama-bcc4.

23. Peter Beinart, "Obama's Foreign Policy Doctrine Finally Emerges With "Offshore Balancing," Daily Beast, 28 November 2011. Available online at: http://www.thedailybeast.com/articles/2011/11/28/obama-s-foreign-policy-doctrine-finally-emerges-with-off-shore-balancing.html#.

24. Jeffrey Goldberg, "Obama to Iran and Israel: 'As President of the United States, I Don't Bluff,'" *Atlantic*, March 2, 2012. Available online at: http://www.theatlantic.com/international/archive/2012/03/obama-to-iran-and-israel-as-president-of-the-united-states-i-dont-bluff/253875/; Barack Obama, "Remarks by the President at AIPAC Policy Conference," Washington DC, 4 March 2012, http://www.whitehouse.gov/photos-and-video/video/2012/03/04/president-obama-2012-aipac-policy-conference#transcript.

25. This section is adapted in part from Dana H. Allin, "Letting Things Go," *Survival: Global Politics and Strategy* 56, no. 4, (2014): 215–24.

26. Robert Kagan, "The World and President Bush," *Survival* 43, no. 1 (2001): 8.

27. Robert Kagan, "Superpowers Don't Get to Retire," *New Republic*, 26 May 2014, http://www.newrepublic.com/article/117859/allure-normalcy-what-america-still-owes-world.

28. Andrew J. Bacevich, "The Duplicity of the Ideologues: U.S. Policy & Robert Kagan's Fictive Narrative," *Commonweal Magazine*, June 4, 2014. Available online at: https://www.commonwealmagazine.org/duplicity-ideologues.

29. Andrew J. Bacevich, "The Duplicity of the Ideologues: U.S. Policy & Robert Kagan's Fictive Narrative," *Commonweal Magazine*, June 4, 2014. Available online at: https://www.commonwealmagazine.org/duplicity-ideologues.

30. Ezra Klein, "The Green Lantern Theory of the Presidency, Explained," *Vox*, 20 May 2014, http://www.vox.com/2014/5/20/5732208/the-green-lantern-theory-of-the-presidency-explained.

31. Peter Beinart, "The U.S. Doesn't Need to Prove Itself in Ukraine," *Atlantic*, 5 May 2014, http://www.theatlantic.com/international/archive/2014/05/us-credibility-fallacy-ukraine-russia-syria-china/361695/2/; Theodore G. Hopf, *Peripheral Visions: Deterrence Theory and American Foreign Policy in the Third World, 1965–1990* (Ann Arbor, MI: University of Michigan Press, 1994); Daryl G. Press, *Calculating Credibility: How Leaders Assess Military Threats* (Ithaca, NY: Cornell University Press, 2005).

32. Washington Post Editorial Board, "The emerging Iran nuclear deal raises major concerns," Washington Post, 5 February 2015, http://www.washingtonpost.com/opinions/the-emerging-iran-nuclear-deal-raises-major-concerns-in-congress-and-beyond/2015/02/05/4b80fd92-abda-11e4-ad71-7b9eba0f87d6_story.html.

33. Gordon M. Goldstein, *Lessons in Disaster: McGeorge Bundy and the Path to War in Vietnam* (New York: Henry Holt and Company, 2008), 40.

34. Gordon M. Goldstein, *Lessons in Disaster*, 39.

35. Gordon M. Goldstein, *Lessons in Disaster*, 40.

36. Andrew J Bacevich, *Washington Rules: America's Path to Permanent War* (New York: Henry Holt and Company, 2010), 87.

37. Goldstein, *Lessons in Disaster,* 40–41.

38. Gordon M. Goldstein, *Lessons in Disaster*, 41.

39. Michael Kazin, "We Don't Need Another JFK: Fifty years later, Kennedy's legend makes life at the White House harder for Democrats," *The New Republic*, 20 November 2013, http://www.newrepublic.com/article/115655/jfks-assassination-made-governing-harder.

40. Peter Beinart, "Pursuing ISIS to the Gates of Hell," *Atlantic*, 4 September 2014, http://www.theatlantic.com/international/archive/2014/09/why-americas-pursuing-isis-to-the-gates-of-hell/379622/?single_page=true.

41. Wesley Lowery, "Biden to Islamic State: We Will Follow You 'To the Gates of Hell,'" *Washington Post*, 3 September 2014, http://www.washingtonpost.com/blogs/post-politics/wp/2014/09/03/biden-to-islamic-state-we-will-follow-you-to-the-gates-of-hell/.

42. Bob Woodward, "McChrystal: More Forces or 'Mission Failure,'" *Washington Post*, 21 September 2009. Available online at: http://www.washingtonpost.com/wpdyn/content/article/2009/09/20/AR2009092002920.html.

43. Barack Obama, "Remarks by the President at the Acceptance of the Nobel Peace Prize," Oslo, Norway, 10 December 2009. Available online at: http://www.whitehouse.gov/the-press-office/remarks-president-acceptance-nobel-peace-prize.

44. Steven Simon, "Staying Out of Syria," *Foreign Affairs*, 26 October 2014, http://www.foreignaffairs.com/articles/142295/steven-simon/staying-out-of-syria.

45. National Security Strategy, February 2015. Available online at: www.whitehouse.gov/sites/default/files/docs/2015_national_security_strategy_2.pdf.

46. President Obama, State of the Union Address, January 20 2015, http://www.whitehouse.gov/the-press-office/2015/01/20/remarks-president-state-union-address-january-20-2015.

BIBLIOGRAPHY

Allin, Dana H. *Cold War Illusions: America, Europe and Soviet Power, 1969-1989.* New York: St. Martin's Press, 1994.

Allin, Dana H. "Letting Things Go." *Survival: Global Politics and Strategy* 56, no. 4 (2014): 215–224.

Allin, Dana H. and Steven Simon. "Ukraine and Obama's 'Credibility.'" *Politics and Strategy* 6, March 2014. Online: http://www.iiss.org/en/politics%20and%20strategy/blogsections/2014-d2de/march-1ef8/ukraine-and-obama-bcc4.

Bacevich, Andrew J. *Washington Rules: America's Path to Permanent War.* New York: Henry Holt and Company, 2010.

Barnes, Robert. "Supreme Court: EPA Can Regulate Greenhouse Gas Emissions, with Some Limits." *Washington Post*, June 23, 2014.

Calleo, David P. *Beyond American Hegemony: The Future of the Western Alliance.* New York: Basic Books, 1987.

Chait, Jonathan. "Obama Promised to Do 4 Big Things As President. Now He's Done Them All." *New York Magazine.* June 2014. Available online at: http://nymag.com/daily/intelligencer/2014/06/obama-has-now-fulfilled-his-4-big-promises.html.

Emmott, Bill. "The world economy is Osama's biggest victim." *The Times.* September 2011. Online: http://www.billemmott.com/article.php?id=333/.

Goldstein, Gordon M. *Lessons in Disaster: McGeorge Bundy and the Path to War in Vietnam.* New York: Henry Holt and Company, 2008.

Hopf, Theodore G. Peripheral Visions: Deterrence Theory and American Foreign Policy in the Third World, 1965–1990. Ann Arbor, MI: University of Michigan Press, 1994.

Kagan, Robert. "The World and President Bush." *Survival* 43, no. 1 (2001).

Kennedy, Paul. *The Rise and Fall of Great Powers.* New York, New York: Random House, 1987.

Klein, Ezra. "Osama Bin Laden Didn't Win, but he Was 'Enormously Successful.'" *Washington Post*, 3 May 2011.

Mann, Thomas E. and Norman J. Ornstein. *It's Even Worse than It Looks: How the American Constitutional System Collided with the New Politics of Extremism*. New York: Basic Books, 2012.

Obama, Barack. *The Audacity of Hope*. New York: Canongate, 2008.

Press, Daryl G. *Calculating Credibility: How Leaders Assess Military Threats*. Ithaca, NY: Cornell University Press, 2005.

Skidelsky, Robert. *Keynes: The Return of the Master*. London: Allen Lane, 2009.

Skidelsky, Robert. "Notes on The Economic Crisis and the International Order." IISS Global Strategic Review, Geneva, September 14, 2009.

Stiglitz, Joseph. "The True Cost of 9/11." *Slate Magazine*, September 2011. Available online: http://www.slate.com/articles/business/project_syndicate/2011/09/ the_true_cost_of_911.single.html/.

Whitaker, Brian. "Al Qaeda is Bleeding US to Bankruptcy, Bin Laden Claims." *The Guardian*. November 2004. Online: http://www.theguardian.com/world/2004/nov/03/usa.alqaida

Wright, Thomas. "Europe's Lost Decade." *Survival: Global Politics and Strategy* 55, no. 6 (2014): 7-28.

Chapter Seven

Germany

Resurgence, Stagnation, or Decline?

Stephen F. Szabo

Germany deemed the sick man of Europe in the first decade of this century has now emerged as the economic power of Europe and a model for the West given its ability to maintain a strong export and industry-based economy at a time when Europe and America have seen deindustrialization and a lack of competitiveness in a global arena against a number of rising nonwestern economies. At the same time it is being asked to take on a stronger leadership role in Europe and beyond as its rise has coincided with the relative decline of the United States, France, and the UK. This development raises a number of questions. First, how deep and stable is the revival of Germany? Second, how does Germany see its role in the West and how will it deal with decline within the West?

FROM SICK MAN OF EUROPE TO WELTMEISTER

Hans Werner Sinn wrote about Germany as the sick man of Europe in 2004.[1] He cited an inflexible labor market, an unsustainable pension system that could not survive a demographically declining population, the economic costs of reunification, and mounting public debt. Labor costs, he contended, were making Germany uncompetitive and investment was leaving for more lucrative locations. High unemployment was one consequence. Heavy subsidies to eastern Germany were undermining growth. German education and research was falling behind its competitors as well. Sinn called for a cultural revolution similar to that of the Thatcher revolution in Britain, which along with France, was out-performing Germany. Sinn's concerns were shared by

Horst Siebert.[2] While Sinn thought immigration would help, it would not solve Germany's problems. However critics like Theo Sarrazin would come later with a withering critique of the costs of Muslim immigration and Walter Laqueur wrote of the last days of Europe due to demographic decline and the immigration of unassimilable Muslims.[3]

Today the narrative has changed dramatically. Germany is now the indispensable nation of Europe. German growth exceeds that of its EU partners, unemployment is down and Germany is held up as a model both in Europe and the United States, as a country which has maintained an upgraded industrial sector and has become the world's leading export economy. Its budget deficit has gone from $103 billion or 3.7 percent of GDP in 2004 to a $7 billion dollar surplus in 2013.[4] All this was symbolized and crowned by the German team's winning of the World Cup in the summer of 2014. How stable are these foundations and what are the prospects for a continued rise?

Germany, like other countries in the G-7, remains in relative economic decline due to the rise of emerging economies. Its 2014 GDP totaled $3.9 trillion which made it the fourth largest economy in the world and represents 5.8 percent of global GDP. This compares to a GDP which comprised about 7 percent of global GDP in the 1980s. However real GDP growth has been impressive, especially given the performance of other western economies over the past decade. The keys to Germany's revival over the past decade can be found in the reforms of the Schröder government in its Agenda 2010 and Hartz Four Reforms. These reforms resulted in wage restraint and cuts in spending on unemployment benefits. The retirement age was gradually raised as well, all of which cut into the generous, but expensive, welfare state. That fact that these reforms were introduced by a Social Democratic-Green government were a German version of Nixon going to China. Labor unions went along with these changes and the consensus oriented system criticized by Sinn and other liberal economists turned out to be crucial to their success. Cooperation between the parties and between labor and management also could be seen in the wise policies associated with *Kurzarbeit*, which meant the German companies kept labor on during the recession with subsidies from the government so that highly trained workers were not lost and were ready when the upswing began. Unit labor costs fell due to a real decline in wages combined with a growth in productivity, although German labor costs remain relatively high.[5] Unemployment is now down to 4.8 percent compared to the eurozone average of 11.4 percent in 2015. The current account had a surplus of €206 billion in 2013, a figure which comprised 7.5 percent of GDP. In short German workers traded wage gains and a decline in their purchasing power for job security. All this added up to a dramatic rise in exports, especially with China, which coupled with stagnant consumer spending at home. An undervalued currency, namely the euro, has been, and will remain, important to this continued export success.

At the same time the costs of unification have finally begun to fall. Germany spent somewhere from $1.5 to $2.5 trillion in transfers to the former GDR since 1990. Some of this came back in terms of increased consumption and tax revenues, but the east continues to be a drain, although at more manageable levels. Germany rode out the financial crisis in better shape than its western partners. German banks were exposed to the subprime market and to bad investments in southern Europe, but the stock and financial markets were not as central to the German economy as in the U.S. or the UK. Home owners and consumers were not as exposed to debt as in the U.S. and the economy was not as vulnerable to the real estate market as was Spain and the U.S. Germany was better positioned in export markets so it could compensate for its exposure to weak western markets via its position in Russia, China, and other emerging economies. Finally Germany kept and upgraded its industrial base so that as Angela Merkel told Tony Blair, "We make things people want." Its stable, consensus oriented, and decentralized political system has been a plus at a time when the American and many European governments are paralyzed by polarization and under great populist pressures. Its foreign policy has avoided the costly and often reckless engagements of the U.S. or the costs of a large defense budget as incurred by France and the UK.

THE DURABILITY OF THE REVIVAL

Yet German success remains extremely fragile. Its exposure to export markets is both a strength and a great potential vulnerability. Germany remains highly dependent on the import of natural resources, especially minerals and energy. Russia is emerging as a major vulnerability. The impact of western sanctions will be felt more deeply in the German economy than in most western countries. Even during the early stages of sanctions German industrial production fell by two percent and the implications of financial sanctions are much more severe. German energy dependence on Russia is especially problematic and cannot be altered for at least the medium term. The move away from nuclear power and toward dependence on renewable energy sources, the *Energiewende*, is a major gamble and risk for the economy. The shale gas revolution in the United States has seriously worsened the competitiveness of German industry due to the high relative costs of energy in Germany leading more German firms to relocate production to the U.S. The major drivers of the German economy, automobiles, chemicals, and machine tools are all highly dependent on the cost of energy. Germany also depends on China for rare earth minerals, which are vital to its high tech industrial products. It is also dependent on its technological advantages that are being undercut by the theft of intellectual property, especially by China. Slowing growth in the Chinese and other emerging markets will likely mean a decline in export growth. Germany's continuing dependence on European markets to which two-thirds of its exports are directed is also a drag given the low growth in this region. Finally the continuing weakness and uncertainty of the Eurozone and of the single currency is a huge question mark.

Demographics have been looming large as a long-term constraint on German growth for decades. The current birth rate of 1.3 children per woman is well below the 2.1 replacement rate. Around 906,000 babies were born the year Germany unified in 1990; by 2010 this figure had dropped to 663,000 and 30 percent of these are to foreign-born parents. Germany will require at least 200,000 immigrants per year at its current replacement rate to limit the drop in population of 7.7 million by 2050.[6] There is special need for trained and highly educated workers. Sarazin and Laquer have argued that Germany will not be able to integrate Muslim immigrants and are creating parallel societies that will undermine German culture and cohesion. However the German record on integration is better than these critics claim and the level of Muslim immigration has leveled off. The European recession has meant that immigration is now coming from southern and Eastern Europe rather than Turkey, which may ease the political and social tensions that have been associated with Muslim immigration.

Aging is a large part of the demographic problem. The current population has 21 percent of people over the age of sixty-five. This proportion will jump to 33 percent by 2050, putting obvious strains on pensions and health care spending. The new Grand Coalition government reversed the trend to increase the retirement age, further exacerbating the problem. When Frank Walter Steinmeier returned to the Foreign Ministry in November of 2013 he noted demography as a major constraint on Germany playing a larger role in foreign policy. An aging society is less dynamic than one with greater proportions of young citizens and the older population is likely to not only drain resources from productive investments but to be more resistant to innovation and change. The dependence of older Germans on savings has reinforced the tough position it has taken not only on inflation but on bailing out southern European countries. This is likely to deepen the tendency toward an already risk-averse culture and possibly will weaken German competitiveness in the future. Add to this the poor showing of German students on PISA scores and the still rather weak university system with the lack of links between research and technology and clearly Germany faces a major obstacle to continued growth and innovation. Germany has only three of its universities ranked among the top one hundred in the world. Its information technology sector is lagging with only six German IT firms among the top three hundred leading firms in this sector as listed by the OECD. Germany ranks behind one hundred and ten countries in the ease of starting a company.[7] Germany's share of gross fixed capital formation is only 17 percent, well below the 21 percent average for industrialized countries. Corporate investment in machinery and equipment has declined since 2011 and German investment is moving increasingly outside of Germany.[8] A contributing factor is the lack of investment in infrastructure which is the result of a fixation on avoiding budget deficits as well as relatively high German energy costs.

Eastern Germany continues to be a drag on unified Germany. In many respects there continues to be two Germanies in terms of economic opportunity and dynamism. Except for some pockets of growth in Thuringia and Saxony, eastern Germany remains a backwater of unemployment, underpopulation, and subsidization. Many of the young have left for the west and out-migration, while down from the highs of the 1990s, continues. The region remains a home for retrograde ideas and ideologies and has a disproportionate amount of violence against foreigners and support for extreme right and left groups, including the successor to the SED, die Linke. The appearance of the anti-immigrant and anti-globalization movement, Pegida, has been a largely eastern German phenomenon. The project of unification will need at least two or three more generations to complete.

The crisis over Ukraine and the imposition of sanctions on Russia highlights another German vulnerability. Although as Hannes Adomeit has observed, Germany's economic dependence on Russia is not great, it is substantial.[9] With 6,167 firms on the ground in Russia at the end of 2013 and with an investment of close to $20 billion in that country, Germany will not be able to escape the implications of a long-term reduction of the Russian market. The first year of sanctions has seen the number of German companies operating in Russia fall to 6,000 by the end of 2014 and a decline in the number of Germans living in Russia drop by 31 percent to 240,113 by January 2015.[10]

Finally the political system, which remains a strength, has some problems. The decline of the two major *Volksparteien* has opened the door to a five or even six party system. Die Linke seem to be a long-term fixture and the rise of AfD (Alternative for Germany) threatens to replace the centrist FDP with a more right-wing and anti-European party. The incentive continues to pull the major parties toward the center but the consensus orientation can become an obstacle to innovation and adaptation in the future. The cautious and tactical leadership of Merkel is likely to be the norm in the future as it has in the past. The Schröder reforms were an important exception to this style but it should be kept in mind that it was a reaction to almost two decades of stagnation and compromise under Helmut Kohl. The Schröder reforms cost him the Chancellorship and cut the SPD back to a party of only 25 percent support in the electorate and ensured that Die Linke will remain a factor in German politics. The electorate is chafing at the stagnation of wages and there are already signs that wages will begin to go up with uncertain effects on German competitiveness. Every society has its vulnerabilities and Germany is certainly better placed than most to deal with these challenges but its future is less in its own control than is the case with the United States or China.

GERMANY AND EUROPEAN DECLINE

Germany's recent economic success stands in contrast to the problems of many of its European partners, especially those in the southern tier of the Eurozone. In fact Germany's economic success has been due in part to its position in the Eurozone and has been a major contributing factor to the problems of the south. As Hans Kundnani, the U.S. Treasury, and others have pointed out, the German export surplus combined with low consumption rates in Germany have resulted in shifting the burden of adjustment to the weaker European economies. Between 1997 and 2007, the German surplus with the rest of the Eurozone went from €28 billion to €109 billion. German banks invested this surplus in property and banks in the south and in sub-prime instruments in the U.S. As Kundnani concludes, ". . . instead of producing convergence, the euro produced divergence." [11]

The dominant narrative in Germany has been one of the superiority of the German model and a tendency to blame the laggards for their lack of discipline and to insist upon austerity for these depressed economies. As Gideon Rachman concludes, " . . . while the country has a positive image in the world at large, where its power is not yet felt, the euro-crisis has seen Germany's image take a battering in its own European backyard."[12] This in turn reinforces a sense of resentment in Germany and only increases its distance in a Europe it is increasingly shaping in its own image, with the prospect of a German Europe rather than a European Germany. At the same time Germany does not want to lead or be seen as a leader or hegemon either in Europe or beyond. What we may be seeing is a return of the German question or problem as described by David Calleo and Ludwig Dehio, that is of a Germany too big for any of its neighbors but not big enough to be a hegemon.[13] It also risks creating encircling coalitions against it within Europe. This new leadership role is due more to default than to initiative, a result of the decline of France and Britain as well as the resurgence of German economic strength.

This opens another old question concerning Germany's role in the West. Is it part of the West or does it follow a different road, a *Sonderweg?* There has been a growing tendency in Germany to begin to separate itself from the West, both in terms of Atlanticism and Europeanism. Already in strategic terms, Germany has begun to further distance itself from the United States, first in the Iraq War and more recently in the case of Libya. The serious rift with Washington over the Snowden NSA revelations and cases of U.S. spying on Germany has accelerated this separation. Germany's reluctance to use military force and to increase defense spending along with its middle position between Washington and Moscow has combined with a contempt for the Anglo-Saxon neo liberal model and its consequences in and after the financial crisis. The hopes many Germans placed in Obama after the George W Bush years have now come back to earth. America is regarded as a powerful country, but one which is weakened by its political polarization, its growing economic and social inequality, its out of control national security state, and its lack of an industrial base.

The energy revolution is one factor working against this general image of decline and is seen as giving the U.S. an important competitive edge over Germany. However the Snowden effect is creating more distance between Berlin and Washington on information technology, cyber and intellectual property rights, and is leading to greater German autonomy in cyber commerce and in cyber security. With the old security ties weaker than during the Cold War, Germany now sees the U.S. as both economic partner and competitor. The fate of the big transatlantic trade and investment treaty, the TTIP, will have important consequences, positive if successful but destructive in the case of failure. The opposition to TTIP in the German public is a result, in part, of the cyber and spying issues. At the same time there have been signs of a return to equidistancing between the U.S. and Russia over Ukraine. An Infratest poll taken as the Ukraine crisis was underway but before the shootdown of the Malaysian airliner, found that half of those polled favored a middle position between Russia and the West, with stronger support for this view in eastern Germany. [14] This has moderated as the crisis intensified but the potential for a return to some equidistancing remains high.

The confluence of left and right into a new form of anti-Americanism is an important result of the split with the U.S. The left sees the Obama Administration pushing for a confrontation with Russia which would threaten peace, while the business sector sees this confrontation as harmful to their deep and profitable economic relationship with Russia. German Atlanticists have been isolated by the actions, or lack of actions, by the Obama Administration over American spying in Germany.

Europe still remains important and the German electorate has not been attracted at this point to the populism which is sweeping through many of its European partners, but the replacement of the FDP by the AfD and the growing attraction of AfD to anti-immigrant groups is an indication that disaffection with the euro and with Europe is becoming a political factor. The combination of disaffection from both Europe and the United States has opened up a new discussion in Germany over whether it is moving away from the West. The historian Heinrich August Winkler, when asked in an interview with *Der Spiegel,* whether Germany's tight links to the West are in question, answered that "There is at least cause for doubt." [15]

GERMANY'S THIRD RISE AND THE NEW GERMAN QUESTION

The first rise of Germany under the Empire, as Calleo points out, took place in a world which had already been colonized and in which Germany had no space to expand. There was also the alliance between steel and barley, between industry and agriculture, which used nationalism to channel democratic forces into supporting an authoritarian system. Germany's second rise during the Third Reich was of a revisionist, highly nationalist, and racist totalitarian system. The current rise is one of a satisfied, rather than revisionist, power firmly based in a mature democracy within a new European system that has sublimated national competition within the structure of the EU. As Winkler observed, the democratic parties are still overwhelmingly western in their values and orientation and German business knows that their key markets are still in Europe. As he stated in the interview, "I don't see a broad rejection of Western values." The NSA controversy is "over different interpretations of values we share." The confrontation with the Putin system should further clarify the importance of values in foreign policy.

This German rise is not a threat to the West but rather a necessity to a reconstituted West. However the weakening of the Atlantic connection, especially in NATO, combined with the fraying of the European anchor with the ongoing European malaise, is pushing Germany into a position where a new German question has arisen. Its main European partner, France, is in a period of stagnation and relative decline and is no longer the balancing partner it has been for Berlin. The United Kingdom is questioning both its internal unity and its role in Europe. The EU remains largely an economic rather than a strategic player and has not created a political union to govern its monetary union. This is all taking place at a time when the western international liberal order is declining in the face of the rise of non-western powers, most notably China. *Exportmeister Deutschland* has become a global geo-economic power that is driven by largely its economic interests and economic sector. As Kundnani concludes, the new German question "has reemerged in geo-economic form."[16] Some prominent German leaders have recognized that Germany now must take a larger leadership role and cannot pretend to be a big Switzerland, but their calls have not been followed up by the Chancellor or the broader leadership.

As Benjamin Rowland's treatment of Spengler in this volume points out, decline follows the "defeat of politics by economics." To this point, German strategy has been largely economically driven and has been, as Josef Janning has observed, one in which "Berlin's foreign policy machine works best when it can support, encourage, help, and reward. It struggles when it has to employ dissuasion, sanctions, or red lines."[17]

The future of the German resurgence is less solid than it currently looks. The external challenges look larger than the domestic ones. The German political class is parochial and needs to think in larger terms and look beyond Germany. Thomas Bagger, Head of the Policy Planning Staff of the Foreign Office under foreign ministers Guido Westerwelle and Frank-Walter Steinmeier, has developed the idea of Germany as a "Shaping Power" (*Gestaltungsmacht*) as the conceptual core of a new German strategy. A *Gestaltungsmacht* is a state that has the power to shape outcomes and events. The term reflects the end of a unipolar era when the U.S. dominated the agenda. This thinking reflects the emergence of a polycentric, highly interdependent, world with rising non-Western powers playing a larger role in global and regional decision-making. The official German government paper on this concept puts it in the following terms: "[T]hese countries are economic locomotives which substantially influence regional cooperation and also have an impact in other global regions and play an increasingly important role in international decision making. . . . We see them as more than developing countries but as new shaping powers."[18] Germany will be a Shaping Power through the use of networks, fashioning networks with new actors both at home and abroad. Germany has to develop networks alongside its traditional fora of the EU, NATO, and the G-8 to develop the global governance needed to deal with the new challenges of globalization.

German foreign policy then will be an important factor in whether the country will be able to maintain its revival. This will entail a number of key policies. First, Germany must do all it can to ensure the success of the TTIP negotiations. Germany will continue to rely on its transatlantic economic base and needs not only to expand its growing investment in North America but also to ensure that western standards continue to undergird a liberal global economic order. Germany has been one of the biggest winners of globalization and has a serious stake in expanding or at least defending this system and TTIP will be key to sustaining this order in the face of rising non-western and often anti-liberal powers. It also must take a more political and strategic view of the Eurozone and move away from its rather narrow and parochial austerity strategy. If it fails to do so the Eurozone and possibly the European project will be in jeopardy, a project in which Germany's has an existential stake. Russia will remain an important but difficult partner for Germany in the future and the continuing policy of balancing economic with larger strategic concerns will need to be maintained for a considerable period of time. Germany understands this is a long-term policy and will need to find the right mix between engagement and containment in its dealing with Russia. Finally a global Germany, led by its global companies, will need to continue to emerge to cope with a less western world. Leadership will require a political as well as an economic vision for a power that holds the future of Europe, once again, in its grasp.

NOTES

1. Hans Werner Sinn, *Ist Deutschland noch zu retten?* (Berlin: Econ Verlag, 2004).
2. Horst Siebert, *Jenseits des Sozialen Marktes: Eine Neuorientierung der deutschen Politik* (Munich:DVA, 2005).
3. Theo Sarazin, *Deutschland schafft sich ab: Wie wir unser Land aufs Spiel setzen (DVA:2010)*. Please also see: Walter Laquer, *The Last Days of Europe: Epitaph for an Old Continent* (Thomas Dunne:2007).
4. Available online at: http://countryeconomy.com/deficit/germany/.
5. Hourly compensation in Germany in 2012 was $45.79 compared to $35.67 in the U.S. and $39.81 in France. Please see: 1) http://www.bls.gov/ilc/ichcc.htm#chart01/. As Paul Krugman notes," Yet Germany is a very successful exporter all the same. How do they do it? Not by producing the latest trendy tech product, but rather, by maintaining a reputation for very high-quality goods, year after year." See article online at: http://krugman.blogs.nytimes.com/2014/06/17/german-labor-costs/?_r=0/.
6. The numbers of immigrants to Germany in 2013 stood at 800,000.
7. Olaf Gersemann, *Die Deutschland-Blase: Das lezte Hurra einer grossen Wirtschaftsnation* (Munich:DVA, 2014), 28.
8. Chris Bryant and Stefan Wagstyl, "German Companies look overseas as domestic opportunities fade," *The Financial Times,* 13 October 2014, 3.
9. Hannes Adomeit, "German-Russian Relations: Change of Paradigm versus 'Business as Usual', *Note du Cerfa* 120, February 2015, http://www.ifri.org/sites/default/files/atoms/files/ndc_120_adomeit_en_0.pdf.
10. Kathrin Hille, "Foreigners quit Russia in droves as sanctions bite, *The Financial Times,* February 5, 2015.
11. Hans Kundnani, *The Paradox of German Power* (New York: Oxford University Press, 2015).
12. Gideon Rachman,"A golden moment for Germany that may not last," *The Financial Times,* July 15, 2014, 11.
13. David Calleo, *The German Problem Reconsidered: Germany and the World Order, 1870* (Cambridge: Cambridge University Press, 1978); Ludwig Dehio, *Germany and World Politics in the Twentieth Century* (New York: Knopf, 1960 and Kundnani, *The Paradox of German Power.*
14. Christiane Hoffmann, "Die Seelenverwandten," *Der Spiegel,* 15/2015, 23. See also a poll commissioned by the Körber Stiftung, *Die Sicht der Deutschen auf die Aussenpolitik* (Berlin: Körber Stiftung, 2014).
15. Christiane Hoffmann and Rene Pfister, "German Leftists Have Not Understood Putin," *Spiegel Online,* June 27, 2014.
16. Kundnani, *The Paradox of German Power;* see also Ulrike Guerot and Mark Leonard, *The New German Question: How Europe Can Get the Germany It Needs* (London: The European Council on Foreign Relations, 2011).
17. Josef Janning, "Germany's summer of discontent on foreign policy," *European Council on Foreign Relations,* June 30, 2014, http://www.ecfr.eu/blog/germanys_summer_of_discontent_on_foreign_policy/.
18. Die Bundesregierung, *Globalisierung gestalten- Partnerschaften ausbauen-Verantwortung teilen: Konzept der Bundesregierung* (German Foreign Office, 2012), 4. See also Thomas Bagger, "The Networked Diplomat," *Internationale Politik,* 3 August 2013; and the joint German Marshall Fund, Stiftung Wissenschaft und Politik paper, *Neue Macht: Neue Verantwortung/* or *New Power, New Responsibility: Elements of a German Foreign and Security Policy for a Changing World* (English version), 2013, http://www.swp-berlin.org/en/projects/new-power-new-responsibility/the-paper.html.

BIBLIOGRAPHY

Adomeit, Hannes. "German-Russian Relations: Change of Paradigm versus Business as Usual." *Note du Cerfa* 120, February 2015. Online at: http://www.ifri.org/sites/default/files/atoms/files/ndc_120_adomeit_en_0.pdf/.

Bryant, Chris and Stefan Wagstyl. "German Companies look overseas as domestic opportunities fade." *The Financial Times,* October 13, 2014.

Calleo, David P. *The German Problem Reconsidered: Germany and the World Order, 1870.* Cambridge: Cambridge University Press, 1978.

Dehio, Ludwig. *Germany and World Politics in the Twentieth Century.* New York: Knopf, 1959.

Gersemann, Olaf. *Die Deutschland-Blase: Das lezte Hurra einer grossen Wirtschaftsnation.* Munich: DVA, 2014.

Hille, Kathrin. "Foreigners quit Russia in droves as sanctions bite." *The Financial Times.* February 5, 2015.

Hoffmann, Christiane and Rene Pfister. "German Leftists Have Not Understood Putin." *Spiegel Online.* June 27, 2014.

Janning, Josef. "Germany's summer of discontent on foreign policy." *European Council on Foreign Relations.* June 30, 2014. Available online at: http://www.ecfr.eu/blog/ germanys_summer_of_discontent_on_foreign_policy/.

Kundnani, Hans. *The Paradox of German Power.* New York, New York: Oxford University Press, 2015.

Laquer, Walter. *The Last Days of Europe: Epitaph for an Old Continent.* Thomas Dunne: 2007.

Leonard, Mark. *The New German Question: How Europe Can Get the Germany It Needs.* London: The European Council on Foreign Relations, 2011.

Rachman, Gideon. "A golden moment for Germany that may not last." *The Financial Times.* July 15, 2014.

Sarazin, Theo. *Deutschland schafft sich ab: Wie wir unser Land aufs Spiel setzen.* Munich: DVA, 2010.

Siebert, Horst. *Jenseits des Sozialen Marktes: Eine Neuorientierung der deutschen Politik.* Munich: DVA, 2005.

Stifung, Körber. *Die Sicht der Deutschen auf die Aussenpolitik.* Berlin: Körber Stiftung, 2014.

Werner Sinn, Hans. *Ist Deutschland noch zu retten?* Berlin: Econ Verlag, 2004.

Chapter Eight

Italy's Decline

A Case Study in Mismanagement

Mark Gilbert

Debates over "decline" arise in a given nation when there is a *combination* of an objective slide in power and prestige and a subjective perception by public opinion, or national elites, that the nation is "counting for less in the world" than it used to, or than it should. There was, for instance, a national debate over "decline" in Great Britain in the early 1960s both for objective reasons—ongoing decolonization, the loss of superpower status, and the superior economic performance of neighboring countries in Western Europe, and for the purely subjective reason that Britain's elites could not accept being diminished to the status of a "greater Sweden."[1] Britain's decline in geopolitical and relative economic terms was inevitable; the question was should Britain aspire to a lesser role in world affairs, or think less of itself, despite its decline in relative wealth and international prestige. Britain's elites—left and right—were not capable of swallowing their pride.

The case of Italy is obviously different in many ways from Britain. Italy has never been a world power and its various attempts to become one—between 1911 and 1943—ended in national catastrophe. For this reason, the country's rebirth after 1945 is the source of great national pride. In 1945, Italy was devastated by fascism and war, at risk of becoming a Cold War battleground, and a country whose economy was dominated by over-protected heavy industries in the North and a Latin American style agricultural economy in the South. The danger that Italy might have become another Portugal was real.

Instead, Italy forged an imperfect but functioning democracy, based upon an intricate constitutional compromise between the major political forces, which was able to deliver substantial social and economic reforms, above all land reform, in the 1950s. The economy boomed. Year after year of 5 percent growth spread consumer goods to all but the poorest in society and created a large prosperous middle class with a stake in the new society. Italy's diplomats, moreover, played a weak hand with skill and by the end of the 1960s, the country actually did count for something in the world. It was a founder member of the EEC (historians are busy showing how much Italy influenced the process of European integration, something which the extant historiography, by focusing on Germany and France's rapprochement, has tended to forget), and of NATO.[2] It produced several leaders—notably Alcide De Gasperi, Amintore Fanfani, and Palmiro Togliatti—who were significant figures on the world stage. Yet it avoided the excesses of national *grandeur* that had marred its own history and arguably marred the foreign policy of its neighbor to the north-west.

The best comparison, possibly, is with Japan. Like Japan, by the end of the 1960s, Italy had emerged from a fascist-imperialist past and military defeat to become one of the world's workshops and to conduct a deferential, though not negligible, role in world affairs.[3] Like Japan, its political system was dominated by a single, pro-American centrist party with a penchant for corruption, low taxes, and using public money for political gain—Christian Democracy (DC). Again like Japan, it was a traditional society whose way of life was being distorted by modernity. But though this made it an unstable polity, upheaval was not perceived as a sign of decline. Modernization was broadly equated with progress.

The social tensions caused by modernity (and the intense ideological conflict within society) also generated another key feature of Italy's postwar success story: its cultural prowess. Italian writers, thinkers, film makers, architects, and designers created a postwar cultural renaissance—a big word, but justified. Norberto Bobbio, Italo Calvino, Giuseppe Tomasi de Lampedusa, Eugenio Montale, Luchino Visconti, Roberto Rossellini, Vittorio De Sica, Federico Fellini were just the highest peaks of an imposing cultural mountain chain. Turin, Milan, and Bologna were intellectual centers of vitality and distinction—far more important than, say, English cities of comparable size such as Birmingham or Leeds, or even German cities like Cologne and Munich. Italian popular culture was well-known across Europe: Giovanni Guareschi's stories sold well in translation; spaghetti westerns revived a movie genre in bloodier guise; in continental Europe, the songs of Totò Modugno and Mina were second in popularity only to Elvis Presley and the Beatles; actors such as Sophia Loren, Marcello Mastroianni, and Alberto Sordi were icons worldwide; Italian fashion was the most chic. Italy's soft power, in short, was immense: where else but Rome would Gregory Peck and Audrey Hepburn have gone for a holiday? In fact, Italy rivaled France as the world's premier tourist destination, with millions of newly wealthy Germans and Scandinavians flocking to its beaches, mountain lakes, and *città dell'arte.*

The 1970s, characterized as they were by terrorism, rampant inflation, political corruption, and social unrest, knocked the gloss off Italy's reputation, but in the 1980s, resurgent economic success put some of it back on (foreigners looked at the headline figures for GDP growth, but didn't look at rising government debt). With a little creative massaging of the figures, Italy briefly became the world's fifth-largest economy, overtaking the UK and all but equaling France. Francesco Cossiga and Bettino Craxi were political figures who backed the West's strategic decisions—notably over the siting of intermediate-range nuclear missiles—even when they were unpopular with public opinion.[4] "Democracy, Italian Style," to borrow the title of Joseph LaPalombara's influential book, was widely perceived to be corrupt, convoluted, and theatrical, but also to be ultimately successful. It met the key test of pragmatism: it delivered the goods.[5]

FROM RENAISSANCE TO DECLINE

In hindsight, Italy's international power and prestige peaked in the mid-1980s. In economic terms, Italy has slipped since then from being the fifth-largest to ninth-largest economy in the world. Of course, this was in part inevitable. The economic success of Brazil, South Korea, Turkey, India, and, above all, China, has reduced the EU-28's share of the world economy, from an estimated 28 percent in 1990 to a projected 16.7 percent in 2018, when the EU is expected to be only the third-largest economy in the world. China will have expanded its share, in the meantime, from just over 3 percent to 17 percent.[6] A smaller share of a bigger pie is not necessarily a bad thing, so long as individual citizens are getting richer, but in the case of Italy, despite the fact that its exporters have done a generally good job of maintaining and even increasing the value of Italian exports, living standards have remained stagnant. Thanks to the Great Recession (and higher taxes), household RDI has slipped back to the same levels as 1988, though gains since that time had not been huge in any case. Only a conspicuous reduction of savings—Italian families used to rival the Japanese and the Belgians as the world's great savers, but now save a mere 6 percent of GDP—has kept consumption from slumping. Italian households remain more convinced than ever of the value of saving, but only a third of them think it is possible to do so. The difficulty that poor and even lower middle class families have in "reaching the end of the month" is by now a well-documented fact, and one that seems bound to lead, in the long run, to social tensions.[7]

The Italian economy is, moreover, clearly underperforming relative to its peers within the EU and its performance has worsened since the introduction of the Euro. Italy has grown less (or shrunk more) than the average of Euro area nations every year since 2003 and has underperformed relative to Germany every year except 2004 and 2005. France has beaten Italy for growth every year except 2010, when both countries bounced back from steep recession by an anaemic 1.7 percent. Belgium, which used to have almost exactly the same level of output per head as Italy, has beaten Italy's rate of growth in all eleven years since 2003, as have the UK (even in 2009, when Italy's economy shrunk by a 5.5 percent to Britain's dismal 5.2 percent), Sweden, and the Netherlands. Spain performed worse only in 2010 and 2011, after the implosion of the housing bubble. The countries of Central and Eastern Europe, obviously, have all caught up considerably with Italian levels of *benessere*. In all, since the introduction of the Euro, Italy has shifted from being a rich country by European standards to a middle income one—and the trend is unambiguously down. [8]

Culturally, Italians fear that they have become provincial—and find the fact hard to digest. A straw in the wind: It was interesting to see how Paolo Sorrentino's *La grande bellezza* (2013), a film which is ostentatiously about Italy's cultural and intellectual decline, was dismissed by many critics when it appeared, with reviewers hastening to compare it unfavorably to Fellini's *La dolce vita*. Of course, it abruptly became a great movie, and was lionized in a hundred patriotic articles, when it won the Oscar for best foreign film. "Italian cinema is not dead," was all of a sudden the theme. The fact is that the film's merciless depiction of the Rome cultural elites' substitution of *mondanità* for *creatività* touched a nerve (because it is true), and the boasting that followed its international success is indicative of a growing inferiority complex.

The question of cultural decline could be discussed in greater detail, but the central point is that decline has become a central theme in Italian discourse in area after area. Type "Italia declino politico ed economico" into Google and you get hundreds of thousands of hits. Type "Italia declino culturale," and the figure is almost as high. Schools and universities are considered to be in terminal decline, with the most brilliant brains fleeing the country and the average level of children's education being poor. [9] Objectively, there is surely something wrong when a nation loses 5,000 top-ranked graduates per year to emigration (one quarter of all engineers graduating with a *summa cum laude* degree is working abroad within one year of graduation). [10] The Italian language itself is held to be in decline, with an invasion of poorly understood and ill-used English words and a general impoverishment of vocabulary. [11]

Perhaps most serious of all, there is a demographic crisis—surely, a glaring symptom of national decline since confident countries beget babies. A bar chart of Italians by age group resembles a column with a bulging middle: since the 1970s, the number of births has been falling steadily, with the result that there are now as many over-seventies as teenagers. Unless migration increases—and there are already appalling racial tensions in some Italian cities, notably Rome, as a result of large-scale immigration by North Africans and East European Roma—it is difficult to see how the Italian state will be able to support the large cohort of people in their early and late fifties who are slated to exit the workforce within the next 15 years. The low birthrate is principally due to the fact that young—and by now not so young—people have for years put off having children because they are un-employed, under-employed, or precariously employed. But it is also due to political ineptitude. To quote Steven Philip Kramer: "The Italian birthrate fell below the replacement level in the 1970s, but only in the 1990s did Rome recognize the extent of the problem, when the underdeveloped welfare state was already stretched to capacity. So the country essentially did nothing."[12]

Last, but in Italy definitely not least, soccer is in precipitous decline: where once Juventus, Internazionale, and AC Milan were the greatest teams in the world, and Serie A by far the most competitive league, with six or more teams that could have won any other league in Europe, Italy is now the fifth-ranked nation after Spain, Germany, England, and France, with Portugal poised to overtake her. This may sound trivial, but it is not, since the decline in soccer teams' prowess reflects a decades-long failure to invest in infra-structure, youth teams, and talent academies, and to impose law and order upon unruly *ultra* whose violence, racism, and criminality deter law-abiding citizens from taking their children to see a game. The decline in the standing of Italy's soccer teams, in short, is a mirror of other pathologies in Italian society that have been bred from the country's economic failure and, above all, its style of politics.[13]

THE ROOT OF THE TROUBLE

Italy's decline is a by-product of its dysfunctional politics. As in the cases of Argentina and Greece, the finger of blame can be pointed nowhere else. To understand Italy's present politics, one has to go back at least forty years. In the mid-1970s, the Communist Party (PCI), led by Enrico Berlinguer, looked briefly as if it would overtake the DC to become the vital center of the Italian political system. There were a number of good reasons for the PCI's growth in support. Berlinguer was a moderate who was willing, in the days before the crucial June 1976 elections, to support NATO. The DC, which had shown courageous leadership in the immediate postwar period, had degenerated by the mid-1970s into an agglomeration of warring factions unable to cope with the challenges thrown up by the country's passage to modernity. Many voters were willing to give the PCI a chance, rather than vote for the DC's venal style of government. Others, however, were still prepared to "hold their noses" to block out the stench of the DC's corruption and place a cross against the same old names. The DC won the 1976 elections with 38 percent of the vote, 4 percent more than the PCI. A government of "national solidarity" was formed by DC boss Giulio Andreotti, with the PCI providing parliamentary support, but no ministers. Washington firmly vetoed PCI participation in the government throughout the remainder of the 1970s. [14]

Why is this old history relevant to today's politics? It is relevant because this so-called "historic compromise" enabled the DC to defeat Red Brigade terrorism and survive the economic crisis of the 1970s without implementing major structural reforms to the country's economy and institutions. In hindsight—but not only in hindsight—the Italian state and its political elites needed a thorough clear-out in the 1970s and did not get one. Italy is paying the price today.

The PCI terminated the government of national solidarity in 1979. Its place as the DC's indispensable ally was taken by the Socialist Party (PSI), whose leader, Bettino Craxi, became the first non-DC premier in June 1983. The DC and the PSI had the numbers in parliament to push through a platform of constitutional and political changes—what was called at the time *la grande riforma*—but never did. The DC had no interest in changing a system that suited it and the PSI—and Craxi personally—soon learned to relish the perks of power. [15]

What would a "great reform" have looked like? First, it would have meant constitutional changes to strengthen the powers of the government in Italy's bicameral parliamentary system. Second, it would have meant an electoral law that "restored the scepter" of sovereignty to the people. [16] Postwar Italy had a highly proportional electoral law that guaranteed a fragmented party system in which no one party could emerge triumphant. Voters cast their ballots and then the politicians haggled over the composition of the government and over which party (and which faction within the parties) would get the various *dicasteri*, or offices of state. Third, ideally a great reform would have attacked the worst abuses of patronage politics. In the 1980s, the political parties held the country in an asphyxiating grip. Their tentacles reached throughout the economy and society, with top jobs in state-owned companies, banks, and cultural foundations being awarded only to individuals with political connections. RAI, the national broadcasting service, whose three channels were explicitly shared out between the DC, the PSI, and the PCI, and whose news services made open propaganda on behalf of their political masters, was almost a parody of the wider problem. [17] RAI 2's cult of Craxi's personality was reminiscent of the Eastern bloc, not of a modern, pluralist democracy.

Rather than embrace a reformist agenda, the PSI and the DC wasted the 1980s in an internecine war of position within the government for greater power and patronage. Craxi's government (1983–87) was held hostage by the DC and although Craxi acquired a spurious reputation among sycophantic journalists for being a *decisionista*, achieved little of substance. Successor governments headed by Giovanni Goria and Ciriaco De Mita, the DC's party secretary, were both sabotaged by Craxi's minions in parliament. A ceasefire was declared only in February 1989, when DC barons led by Andreotti ditched De Mita and came to terms with the PSI boss. [18]

Once again: why is this old history relevant? It is relevant because the war of position was largely fought with public money. Prudent management of the public purse went by the board as Craxi wrestled for power with the DC. The single largest factor conditioning Italian politics today—the debt trap the country has fallen in—was created when Premier Matteo Renzi was still a schoolboy. It is vital to understand this point. At a time when Margaret Thatcher was imposing supply-side reforms on Britain, Ruud Lubbers was squeezing public spending until the pips squeaked in the Netherlands, and even François Mitterrand's goal of constructing socialism in one country had given way to Bundesbank-imposed austerity, Italy engaged in a binge of unproductive public spending. In borrowing terms, the 1980s were like war years; a decade in which the Italian state typically paid out 10 percent or more of GDP every year than it raised in taxes. [19] Much of this vast increase in expenditure (overall, the national debt rose from under 60 percent of GDP in 1980 to 121 percent in 1994) was siphoned off in corruption, or used to finance generous pensions (it was possible to retire, in some cases, after only 15 years' work, and pensions were based upon final salary, not contributions paid), or frittered away on the cost overruns of prestige projects.

This dangerous debt increase occurred despite the fact that taxes also increased sharply during the 1980s as a share of GDP. They reached 40 percent of national income by the early 1990s: a hitherto unheard of figure. Taxes were raised, moreover, disproportionately from the salary and wage-earning classes who could be taxed at source. Evasion of taxes among entrepreneurs and professionals was (and is) rife. In the dying days of the DC-PSI "regime," the Italian state in effect contrived an unjust redistribution of wealth from the middle class to those with good political connections, or to those who were directly living off politics. A lot of millionaires made their fortunes in the 1980s, which became renowned as a decade of excess. For sheer bling, Milan in the 1980s rivaled the follies of Russian oligarchs or Chinese property dealers today. Silvio Berlusconi, with his media empire and jet-set lifestyle, was the single individual, Craxi aside, who most epitomized the entire epoch. Craxi was, in fact, Berlusconi's political protector and sponsor. [20]

Such a state of affairs could not go on, especially when the end of the Cold War robbed Rome's politicians of their anticommunist rationale. Between 1990 and 1994, Italy experienced the worst crisis of any contemporary democracy since the collapse of the French IV Republic in 1958. The DC and the PSI were swept away in 1992–93 by corruption investigations in Milan, Venice, and other cities, and by a crackdown on the mafia links of politicians in the country's South. Literally thousands of politicians were investigated (over 2,500 by the Milanese prosecutors alone) and most were either sentenced or took a plea bargain.

The turmoil in the political sphere spilled over into the markets: during the September 1992 crisis in the European Monetary System, only a savage austerity package, featuring tax raises and a levy on bank accounts, saved Italy's creditworthiness. Out of the EMS, the lira plunged against the German mark and Italy's formidable exporters were able to capitalize for the remainder of the decade upon the advantage given to them by a devalued currency (Italy ran substantial trade surpluses in the mid-1990s). The memory of the spurt of rapid economic growth brought about by the devaluation of 1992 lives on today; the fact that it suddenly made Italians poor relatives of the Germans is remembered less well.

What is not sufficiently appreciated outside Italy, however, is that the economic consequences of the end of the so-called "First Republic" were enormous for the mass of Italian voters. When Eurozone politicians preach the need for fiscal rigor to the Italians, they are ignoring—willfully or otherwise—the fact that most Italian citizens consider that they have been enduring austerity since the summer of 1992. Ever since then, the Italian state, in order to keep the financial markets quiet, has been underinvesting in national infrastructure (and thus deflating the economy) and taxing too many of its citizens too much. While Italians pay, as a percentage of national income, little more tax than most Eurozone citizens, their hospitals, welfare provision, universities, roads, and railways are for the most part worse than in the rich countries of northern Europe.[21] Those countries have invested their wealth wisely: Italy, when it was wealthy, squandered a patrimony. And this is the root cause of Italy's present mood of decline, and of its objective slide down international rankings in many areas of life, not just output per head.

TARNISHED SAVIORS

Despite the commonplace metaphor, debt is more like a slag heap than a mountain. That is to say, it is a human-constructed, potentially poisonous mound, and it can be eliminated by political action, in a way that a mountain cannot. The debt-slag can be shifted, (A) in an ecologically sound way, by sensible policies that boost growth, cut government waste, and inspire the confidence of the international markets (and hence reduce the costs of financing the debt). It can also be reduced by raising taxes on those who have done well during the boom years and redistributing wealth to help working and middle class incomes and consumption. Alternatively, one can (B) try and leach the slag away through inflation, a process that has harmful effects by the dozen on the environment, but which can be less politically damaging for those doing the leaching.

The second way Italy's politicians have contributed to driving Italy's decline is in their attitudes to the debt burden after it had been created by the 1980s binge. The politicians of the Second Republic, above all Silvio Berlusconi, though we should not demonize him in this regard, proved incapable of virtuous method A, and were not allowed, because of their treaty commitments to their partners in the European Union to adopt method B, especially after 1999. As a result, they have done neither one thing nor the other; have temporized, and have arguably got the worst of both worlds.

More generally, the political class—left and right—has failed to adjust the Italian state to the rigors imposed by Euro membership. Two *toccasana* (cure-alls) for national renewal have been proposed to the Italian people since the collapse of the early 1990s. The first of these is a single individual: Silvio Berlusconi. In the 1994 election campaign, and in several subsequent electoral tests, Berlusconi depicted himself as a man of destiny who would save Italy from the ineptness of squabbling politicians. He would bring to the premiership skills honed in the business world to meet the national balance sheet and deliver the goods (the clichés are deliberate: Berlusconi has never made the mistake of overestimating the intelligence of the average Italian voter). The entire Italian right-wing—a motley crew of so-called liberals, reactionary Christian Democrats, former and actual fascists, the *Lega Nord*, and southern Italian notables with murky acquaintances—have found an instrument of uneasy unity by backing Berlusconi's claim to be the *salvatore della patria*. Without him, they could never have assembled a winning coalition and obtained the fruits of office. For his more idolatrous followers, Berlusconi, like Mussolini, is always right, perhaps especially when he is obviously wrong. A savior's judgment cannot be called into question.

The second cure-all for national renewal was offered by the center-left, by Catholic centrists and by influential *professori* with a pulpit in the national newspapers: more Europe. For many educated Italians, the Process (capital letters are obligatory) of European Integration is nothing less than a historical destiny whose end is a federal United States of Europe that will bring social justice to all European peoples. It was a crucial question of national pride for men like Romano Prodi (premier 1996–1998 and then president of the European Commission, 1999–2004), Mario Monti (technocrat premier from November 2011 to April 2013 and former EU commissioner for the single market), Carlo Azeglio Ciampi (president of Italy 1999–2006 and before that treasury minister in Prodi's 1996–1998 government), Tommaso Padoa-Schioppa (Prodi's economy minister during his second premiership 2006–2008 and a member of the executive committee of the ECB before that), and Giorgio Napolitano (president of the republic from 2006 to January 2015)

that Italy should be in the forefront of this process.[22] Membership of the Euro
was also expected to bring concrete immediate economic benefits, too. The
neo-liberal side of the Maastricht Treaty was perceived as a *vincolo esterno*
(outside constraint) that would compel Rome to follow budgetary discipline,
implement necessary supply-side reforms and, in general, "Europeanize" the
state. Between 1996 and 1998, Prodi and Ciampi worked like Trojans to get
Italy's accounts in order.[23] A special tax was imposed upon higher earners
and state-owned industries were privatized. Italy made the grade and was
accepted into the Euro-club in 1998. Prodi's parliamentary majority sacked
him a few months later.

The great fact of the improperly named Second Republic (i.e., the period
since the democratic collapse of the early 1990s) is that both putative saviors
have been tarnished—Berlusconi irredeemably so. Berlusconi governed Italy
for five years between June 2001 and May 2006 and for over three years
between May 2008 and November 2011. He was premier longer than any
other statesman in the history of postwar Italy—more than De Gasperi, more
than Craxi, more than the imaginative Amintore Fanfani, whom de Gaulle
admired, and more than Aldo Moro, whose cruel "execution" at the hands of
the Red Brigades epitomized the breakdown of the Italian state in the 1970s.
Yet the accomplishments of Berlusconi's governments were negligible. It
was on his watch that the decline occurred. The style of politics, moreover,
remained the same as always. Despite the substantial majorities Berlusconi's
coalitions enjoyed in parliament, his governments always seemed to be hang-
ing by a thread. Far from being a chief executive making tough decisions
fast, Berlusconi often had to act as mediator-in-chief between the big beasts
of his coalition. Above all, hundreds of days were spent on Berlusconi's own
private affairs; on laws that succeeded in keeping him out of jail, and in
frenzied speculation about his complicated sex life.

In 2011, swamped with personal and political problems, Berlusconi's
government lost the plot. Foreign owners of Italian debt began dumping
bonds, the "spread" with German bonds widened dramatically, and a Greek-
style crash loomed. After pressure from horrified EU leaders, President Giorgio Napolitano told Berlusconi it was time to go.[24] The would-be savior was
condemned to four years' imprisonment for embezzlement in July 2013 and
is currently facing other criminal charges of a serious nature. Although his
hardcore supporters continue to insist that he alone can revive Italy, and rant
against the "judicial terrorism" of which he has been a victim, Berlusconi
will never be premier again—although *Forza Italia* remains a political force
of some weight. The enchantment binding millions of middle class Italians to
his personality has been broken.

The tarnishing of the EU has been less lurid, but is perhaps potentially
more important. It is now widely asserted—notably by the populist *Lega
Nord* and comedian Beppe Grillo's "Five Star" Movement (M5S)—that the

EU's commitment to fiscal rigor has been the primary cause of Italy's economic decline and that only exit from the single currency can save the Italian economy from more decades of slow or nonexistent growth.[25] More than 50 percent of Italians think EU membership is a bad thing: an unprecedented number. The truth is that, unlike Great Britain, Italy has never had a grown-up conversation about the merits of Euro membership. Italians joined the single currency as a leap of faith, without serious discussion of membership's merits and demerits.

In hindsight, Euro membership saved Italy from a brutal millennium devaluation: Eurozone convergence toward German bond yields made it easier for Italy to finance its public debt and put off therapeutic reforms. On the other hand, the fact that the *vincolo esterno* turned out to be a pair of elastopants, not a corset, allowed Italy's politicians to live in a fools' paradise. The post-Euro decade should have been the moment for Italy to get into the gym and sweat: instead, it will pass into history as a period in which the political class (above all the Right, but the Center-Left are not innocent) sat on the sidelines and gossiped idly about Berlusconi's crimes and misdemeanors while others pounded the treadmills of supply side reforms. The debt disaster of the 1980s was compounded by a culpable failure to take hard decisions in the 2000s. The politicians of the Second Republic have as much responsibility for the decline as their predecessors in the First (and, of course, there were many politicians who were influential in both Republics).

NOT OUR FAULT

If Italy is in decline—and it is hard to dispute that its problems go beyond the slide in importance, prestige, and relative wealth common to European countries—the question becomes what can be done to stop or, better, reverse the decline? This is the central question in Italian political debate today.

One thing that ordinary Italian voters have done is "kick the rascals out." The analysis of this chapter, by laying the blame for the disastrous decline of Italy since the 1980s squarely on the shoulders of its political class, is conforming to the judgment that the Italians themselves have made upon the men (and the few women) who have ruled them. The sheer scale of political change in Italy since the downfall of Berlusconi in November 2011 is startling. First and foremost, the M5S has mobilized a huge slice of the population *schifato* by the dishonesty, corruption, and incompetence of the political class. The M5S, alas, is a hysterical, wayward, querulous creature whose militants are already showing signs of careerism and whose leader, Grillo, has a distinct fascist tinge. Yet its popularity obstinately remains around 20 percent of the electorate. There are millions of young and early middle-aged people who will vote for it: such people regard the parties of the Second

Republic literally as criminal gangs. The *Lega Nord*, which seemed like a dead man walking in 2011 after its charismatic founder and leader, Umberto Bossi, and his family were charged with misuse of public funds, has bounced back dramatically by adopting a policy stance that is openly influenced by Marie Le Pen's *Front National*. Its new leader, Matteo Salvini, is a shrewd populist in his early forties with a knack for reducing even the most complex questions to their lowest common denominator.[26] It works: the *Lega* is taking over 12 percent in the opinion polls—higher even than its glory days in the mid-1990s—and is for the first time showing signs of breaking out of its northern heartland to take votes in central and even southern Italy. Its new supporters have largely come at the expense of Berlusconi's Forza Italia, which now runs a serious risk of being relegated to second position among the parties representing the Italian right.

On the center-left, the turmoil has been scarcely less. The rise of the current premier, Matteo Renzi, to power in 2013–2014 was an unprecedented event in modern Italian politics. In effect, following the demoralizing electoral failure of the principal party of the left, the *Partito Democratico* (PD), in the 2013 general elections, there took place an emotional generational revolt by the party's younger activists and supporters against an older generation of leaders that had been too incompetent to beat Berlusconi and that had allowed the Right to let the country drift into disaster. Renzi rode the wave of revolt with consummate political skill (and not a little ruthlessness) by pledging to *rottamare* (junk) the old guard and bring about national rebirth.[27] The PD is now mostly in the hands of a new generation of politicians who are mostly in their early forties. They believe, in the face of the evidence, that the existing institutions of Italian representative democracy, and the existing political process, can still deliver positive outcomes—though how long their optimism and political idealism will last if Renzi's ambitious reform agenda is defeated is anybody's guess.

This chapter has argued that Italy's decline has largely been due to the ineptness and venality of its political leadership. It *may* follow from this that only better political leadership—a generation of leaders who consistently put the collective good ahead of the desires of sectional interests, who prize education and hard work over the favor-networks, and who are prepared to take hard, unpopular decisions now for the sake of Italians still in school or as yet unborn—can halt and reverse the country's increasingly demoralizing decline. Certainly, only a generation of leaders (and not a few isolated individuals) that are honest, competent, and fair will restore the confidence of the under-40s in Italy's political institutions.

Whether the new political class that has emerged since the downfall of Berlusconi in 2011 is capable of rising to this challenge is an open question to which nobody has a convincing answer. The experience of the Renzi government, which has begun an ambitious program of reforms to the constitution, labor market, and public administration, seems to indicate a negative response. All the proposed reforms have run into a wall of opposition in parliament and civil society, and very often the opposition has been anything other than constructive. The government has also failed to get a grip on public spending, which continues to rise inexorably.[28] This is in part because the economy remains mired in recession, but it is also due to the government's unwillingness (and inability) to reduce what the state does and to make the state do things better.

Adam Smith notoriously tells us that there is a great deal of ruin in any nation, but that does not mean that nations cannot be ruined by the stupidity and cupidity of their rulers—the examples of Argentina and Greece are before us all. Over the past thirty years, Italy's political class has steered *il bel paese* to a point where either renewal begins soon, or decline will quicken. Given Italy's economic weight in Europe, and its history of political instability, it is in nobody's interest that its decline should become a rout. For any acceleration in Italy's decline would quickly spill over into the political systems of its neighbors.[29]

NOTES

1. For the contemporary debate over British decline, see especially the symposium on "Suicide of a Nation," *Encounter* 118 (July 1963), edited and introduced by Arthur Koestler.

2. Readers of Italian should consult Antonio Varsori, *La Cenerentola di Europa* (Rome: Rubbettino, 2010) for a good summary of the scholarship on this subject.

3. The comparison with Japan might surprise, but the similarities between Italy and Japan's political cultures, and their leadership styles, has been explicitly made by Richard J. Samuels, *Machiavelli's Children: Leaders and Their Legacies In Italy and Japan* (Ithaca N.Y.: Cornell University Press, 2005). This interesting exercise in comparative history is also worth reading for the sophisticated and thought-provoking thesis it advances about the types of political agency.

4. On this subject, see Leopoldo Nuti, *La sfida nucleare. La politica estera italiana e le armi atomiche, 1945–1991* (Bologna: Il Mulino, 2007), especially ch. 8.

5. Joseph LaPalombara, *Democracy, Italian Style* (New Haven CT: Yale University Press, 1987).

6. IMF, *World Economic Outlook*, October, 2013, figures at PPP.

7. On savings rates, see Daniele Franco, "Il risparmio delle famiglie italiane," http://www.astrid.eu/Regolazion/Studi--ric/Archivio-25/Franco_-risparmio-19-giugno-2012.pdf.

8. http://epp.eurostat.ec.europa.eu/tgm/table.do?tab=table&plugin=0&language=en&pcode=tec00115).

9. Readers of Italian might like to consult Graziella Priulla, *L'Italia dell'ignoranza: crisi della scuola e declino del paese* (Milan: Angeli, 2011).

10. http://espresso.repubblica.it/opinioni/libero-mercato/2014/02/27/news/fermate-l-esodo-dei-laureati-migliori-1.155235.

11. My particular antipathy is "briffing" (briefing), a word much used by imperfectly educated yuppies wishing to sound like West Wing whizzkids. Almost all political initiatives in Italy nowadays seem to be given an English title: examples are "Jobs Act," "Family Day," "devolution." Premier Matteo Renzi candidly admits he speaks "Globish" rather than English; his comical speech to the Council on Foreign Relations in New York on 24 September 2014 amply confirmed his deficiencies in this regard.

160 Mark Gilbert

12. Steven Philip Kramer, "Baby Gap: How to Boost Birthrates and Avoid Democratic Decline," *Foreign Affairs*, May-June 2012.

13. The decline of Italian soccer has even sparked the interest of one of the country's leading economists: see Tito Boeri and Battista Severgnini, "The Decline of Professional Football in Italy," Forschungsinstitut zur Zukunft der Arbeit, Discussion paper No. 7018, November 2012.

14. U.S. policy toward Italy in this period is explained by Ambassador Richard N. Gardner, *Mission Italy: On the Front Lines of the Cold War* (Lanham MD: Rowman & Littlefield, 2005).

15. A point strongly made, of course, by Patrick McCarthy, *The Crisis of the Italian State* (New York: Saint Martin's, 1995 and 1997).

16. The phrase is taken from Gianfranco Pasquino, *Restituire lo scettro al principo: proposta di riforma istituzionale* (Rome: Laterza, 1986). Pasquino, a Bologna University professor, was elected to parliament in the 1983 elections and took an active role in pushing for a change to Italy's then narrowly proportional electoral law.

17. On this issue, Gianni Cuperlo, *Storia e futuro della politica in televisione* (Rome: Donzelli, 2004) is very interesting. Cuperlo has since become Matteo Renzi's chief rival within the PD.

18. The most detailed account in English of these political intrigues is Mark Gilbert, *The Italian Revolution: The End of Politics, Italian Style* (Boulder, Colo: Westview Press, 1995), ch. 1 *passim*.

19. See Maura Francese and Angelo Pace, *Il debito pubblico italiano: dall'Unità a oggi. Una ricostruzione della serie storica* (Rome: Banca d'Italia, 2008), 28.

20. The best book on Craxi's role in the end of the First Republic is Simona Colarizi and Marco Gervasoni, *La Cruna dell'ago: Craxi, il partito socialista e la crisi della repubblica* (Rome: Laterza, 2006).

21. According to Eurostat figures (June 2014), the Italian state absorbs 44 percent of GDP in taxes. This is slightly less than Denmark (48.1 percent), Belgium (45.4 percent), France (45 percent), and about the same as Sweden, Finland, and Austria. The EU-28 average is 39.4 percent; the EU-18 average is 40.4 percent. Available online at: http://ec.europa.eu/taxation_customs/resources/documents/taxation/gen_info/economic_analysis/tax_structures/2014/pr_92-2014_en.pdf.

22. See, by way of illustration: Padoa-Schioppa's *L'Europa: Forza Gentile* (Bologna: Il Mulino, 2001), or Prodi's *Europe As I See It* (Cambridge UK: Polity, 2000). President Napolitano's collected speeches on the EU are available at: http://www.quirinale.it/elementi/Continua.aspx?tipo=Discorso&key=2821.

23. On this effort to make the Euro grade, see Alberta Sbragia, "Italy Pays for Europe: Political Leadership, Political Choice and Institutional Adaption," in *Transforming Europe: Europeanization and Domestic Change* (eds.) Maria Green Cowles, Jim Caporaso and Thomas Risse-Kappen (Ithaca NY: Cornell University Press, 2001), 79–96. See also, in English, Kenneth Dyson and Keith Featherstone, "Italy and EMU as a 'vincolo esterno': Empowering the Technocrats, Transforming the State," *Southern European Politics & Society* 1 (1996): 272–99.

24. Background to the 2011 crisis is reported in Alan Friedman, *Ammazziamo il gattopardo* (Rizzoli, 2014).

25. The Lega Nord has created a website from which interested citizens can download anti-Euro pamphlets and posters and has organized several protest days against the single currency: http://www.bastaeuro.org/ Beppe Grillo is promoting a referendum to leave the Euro (the two movements may yet end up cooperating): http://www.beppegrillo.it/.

26. See his Twitter account: https://twitter.com/matteosalvinimi. One good indicator of Italian decline is the fact that the new generation of politicians communicate almost entirely in semi-literate messages embodying banal, when not actually downright offensive, slogans.

27. For an idea of what Renzi stands for, see his short book, *Oltre la rottamazione: nessun giorno è sbagliato per provare a cambiare* (Milan: Mondadori, 2013).

28. The Italian state spent €825 billion in 2014: an increase of 7.8 percent on the previous year at a time of near deflation. See: Gianni Trovato, "Spesa pubblica: balzo del 7.8% nel 2014," *Il Sole 24 Ore*, 6 August 2014.

29. The author would like to thank Tom Row and John Lamberton Harper for their very thoughtful and helpful comments on the draft version of this chapter. He would also like to thank Dana H. Allin for allowing him to reproduce material from a previous publication, "Italy's Forty Years' Crisis," *Survival: Global Politics and Strategy*, 56: 5, 129–42.

BIBLIOGRAPHY

Ambassador Gardner, Richard N. *Mission Italy: On the Front Lines of the Cold War*. Lanham MD: Rowman & Littlefield, 2005.

Boeri, Tito and Battista Severgnini. "The Decline of Professional Football in Italy." *Forschungsinstitut zur Zukunft der Arbeit*. Discussion paper No. 7018, November 2012.

Dyson, Kenneth and K. Featherstone. "Italy and EMU as a 'vincolo esterno': Empowering the Technocrats, Transforming the State." *Southern European Politics & Society* 1 (1996): 272-299.

Francese, Maura and Angelo Pace. *Il debito pubblico italiano: dall'Unità a oggi. Una ricostruzione della serie storica*. Rome: Banca d'Italia, 2008.

Friedman, Alan. *Ammazziamo il gattopardo*. Rizzoli, 2014.

Gilbert, Mark. *The Italian Revolution: The End of Politics, Italian Style*. Boulder, Colo: Westview Press, 1995.

Kramer, Philip. "Baby Gap: How to Boost Birthrates and Avoid Democratic Decline." *Foreign Affairs*. May-June 2012.

LaPalombara, Joseph. *Democracy, Italian Style*. New Haven CT: Yale University Press, 1987.

Nuti, Leopoldo. *La sfida nucleare. La politica estera italiana e le armi atomiche, 1945-1991*. Bologna: Il Mulino, 2007.

McCarthy, Patrick. *The Crisis of the Italian State*. New York: Saint Martin's, 1995 and 1997.

Pasquino, Gianfranco. *Restituire lo scettro al principo: proposta di riforma istituzionale*. Rome: Laterza, 1986.

Priulla, Graziella. *L'Italia dell'ignoranza: crisi della scuola e declino del paese*. Milan: Angeli, 2011.

Samuels, Richard J. *Machiavelli's Children: Leaders and Their Legacies In Italy and Japan*. Ithaca N.Y.: Cornell University Press, 2005.

Sbragia, Alberta. "Italy Pays for Europe: Political Leadership, Political Choice and Institutional Adaption." In *Transforming Europe: Europeanization and Domestic Change*. Edited by Maria Green Cowles, Jim Caporaso and Thomas Risse-Kappen. Ithaca, New York: Cornell University Press, 2001.

Varsori, Antonio. *La Cenerentola di Europa*. Rome: Rubbettino, 2010.

Chapter Nine

Russia as a "Great Power"

Revival, Stagnation, and Decline

Hannes Adomeit

"If we were to continue treading on the current path we will not make the necessary progress for an increase in the standard of living. We also will not be in a position to safeguard the security of our country or its normal development. We would even jeopardize its existence. I say this without any exaggeration."

—Vladimir Putin [1]

"We have to draw lessons from recent events. So long as oil prices were growing many, almost all of us, to be honest, harbored the illusion that structural reforms could wait. [. . .] But we can tarry no longer. We must begin the modernization and technological upgrading of our entire industrial sector. I see this as a question of our country's survival in the modern world."

—Dmitry Medvedev [2]

The statements by the two top Russian leaders seem to have been made just recently and, given their frankness, in private. They were, however, uttered in 2008 and 2009, respectively, and in public. They also underline the fact that what Vladimir Putin and Dmitry Medvedev had to say six and seven years ago still applies today. Not only did the decision-makers in the inner circle of the Kremlin continue to cling to the illusion that major structural reforms can wait but their policies have accelerated Russia's march along the path leading from revival via stagnation to decline. Even shortly before Putin's return to power for a third term in office as president, the term "modernization," no matter whether its content was understood as being limited to "technocratic" solutions or to have social, economic, and political dimensions, has for all practical purposes disappeared from public discourse. The stark image of the country's survival and its very existence being at stake has been replaced by the arrogance of power, neo-imperialism, and strident anti-Westernism. This constitutes a complete reversal of the idea that Russia's road to a post-modern economy and society with a flexible political system depended on close cooperation with the United States and Europe.

The astounding reversal needs explanation. This is true, literally and figuratively, not only for "academic" reasons but for policy making as well. The corresponding endeavor will be undertaken by focusing on four distinct phases of development.

The *first* briefly covers the effects of the collapse of the Soviet Union on Russia. This is the era with Boris Yeltsin as president, extending from the dissolution of the USSR in 1992 to the financial crash of 1998. The *second* is Russia's economic revival and ascendancy to self-proclaimed "Great Power" status under Putin during his first two terms in office, stretching from his election in 2000 to the global financial and economic crisis of 2008–2009 with its effects on Russia. The *third* is contemporaneous with the major part of Medvedev's presidency in tandem with Putin as prime minister. This phase, ranging from 2009 to 2012, is characterized by Russia's ambiguous and inadequate recovery from the crisis with economic growth rates failing to return to the high level enjoyed in the preceding period and the realization not only by Russian economic experts but also, as quoted above, the top political leaders that comprehensive structural reforms were urgently required to arrest stagnation and decline. The *fourth* is that of Putin's return to the presidency in 2012 and is marked by the above-mentioned arrest of the "modernization" discourse (in any case, always a discourse, never a policy or strategy) as well as the adoption of policies reminiscent of the stagnation (*zastoy*) era under communist party leader Leonid Brezhnev which are almost certain to accelerate decline.

SOVIET COLLAPSE AND RUSSIAN DECLINE

In the period from the collapse of the Soviet Union in 1992 to Putin's ascendancy to power at the end of 1999, Russia underwent a radical transformation through "shock therapy," moving from a centrally planned economy to a globally integrated market economy. In a corrupt and haphazard privatization process, politically well connected "oligarchs" gained control over major state-owned firms and left equity ownership highly concentrated. In that period, real GDP fell by more than 40 percent. Hyperinflation wiped out personal savings. Crime and destitution was spreading.

By 1997, with the first (slight) GDP increase since the collapse of the Soviet Union, it seemed that Russia had finally begun to live up to the precepts of transition theory, that is, transition from a one-party state, command economy and controlled society to a democratic and pluralist political system, a market economy with more or less fair competition, a law-based state, civilian rather than military priorities, and an active civil society.

However, the crash of the financial market, including government default, the devaluation of the ruble by close to 200 and the contraction of GDP by 5.3 percent in 1998 demonstrated that transformation theories were inapplicable to Russia. Russia, as a perceptive Russian expert wrote, got "lost in transition."[3] The path chosen and the system that developed under Yeltsin did not replicate the experience of the Baltic States and Poland. Under his successor, put in power through a blatantly corrupt and conspiratorial process, who guaranteed the, in the wider sense, "Yeltsin family" immunity from prosecution, a system *sui generis* was to develop: the "Putin system."

ASCENDANCY TO SELF-PROCLAIMED "GREAT POWER" STATUS

When Putin assumed the presidency in 2000, the top priority of his rule became—in the Kremlin's narrative—overcoming the "chaos" and "disorder" of the Yeltsin era and making sure that Russia would "rise from its knees" and resume its "rightful" place as a "Great Power" in European and world affairs. The image of Russia's current and future status was aptly expressed by foreign minister Evgeny Primakov in his article upon the 200th anniversary of his nineteenth century predecessor, Prince Alexander Gorchakov. "Be it declared," the Czarist foreign minister had written after Russia's disastrous defeat in the Crimean war of 1853, "that in matters of domestic and foreign policy alike, Russia has liquidated her accounts with the recent past." It was not disappearing as a major European power. It was not sulking. It was simply "gathering strength."[4]

In fact, Putin's record for the achievement of the aim of restoring Russia to the position of a Great Power in the first two terms of office was impressive: The Russian economy started to grow, with an average annual growth rate of about 7 percent in 1999–2007.[5] Inflation decreased substantially, from 84 percent in 1998 to 10–12 percent in 2004–2007. Economic reforms were introduced, including a new tax code with lower and fewer taxes, notably a flat income tax of 13 percent. This helped to alleviate the chronic budget deficit of on average 9 percent of GDP and to change it into a budget surplus amounting to 7.5 percent of GDP. The current account (i.e., balance of payments) deficits turned into current account surpluses. Public foreign debt dwindled from 100 percent of GDP to 4 percent. The large trade surpluses led to the accumulation of hard currency reserves that reached approximately $600 billion in August 2008—the third largest after China and Japan. Part of this sum was used for the creation of a stabilization fund in the amount of $180 billion. The Kremlin confidently took up the idea developed in 2001 by Goldman Sachs' chief economist, Jim O'Neill, that Russia was in the same league with China, India, and Brazil; that this "BRIC" configuration had to be considered an emerging economic powerhouse; and that, by 2037, the combined GDP of those four countries could be bigger than that of the G7.[6]

In February 2008, Putin looked back at his two terms in office as president and, predictably, provided a favorable assessment of his achievements. Over the last eight years, total investment in the Russian economy had risen seven-fold, he said. Stock market capitalization had undergone a 22–fold increase compared to 1999. The stock market was worth $60 billion at the end of 1999 but by the end of 2007 it had risen to $1.330 trillion. In 2007, capital inflow amounted to a record $82.3 billion. In that year, Russia achieved its best GDP growth result yet—8.1 percent. As a result, he continued, Russia had moved ahead of G8 countries such as Italy and France in terms of GDP as calculated on a purchasing parity basis and had become one of the world's seven biggest economies. Unemployment and the level of poverty had decreased, and demographic problems had been alleviated as the falling birth rate and rising death rate had been checked.[7]

The Kremlin's self-confident mood was evident in the speech by the then Russian finance minister, Aleksey Kudrin, at the World Economic Forum in Davos on January 23, 2008. He stated that the U.S. economy was at the verge of a recession and that global economic growth was slowing down. In such a situation, he thought, interest in Russia would be growing because the country was "an island of stability in the ocean of a global crisis" and that, therefore, "investors will continue to invest billions of dollars into the rising Russian economy."[8] In June 2008, that is, shortly after he had been installed as president, Medvedev promised to elevate the ruble to one of the world's reserve currencies and to turn Moscow into an international financial center.[9] Such assessments conformed to the predictions expressed by Igor Shuvalov, one of the deputy chiefs of the presidential administration, in the same month that "by the end of the year, Russia will occupy sixth place among the world's national economies."[10]

The economic success story was portrayed by the Kremlin as being part and parcel of the establishment of "political stability." Western criticism to the effect that Russia was moving in the "wrong direction," away from democratic, law-based, and free-market principles to an authoritarian system with increasing influence of the *siloviki*—the representatives of the "power" institutions and agencies, notably the secret police—in decision-making, was met with scorn.[11] The Kremlin's public relations experts countered with the argument that democracy had many variants but that the model Putin had developed, that of "managed" or "sovereign" democracy, perfectly well fit Russian society. No replica of Western models was needed.

Not surprisingly, the self-confident mood manifested itself also in Russia's foreign policy stance. One major example was Putin's speech at the February 2007 Munich International Security Conference. In essence, he called for a comprehensive reconsideration and restructuring of international relations. In obvious reference to the United States, he considered "the unipolar model not only unacceptable but also impossible in today's world [. . .] because at its basis there is and can be no moral foundations for modern civilization."[12] Russia, in other words, should have a greater say in European security and world affairs. As also the substantial modernization efforts made in the strategic nuclear sphere demonstrated, Moscow returned to the Soviet-era axiom that, in the relationship with the United States, the inalienable corollary to strategic parity is political equality.

FROM CRISIS TO STAGNATION

The confident assumptions about Russia as an "island of stability" and one of the emerging powerhouses of the world economy were shattered in the 2008–2009 global financial and economic crisis. The crisis underlined that Russia was firmly integrated in the world economy and could not be insulated from its ups and downs. It also showed that there was a significant gap between the C, I, and B of the BRIC, on the hand, and Russia, on the other, in terms of the ability to react to external shocks. The following developments testified to this state of affairs:[13]

- Whereas, in the first three quarters of 2008, Russia maintained high GDP growth rates, the last quarter heralded the coming stagnation and decline: GDP growth reached a mere 1.1 percent. During the first half of 2009, the average *fall of its GDP* was 10.4 percent—9.8 percent in the first quarter and 10.9 percent in the second. The aggregate decline in 2009 compared to the preceding year amounted to 8.7 percent.
- In the last quarter of 2008, *industrial output* declined by 6.1 percent. Even steeper plunges were recorded in 2009: 14.3 percent, 15.4 percent, and 11 percent in the first, second, and third quarters, respectively. Decreases occurred in all sectors of industry. However, the worst situation obtained in the manufacturing industry, which was down by 20.8 percent in the first quarter of 2009; automotive manufacturing fell by 55.9 percent.
- In October 2008, the Russian *stock market practically collapsed*. The Russian Trading System (RTS) fell by 75 percent as compared to its peak in May 2008. This fall was larger not only than that of the other three countries of the BRIC group but of all the other main industrialized countries.

- The country's fiscal position *worsened*. The budget surplus again turned into deficit. It fell from 4.1 percent of GDP in 2008 to −7.4 in 2009 and −7.5 percent in 2010.
- The significant contraction of economic activity was also reflected in Russia's *foreign trade*. The value of exports fell from $137 billion in the third quarter or 2008 to 68.1 billion in the second quarter of 2009; imports in the same period decreased from $82.9 billion to $43.8 billion.
- Until the 2008 crisis, Russia had been able to increase its currency reserves largely because of its huge incomes from the sales of raw materials (oil, gas, and metals). This trend was now reversed. Russian *currency reserves decreased* by more than one third: from $597 billion in August 2008 to $384 billion in February 2009.
- In the same period, the Central Bank had to spend over $200 billion in order to halt the *devaluation of the ruble*. This action, however, was unsuccessful. The ruble lost 40 percent of its value compared to the U.S. dollar. Nevertheless, the significant currency reserves accumulated and transferred to the Reserve Fund helped Russia weather the worst of the crisis.

There are two major reasons why the effect of the global financial and economic crisis was felt more acutely in Russia than in the other BRIC countries and in most of the OECD member states. The first is the drastic fall of the oil price from $150 per barrel in July 2008 to about $50 in January 2009 ($53 on average in 2009). Prior to the crisis, the oil and gas sector of the economy accounted for almost one third of GDP; fossil fuels amounted to almost two-thirds of Russian exports; corresponding receipts covered almost one-half of the national budget. It was, therefore, inevitable that the oil price decrease would produce extraordinary shock effects on the Russian financial system and the economy.

Second, foreign creditors withdrew large amounts of money from the massively indebted Russian corporate sector—more than $140 billion in 2008 and $150 billion in the following year—so as to improve their own liquidity, and they refrained from extending new credit which had fed the Russian economic engine. The two factors point to serious structural deficiencies of the Russian economy. Russian economists compiled some of them. These were held to include the following:

- *Lack of "long-term money"* by Russian savers to be transformed into investments.
- *Lack of labor market efficiency and labor mobility*. Employment is excessive in the private industrial sector, and in the 2008–2009 crisis it increased in the state sector.

- There are numerous *unprofitable enterprises* with out-of-date technology, and these are often based in *monogoroda*—single industry towns built around one main enterprise.
- *Investment risks are high* as potential Russian and foreign investors have to overcome bureaucratic barriers and contend with organized crime that, in turn, acts in conjunction with corrupt government officials.
- Such risks are compounded by a *corrupt and inefficient legal system.* Business arbitration procedures are inadequate and out of date. Many businessmen, therefore, prefer British or Dutch legislation for the conclusion and adjudication of contracts.
- There are *powerful cartels* that exert control over regional and sector markets, limiting fair competition in the market place. [14]

Putin himself acknowledged some of these deficiencies even before the onset of the crisis. In his February 2008 presentation of the Development Strategy for Russia until the Year 2020, for the main part, as noted above, he provided a favorable assessment of his two terms in office as president. [15] However, he was—in his own words—also willing to take "an objective and realistic look at the situation and adopt a resolutely self-critical approach." Russia, he acknowledged, had not succeeded in breaking away from the inertia of development based on energy resources and commodities. Only fragmentary attempts had been made to modernize the economy. As a result, Russia's dependence on raw materials exports and imported goods and technology was *increasing.* For him, this was evidently a nightmare.

> In the future, this could lead to us lagging behind the world's big economic powers and could push us out from among the world leaders. If we were to continue on this road we would not make the necessary progress in raising living standards. Moreover, we would not be able to ensure our country's security or its normal development. *We would be placing its very existence under threat.* I say this without any exaggeration. [16]

The country had to choose "between the opportunity to become a leader in economic and social development and *the threat of losing our economic standing, losing our security and ultimately even losing our sovereignty."* [17] What was to be done? Deep changes had to be made in all dimensions of the state management, the economy, and society. Russia, according to Putin, had to:

- achieve the transition to a new generation of education standards that would meet the needs of the modern innovative economy;
- improve interaction between scientific and educational organizations, the state, and the business community;

- encourage the business community to invest more in research and development;
- make more effective use of state resources invested in science and concentrate them on fundamental and cutting-edge areas of research;
- change the healthcare system and modernize healthcare facilities;
- create a national innovative system based on all of the different state and private institutions supporting innovation;
- embark on the large-scale modernization of production facilities in all economic sectors;
- develop new sectors able to compete globally, above all in the high technology sectors that are leaders in the "knowledge economy," including aircraft manufacturing, shipbuilding, energy, information technology, and medicine;
- build new and modernize existing roads, railway stations, ports, airports, electricity stations, and communications systems;
- develop market institutions and a competitive environment that would motivate companies to cut costs, modernize production, and respond flexibly to consumer demand;
- eradicate the "excessive administrative pressure" on the economy that had become one of the biggest brakes on development;
- establish competitive conditions for attracting the best and the brightest into the civil service and make it more accountable to society;
- do away with the "excessive centralization of state management" because the government took months and even years to make even the most elementary decisions;
- make use of the possibilities that existed for bringing private capital into the state sector, whether in industry or in the social sector;
- continue the work to "establish an independent and effective judiciary that unquestionably guarantees entrepreneurs' rights, including the right to protection from arbitrary action by bureaucrats."

Given the long list of economic ills and the numerous requirements to remedy them, one is left to wonder as to whether the "Putin system," including its very political foundation, wasn't in "urgent need" to be abolished altogether and an entirely new one to be constructed. Putin obviously was far from contemplating such a radical remedy. Furthermore, he exempted the political sphere from the demands for major change. Thus, he merely spoke of the need to transform the (presumably existing) "democratic state into an effective instrument for civil society's self-organization," "raise the role of non-governmental organizations, human rights ombudsmen and public councils," and further "develop the multiparty system." But in the same breath, almost in a violent outburst, he warned the political parties that they "must not forget their immense responsibility for Russia's future." No matter how fierce the political battles and no matter how irreconcilable the differences between parties might be, they should "not bring the country to the brink of chaos" and they should avoid "immoral and illegal, irresponsible demagogy and attempts to divide society and use foreign help or intervention in domestic political struggles."

It is more than doubtful that Putin himself was the author of the comprehensive diagnosis of what was wrong and what needed to be done. What is of significance here is that he lent his name to the call for major change and that the measures he suggested essentially coincided with those of "his" president. Medvedev, when he was president in the tandem arrangement with Putin as prime minister in 2008–2012, was even more critical of the system as it had developed.[18] Probably the most well-known of his assessments was the complaint that Russia had a "culture of legal nihilism that in its cynicism has no equal anywhere on the European continent." Russians needed to understand clearly that "if we want to become a civilized state, first of all we need to become a lawful one."[19] Further on social affairs, he pointed to "chronic corruption," a "semi-Soviet social system," and "demographic decline" that needed to be overcome. In economic affairs he decried Russia's "chronic inefficiency," "primitive raw materials economy," and "humiliating dependency on raw materials." The scathing criticism culminated in the message that, in essence, replicated the one conveyed earlier by Putin.

> We have to draw lessons from recent events. So long as oil prices were growing many, almost all of us, to be honest, harbored the illusion that structural reforms could wait . . . But we can tarry no longer. We must begin the modernization and technological upgrading of our entire industrial sector. *I see this as a question of our country's survival in the modern world.*[20]

Russia had to aim at the creation of a modern, diversified economy based on high technology and innovation. In contrast to previous such efforts, modernization this time had to be achieved not through coercion but via the development of the creative potential of every individual, through private entrepreneurship and initiative. What, in Medvedev's view, was the model that was to be emulated in such efforts to ensure the country's survival? As a world leader in technological innovation and its practical application to the economy, the example to emulate evidently was the *United States*. His attempt to transfer and replicate the U.S. experience in Russia is apparent in such proposals of his as the transformation of universities into "business incubators." These were to provide graduates from science and engineering departments with the possibility to apply research results in commercial enterprises. For such a purpose, he proposed:

> The foundation of an advanced research and development centre concentrated on the support of all priority spheres [. . .], a modern technology centre *mod-*

eled, if you like, after Silicon Valley and other foreign centers. The conditions
will be created there, to offer an attractive environment for leading scientists,
engineers, designers, programming specialists, managers and financial experts;
new technologies would be developed there, which would be able to compete
successfully on the world market.[21]

In March 2010, he announced that such a research and development "innovation centre," soon to be referred to as "innovation city," would be established in Skolkovo, not far from the capital.[22] Medvedev's modernization
campaign also had an important international dimension. Russia, he stated,
should attract foreign capital and make sure that "new technologies and
modern ideas would flow into the country."[23] Russian foreign policy had to
be put to the service of the country's modernization. It should "not only [help
to] provide practical assistance to Russian enterprises abroad and facilitate
the introduction of indigenous [Russian] quality brands of products and services [abroad] but also attract foreign investment and modern technologies to
Russia." For that very purpose, he called on the foreign ministry "to develop
a program for the effective utilization of foreign policy factors for the purpose of [accelerating] Russia's long-term development."[24] The foreign ministry duly obliged.[25]

One of the forms the foreign policy dimension of Medvedev's modernization campaign took was the so-called Partnerships for Modernization. The
idea had its origins in May 2008 when the German foreign ministry under the
auspices of the then foreign minister and vice-chancellor Frank-Walter Steinmeier proposed such a partnership—to supplement the German-Russian Strategic Partnership. Two years later, at the EU-Russia summit in Rostov on the
Don River, a corresponding EU-Russia Modernization Partnership was
founded and subsequently also a plethora of corresponding partnerships by
EU member states.

The drive to create favorable conditions for modernization was not just so
much hot air but was applied to practical foreign policy issues. Thus, Russia
responded positively to Obama's "reset" in U.S.-Russian relations; it cooper-
ated with the U.S. on the Iranian nuclear issue; it helped ISAF and anti-terror
operations in Afghanistan; and it abstained on the Libyan resolution. However, as for the domestic dimension, Medvedev's diagnosis and treatment of the
structural deficiencies impeding modernization, just like Putin's, almost
completely neglected the political obstacles. The ills, like corruption and
cynical regard for the law, were held to be social in origin, not political.
Thus, Medvedev decried Russia's "centuries'-old backwardness" and its "archaic society," where a few leaders "think and decide for everyone" but
whose actions were "chaotic and dictated by nostalgia and prejudice."[26] But
even the mere question as to whether such phenomena could be connected
with the political realm and reinforced by it failed to be posed.

In significant part as a result of such deficiencies and the lack of meaning-ful reforms, not just in the economic sphere but also in political and social dimensions, the "humiliating dependency" on raw materials deepened. Eco-nomic growth rates declined. In December 2011, when he was still prime minister, Putin said: "We are setting ourselves the goal of accelerating eco-nomic growth to 6 percent, better to 6–7 percent, and join the list of the world's top five economies in five years but not only because advanced economies will be falling but also because we'll be growing."[27] However, not only did Russian GDP growth rates fail to reach pre-crisis proportions, they went into steep decline. Thus, the economy grew by only 4.3 percent in 2011, 3.4 percent in 2012, and 1.3 percent in 2013.[28] Significantly for this study, according to Kudrin's definition, *economic growth in Russia of less than 3 percent is stagnation.*[29] This raises the question as to the reasons for such stagnation and decline, and whether the slide downhill is likely to be arrested, or continue and perhaps even accelerate.

DECLINE

In retrospect, six events that took place in the period from fall and winter 2011 to spring 2012 can, in their entirety, be regarded as producing a major turning point in Russia's political, economic, and social development. They also serve to provide answers to the question about the causes of stagnation and decline. The events to be enumerated, ordered according to time se-quence, are (1) the announcement by Putin on September 24 that Medvedev would not run in the upcoming presidential elections; (2) the resignation or dismissal, two days later, of finance minister Kudrin; (3) the publication, on October 3, of Putin's initiative for the creation of a Eurasian Union on the basis of the Customs Union Russia, Belarus, and Kazakhstan; (4) the whis-tles, catcalls, and booing in Moscow's Olympic Stadium, on November 20, as Putin entered the ring to congratulate a victorious Russian heavyweight martial arts fighter; (5) the December 4 parliamentary elections; and (6) the March 4, 2012, presidential elections.

Putin's announcement of his decision to run for president and Medvedev to step back into the role of prime minister was made in front of about 11,000 activists of the president's United Russia party in preparation for the upcom-ing parliamentary elections. It evoked tremendous disappointment among democratically minded and reformist elements in Russian politics and society as well as among Western political leaders and public opinion. It was not simply the decision itself that accounted for the disillusionment but Putin's revelation that the "agreement" between him and Medvedev "over what to do in the future was reached between us several years ago [. . .] at the time when we formed our comradely union."[30] Those who had thought that Medvedev's "modernization" drive, even though it had not yet produced tangible results, had at least pointed Russia in the right direction and that it would continue, felt that they had been fooled in a cynical game of musical chairs.

Part of the disappointment and disillusionment surfaced on November 20 when Putin entered the ring of Moscow's Olympic Stadium to congratulate a Russian martial arts fighter for his victory. The stadium was filled with about 20,000 spectators who could be expected to be favorably inclined toward him yet he was greeted by whistles, catcalls, and boos—all of which, embarrassingly for him and his entourage, carried live on television.[31]

The depth of dissatisfaction with the political system was revealed in the aftermath of the elections to the Duma on December 4 and to the presidency on March 4. Tens of thousands of people, many of them young, took to the streets in Moscow, and dozens of smaller rallies took place in other cities across Russia with a crowd of 3,000 reported in Tomsk, and 7,000 in St. Petersburg, according to police reports.[32] The protests were directed against the United Russia party, denounced as the "party of thieves and rogues," and against Putin as a "thief" and for a "Russia without Putin." Protesters said that they were "tired of absolute rulers and the police state," "the pervasive lawlessness and corruption," "the lack of civil freedoms," and "the absence of independent courts and social justice."[33] The scale and persistence of the protests were a complete surprise because in previous demonstrations a few dozen or at best hundreds of demonstrators had been vastly outnumbered by police and easily been dispersed so that Western observers and apparently also the Kremlin had come to the conclusion that apathy was the defining feature of Russian society.

Putin and his entourage in the Kremlin drew the conclusion from the unexpected mass protests that the pursuit of a reformist path of development would undercut their power. They decided to base their rule on the "conservative" majority composed of the huge army of officers and rank-and-file of the armed forces and the security agencies; the bloated corps of government bureaucrats; the employees of the (mostly unproductive) enterprises with (mostly obsolete) equipment; and the millions of pensioners. The very term "modernization," as mentioned above, disappeared from public discourse. Instead of embracing Western models and providing substance to the many modernization partnerships, the Kremlin denigrated and vilified the Western experience. In demonstrative alliance with the Russian Orthodox Church, it put itself forward as the mainstay of traditional Christian values in the face of Western "decadence."

One of the reasons for the discontent that had manifested itself in the large-scale demonstrations lay in the fact that, after the constitutional change signed by Medvedev three years earlier for the extension of the term in office of the president from four to six years, Putin would be able to rule until 2024. Young, Western-oriented, and successful representatives of the middle class feared that this would keep him in power longer than Brezhnev and that, indeed, it would mean the return of political and economic stagnation.

Such concerns were well in place given the circumstances of Kudrin's resignation or dismissal from the post of finance minister on September 26, 2011. Essentially, he had argued that planned increases in military expenditure could be realized only at the expense of spending on education and welfare. Funds would be diverted from the urgently required modernization of the economy and make Russia even more dependent on oil and gas exports. "We have neither the ability nor the money to increase military spending," he said.[34] The Kremlin, as will be shown below, disagreed with such views and continued to increase allocations for external defense and internal security.

The turn away from modernization partnerships with the West went hand in hand with the publication of Putin's initiative for the creation of a Eurasian Union on October 3, 2011—evidently the definition of his political priorities until 2024.[35] On the basis of the Customs Union and the Single Economic Space, "a qualitatively higher level of integration" should be reached and "a full-fledged economic union" be created. Goods, capital, and labor would move freely, and economic and monetary policy of its member states would be coordinated, as Putin outlined. He saw no contradiction between participation of neighboring countries in "advanced projects of integration" on post-Soviet territory and the pursuit of the "European choice." The Eurasian Union would be based on universal principles of integration and form an integral part of a larger Europe united by common values such as freedom, democracy, and the market.

In reality, however, at issue were two diametrically opposed concepts of integration—one that would link the countries of Eastern Europe and the Southern Caucasus to the EU by virtue of their participation in the Eastern Partnership and the conclusion of Association Agreements to lead to the creation of a Deep and Comprehensive Trade Area (DCFTA), the other that of the Eurasian Union which, in essence, would amount to the confirmation of a Russian sphere of interest where values are secondary but Moscow's influence and control preeminent. In his capacity still as premier, Medvedev made this perfectly clear. "If Ukraine were to take the road of European integration," he stated, "it would be more difficult for the country to integrate with the Single Economic Space and the Customs Union. *You cannot sit on two chairs.*"[36]

Putin's course for the increase of military expenditures and the modernization of the armed forces rather than the economy and the pursuit of Eurasian integration rather than building "common spaces" with the European Union is one of the main factors for Russia's stagnation and decline—for two reasons. The first is related to the Eurasian Union project itself. It binds together countries with undemocratic, authoritarian, and corrupt systems, unfair competition, central control over or interference in the market, arbitrary application of the law, repression of the freedom of expression, and limitation of the activities of non-governmental institutions. Kazakhstan, by far the bigger of the thus far two partners of the Eurasian Economic Union, has a similar economic structure as that of Russia. It is equally heavily dependent on the production and export of raw materials. It can contribute practically next to nothing to the modernization and diversification of Russia's economy. Russia's "humiliating dependence" on raw materials production and exports will not be lessened. The same is true for its conclusion in May 2014 of a $400 billion deal with China for the construction of gas pipelines and other infrastructure over the next 30 years. Belarus, too, will not provide any impetus to reform and in all likelihood only agreed to join the Customs Union because it is dependent on the provision of cheap Russian oil and gas. Moreover, the Customs Union is not working, as shown, for instance, in the re-export of agricultural products by Belarus to Russia in contravention of the sanctions that the Kremlin decreed.

The second reason derives from Putin's determination to prevent not only membership of Ukraine in NATO but also any significant cooperation of the country with and integration into the EU. In fact, the Eurasian Union project would be meaningless without the participation of Ukraine. This is due to the country's large territory, the second biggest country on the European continent after Russia; its large population; its economic importance for Russia, including in military industry; its role as a transit country for Russian gas; and its strategic location between the Baltic and the Black Sea. Moscow's uncompromising opposition to Kiev's course toward the conclusion of an Association Agreement with the EU precluded any "win-win situation," that is, the idea that an independent, democratically oriented, prosperous, and economically dynamic Ukraine would not only be in the best interest of the Ukrainians and the EU but also of Russia. Conversely, as Putin's utterly determined and uncompromising path of preventing Ukraine from pursuing the European option demonstrated, all three "players" in the Moscow-imposed "zero-sum" game are losers, yet the biggest loss is probably that suffered by Russia: Ukraine, whatever its territorial extent after the loss of control over Crimea and eastern parts of the country, is lost for Russia. Crimea and whatever other parts of eastern and potentially southern Ukraine Moscow will be able to control are likely to be basket cases of subsidization rather than viable and vibrant trade partners.

The domestic developments, that is, the stridently anti-Western campaign and the abandonment of the modernization drive, the vigorous pursuit of Eurasian integration, the annexation of Crimea, and the military intervention in eastern and southern Ukraine with a view to creating, if possible, a separatist Novorossiya stretching from Kharkov and Dnepropetrovsk via Mariupol, the Crimea, and Odessa to separatist Transnistria, are all interrelated. In turn, they have produced a dynamic that has given rise to several subordinate factors that are bound to not only lock the country into stagnation but to accelerate decline.

First and foremost, the Kremlin's neo-imperialist policies have evoked a plethora of Western sanctions which, in turn, have produced direct and indirect effects ("collateral damage") on the Russian economy. Methodologically, it is almost impossible to distinguish between the two. What is certain, however, is that they have severely affected Russian growth prospects. The negative effects of direct and indirect sanctions as well as other costs of neo-imperialism include the following:

SHRINKING RESERVES

The sanctions imposed by the United States and the EU as well as Australia, Canada, Japan, Norway, Switzerland, and other countries have targeted Russian financial institutions, limiting their access to capital markets. U.S. and European nationals and companies may no longer buy or sell new bonds, equity, or similar financial instruments with a maturity exceeding 30 days, issued by major state-owned Russian banks, including Sberbank, VTB Bank, Gazprombank, Russian Agricultural Bank (Rosselkhozbank), and Vnesheconombank (VEB), their subsidiaries outside the U.S. and entities acting on their behalf.[37]

According to some analysts writing at the time when financial sanctions were put in place, the measures would only have a limited impact on the credit profiles of either Russia or the banks directly affected. Their foreign-currency, short-term maturities were moderate and liquidity comfortable. This reduced the possibility of a sharp increase in refinancing risk. In case of need, the banks could also benefit from Russian government support. Russia's total international reserves after all amounted to $472 billion.[38]

Other analysts have disputed such calculations and wondered how long, if sanctions continued, Russia's strong reserve position could last. They base their assessments on the fact that, on November 9, 2014, the Central Bank of Russia (CBR) provided figures to the effect that total international currency reserves amounted to $421 billion.[39] While that sounded reassuring, the figures meant that reserves had fallen from $524 billion on October 31, 2013. Thus, Russia had lost $103 billion of reserves in a single year. Furthermore, not all the reserves are actually liquid, a significant part of these is committed to co-financing voluntary pension savings of Russian citizens, balancing the budget of the state pension fund and the financing of infrastructure projects. Assuming, therefore, that nothing extraordinary would happen, Russia's international reserves in 2015 are likely to shrink by $90 billion (foreign repayments of $150 billion minus an estimated current account surplus of

$60 billion), leaving Russia with only some $100 billion of usable reserves by the end of the year, covering about four months of imports. [40]

DECLINING THE OIL PRICES, DEVALUATION OF RUBLE, AND CAPITAL FLIGHT

The Kremlin and the government failed to heed its own warnings about the "humiliating dependency" on raw materials and dangerous reliance on high oil prices, and that major structural reforms were required in order to safe-guard Russia's very "existence" and "survival."[41] That basic deficiency turned into a serious crisis in 2014 as oil prices tumbled from monthly averages of about $105 per barrel from January to July, with a high of $115.75 in June, to $47.43 on January 13, 2015.[42] Given the fact that the price for natural gas is tied to that of oil, that oil and gas account for half of Russia's budget (pegged to an oil price of $96 per barrel for fiscal 2015) and two-thirds of its total exports, the huge fall of oil prices produced shock waves throughout the economy and the fiscal system. A vicious circle was set in motion, consisting of the loss of confidence of domestic and foreign economic actors in the economy and the ruble; its devaluation; massive capi-tal flight; and sanctions limiting the ability of the big state banks to raise credit.

To provide some data, the transfer of funds by Russian companies and individuals in the first half of 2014 amounted to $75 billion—an outflow that surpassed the $62.7 billion drain in all of the preceding year. For the whole year, the net capital drain reached a disastrous $151.1 billion, twice the amount of the preceding year.[43] Evidently, the sums that are leaving the country are not available for investment in the domestic economy. To this has to be added the disinclination of potential foreign investors, credit pro-viders, and foreign companies active in Russia to commit themselves to any new investments in the light of the deterioration of political relations with Russia and economic and financial sanctions. The aversion to the taking of financial risks was reinforced in January 2015 as Fitch Ratings and Moody's Investors Service downgraded Russia to its lowest investment grade and Standard and Poor even went further and cut Russia's credit rating to "junk" status.

The devaluation of the ruble in conjunction with the credit crunch is yet other factor that has a negative impact on economic growth. In 2014, the Russian currency lost 46 percent of its value against the U.S. dollar and more than 17 percent since the beginning of 2015.[44] As a result, the import of foreign technology, either for the replacement or the purchase of new equip-ment, has become prohibitively expensive. The problem is heightened by the high interest rates. In December 2014, in order to try to stem the fall of the ruble, the Central Bank increased its key interest rate from 11.5 percent to 17 percent—a move that did not help the ruble but threatened to deepen the recession expected for 2015. In recognition of the stifling effect on investment and production, at the end of January, the Russian Central Bank cut its interest rate to 15 percent.[45] That small reduction, however, is unlikely to have much of an impact on the economy.

INCREASING STATE CONTROL, INTERVENTION, AND MANAGEMENT

As external sources of internal financing and FDI are drying up, the government is forced to step in to assume a larger role in the management of the economy. This is yet another development that has preceded the imposition of Western sanctions—and its significance is also set to increase. According to the Yegor Gaidar Economic Policy Institute, the state sector of the economy in 2006 constituted 38 percent of Russia's GDP and rose to almost 40 percent in 2008. That percentage, according to the Ministry of Economy, grew up to 50 percent. In comparison, the world average of the government's ownership of the economy amounts to 30 percent.[46]

In most countries government has a bad record for stimulating growth, and Russia, to put it mildly, is no exception. Corruption is bound to increase as a result of more government regulation. It will in all likelihood also negatively affect the climate for doing business in Russia. The country made considerable progress in 2013–2014 toward improving conditions, climbing from 92nd place in the World Bank's "Ease of Doing Business" survey of 2013 to 62nd place in the 2015 survey (latest data of June 2014).[47] Now, however, Russia is highly unlikely to meet Putin's stated goal of entering the rating's top 20 economies by 2018. It may substantially slip back.

RISING OUTLAYS FOR ARMED FORCES, INTERNAL SECURITY, AND THE MILITARY-INDUSTRIAL COMPLEX

The trend toward recentralization and more government regulation will also increase because of rising defense expenditure, the effects of the Western sanctions policy on the Russian defense industry and the cut-off from Ukrainian military supplies and services. Between 2004 and 2014, Russia doubled its military spending. The national defense budget for 2015 will reach a record 3.3 trillion rubles ($50 billion), or 4.2 percent of the country's GDP.[48] This represents an 812 billion ruble ($12 billion) increase over the preceding year, and portends a proportionally larger defense budget over the next several years. The share of defense expenditures in GDP had previously risen from 3 percent in 2012, to 3.2 percent in 2013, and 3.4 percent in 2014. In 2016, that share, under the (illusionary) assumption of a 1 percent GDP growth, was projected to decrease from the 4.2 percent of GDP of the preceding year to 3.7 percent but with the contraction of the economy the share will be higher. The "anti-crisis plan" developed by the finance ministry in January 2015 provides for an expenditure cut of 10 percent for most budgetary line items except, however, among some other outlays, for "national defense."[49]

Plans are still in place for the implementation of an ambitious, far-reaching rearmament program for the period 2011–2020 in the amount of 20 trillion rubles ($308 billion). In accordance with the program, the state defense order will grow by more than 20 percent year on year in 2015 and by more than 40 percent in 2017. These expenditures, Russian officials claim, also will not be cut "regardless of the current economic situation."[50] Considering that the procurement effort in part relies on the import of foreign technology but that their costs have risen as a result of the depreciation of the ruble, there will be cuts *de facto* unless the government increases the ruble allocations.

The budgetary line item of "national defense," however, understates the burden of outlays for, in the broader sense, national and international *security*. According to Russian defense experts, the corresponding expenditures for 2014 were estimated to increase from 4.6 trillion rubles in 2013 to 5.5 trillion rubles ($84.6 billion or 6.8 percent of GDP) in 2014 and stay at that level nominally with a slight reduction of the share of these expenditures to GDP (6.7 percent) in 2016.[51] The costs for the modernization of the Russian armed forces are rising not only because of the depreciation of the ruble and the attendant increase in ruble terms but because of the United States and EU prohibitions for the export of military and dual use goods and technology. The sale to any individual or legal person in Russia of equipment and technologies included in the list of dual use goods now requires prior authorization by competent authorities in the United States and the EU. Even before the EU's export control decisions, the government in Berlin had revoked the permission given to the Rheinmetall Corporation to build a combat training center in Russia. France has put on ice its contract with Russia for the delivery of two Mistral helicopter ships to the Russian Navy. Thus, for the foreseeable future, military-technological cooperation between Western and Russian companies can well be ruled out. The Kremlin must therefore mobilize its own resources.

This also concerns military-industrial cooperation between Russia and Ukraine. Until Russia's annexation of Crimea, this was an important aspect of their relationship going back to Soviet times and covering such areas as airplane, helicopter, and naval engines, space launchers, airborne guided missiles, radars, aircraft components, and avionics. Ukraine and Russia were also pursuing several projects in the aerospace industry, space launchers, aircraft and naval engines, radio-electronic equipment, precision machinery, and instrument making. In mid-June 2014, however, Ukrainian president Petro Poroshenko was reported to have forbidden all military cooperation with Russia. Evidently, Ukrainian inputs to Russia's armed forces modernization can be replaced by domestically produced systems, components, and materials, but Russia will at least need two and a half years to achieve this, and it will be very costly.[52] For those in Putin's coterie, who have been pushing for independence and development of the domestic military-industrial complex, the decoupling of Russia from foreign technology is good news. It promises a windfall of fresh money. But whether the Russian defense industry can successfully meet the new challenges is an entirely different matter.

Even more importantly, Putin is on record several times as having supported the idea that the defense industry can be turned into a "locomotive" or "engine" for the modernization the whole economy.[53] The idea goes back to the beginning of his rule. For instance, the national security concept that was developed under his aegis as secretary of the National Security Council and published in January 2000 stated that it was necessary "to transfer new military technologies to stimulate the civilian economy" and "to develop mechanisms to ensure the competitiveness of Russian companies on the world market."[54] Putin himself asserted that military industry was a "priority sector" of the Russian economy in which "advanced technologies and highly competent personnel has accumulated."[55] That sector, therefore, "must be the locomotive for [economic] development and help Russia to get rid of all [!]its problems."[56]

It would be difficult to find an example among industrialized or industrializing countries where modernization of the economy was achieved through the expansion of defense industry. If the Soviet experience is any guide, pouring money into the military-industrial complex is likely to contribute to imperial overstretch rather than to innovation and improvements of the civilian economy.

THE "COSTS OF EMPIRE": SUBSIDIES ON OIL AND GAS EXPORTS AND COSTS OF PIPELINES

One of Russia's main instruments to pressure post-Soviet states into its Eurasian Economic Union project is cheap oil and gas as carrots, and high prices as sticks. As for income and profits lost in the export of natural gas, starting from January 2012, the price of gas sold to Belarus was lowered from $244 per 1,000 cubic meters (tcm) to $164. Presumably using the price charged by Gazprom to European customers then in the range of about $415, Putin concluded: "This means that at least US$2 billion [annually] will stay in Belarus," that is, Russia is forfeiting that amount per annum.[57] Russia is forgoing income and profits also because of the preferential prices charged to other countries. Thus, in 2013, the price for a thousand cubic meters of natural gas for Armenia amounted to $189, Georgia—$235, and Moldova—$365. Poland and the Czech Republic, in comparison, had to pay more than $500.[58]

Subsidization and lost income are also an important feature of the oil export business. The establishment of a single economic space in the shape of the Eurasian Economic Union requires common regulations for a wide range of issues.[59] Adjustment of tax rates, in particular export duties, is of primary importance. This first and foremost applies to crude oil export duties which were considerably lower in Kazakhstan ($80 per ton) and Belarus ($278) than in Russia ($350–370 per ton). If the differences had not been adjusted, Russian oil companies would have been tempted to export crude oil through Kazakhstan and Belarus, which in turn would seriously have damaged the oil-dependent Russian budget, with estimated losses of $40–50 billion annually. In order to forestall this, Moscow introduced a so-called "big tax maneuver" in the oil industry, with a gradual reduction of export duties on oil and light oil products over the course of three years and a simultaneous increase in mining extraction tax (MET). The "maneuver" should in theory balance budget losses from export duties with new gains from the MET. However, according to Russian finance minister Anton Siluanov, the tax changes will nevertheless negatively affect the budget since an increase in MET leads to a reduction in corporate profits inflicting lower tax collections; such losses are estimated to be in the range of about $5 billion in 2015.[60]

The "maneuver" has repeatedly been criticized by Igor Sechin, CEO of the Russian state oil giant Rosneft and a close Putin ally, who has complained that the tax changes will undermine new oil refinery projects, including Rosneft's huge Far East Petrochemical Company, which will cost 1.3 trillion rubles ($20 billion). Since his lobbying did not stop the bill, Rosneft is seeking compensation in the amount of up to 2 trillion rubles ($31 billion) from Russia's national sovereign funds. A clear beneficiary of the "maneuver" again is Belarus. Moscow agreed to a deal whereby Minsk will keep proceeds from oil product exports, which will effectively add $1.5 billion to the Belarusian budget at Russia's expense.[61]

Gazprom is engaged in politically motivated projects that are commercially unprofitable. One major example has been the Kremlin's determination to circumvent Ukraine in the gas supply to Europe. Until December 1, 2014, the intended means to do so was the *South Stream* gas pipeline, a project slated to run from Russia's Black Sea coast to Austria. In November 2010, Gazprom claimed that costs would amount to €15.5 billion ($17.7 billion), which was even then well above previous estimates of around €10 billion; the seabed portion would cost €10 billion, and the on-land portion in

Europe around €5.5 billion.[62] According to Western estimates, however, this was a vast understatement, total project implementation cost, including infrastructure in Russia, to reach €26.6 billion ($30.1 billion)[63] —according to some estimates even $40 billion.[64] The wide discrepancies in the estimates were due, among other things, to sketchy and unreliable figures for the costs of the South Stream sections in individual transit countries. To take Bulgaria as an example, ever since Gazprom and the Bulgarian government-controlled energy holding BEH began negotiations, the estimated costs for the construction of the Bulgarian section doubled to more than €4.2 billion ($4.8 billion). How much of that sum Gazprom was to pay no one knew. Unknown was also the amount handed out in bribes over the years. Energy experts, including the previous Bulgarian ambassador to Moscow, proceeded from the assumption that it involved a sum amounting to €2 billion ($2.3 billion).[65]

Bulgaria, however, was also the ultimate stone over which Gazprom stumbled and fell. Sofia adhered to the EU's anti-trust legislation and the provisions of the EU's Third Energy Package for the "unbundling" of production, supplies, and sales. Putin's and Gazprom CEO Aleksey Miller's announcement in Ankara on December 1, 2014, of South Stream's termination did not, however, mean the abandonment of the Kremlin's determination to circumvent Ukraine. On December 2, still in the Turkish capital, Miller and his Turkish counterpart of Botas Petroleum Pipeline Corporation, in the presence of Putin and Turkish Prime Minister Recep Erdogan, signed a Memorandum of Understanding for the construction of an offshore gas pipeline across the Black Sea to Turkey. The new gas pipeline is to have a capacity of 63 billion cubic meters, with 14 billion cubic meters slated for Turkish consumers and nearly 50 billion cubic meters to be transported to the border between Turkey and Greece. From there, gas could be shipped to customers in that country and beyond.[66] Costs are attached also to Putin's attempt to herd all the countries of the post-Soviet space into the projected Eurasian-Economic-Union pen and to perform a twenty-first century version of the sixteenth century "gathering of lands." In addition to opportunity costs, there are many current and future direct costs to that policy. These would deserve a separate study and carry lots of uncertainties as to precise figures. Some general idea as to the costs attached to the neo-imperial policies, however, can be provided.

THE "COSTS OF EMPIRE": SUBSIDIZATION OF CLIENT STATES, SEPARATIST ENTITIES, AND THE CRIMEA

All three separatist entities on post-Soviet space, Abkhazia, South Ossetia, and Transnistria, have received significant budgetary and other support. Russia is estimated to have helped *Abkhazia* to the tune of one billion dollars over the six years after Moscow's recognition of the breakaway republic as an independent state.[67] In 2010 to 2012 alone, it earmarked $350 million for supporting the budget and infrastructure projects, with that number expected to triple to $1 billion between 2013 and 2015.[68] The costs are likely to rise. This is due to the fact that, in November 2014, Putin and the Abkhaz "president" Raul Khadzhimba signed instruments for the establishment of a "strategic partnership" and "alliance" between the two countries. In addition to the cost for maintaining its military bases there and an estimated 4,000 troops, Putin committed Russia to doubling the economic and financial assistance provided to Abkhazia.[69]

South Ossetia, the other Georgian breakaway republic, has also received substantial aid. For instance, Russian subsidies to its 2009 budget, the first after "independence," amounted to 8.5 billion rubles ($280 million). Tskhinvali's own revenues, however, only amounted to 139 million rubles, that is, 98.4 percent of the local budget came from the Russian treasury. In the following years, the ratio of Russian and local taxes in the budget has remained roughly the same.[70] To provide another figure of the often nontransparent and unreliable accounting of allocations and expenditure, in the period from August 2008 to June 2010, Russia is said to have expended 26 billion rubles ($858 million), that is, about $28,000 for each South Ossetian resident. This included, in addition to budgetary assistance, rehabilitation aid, as well as Moscow city budget support for a large housing project and Gazprom-funded construction of gas pipelines between Russia and South Ossetia.[71] Russia furthermore bears the cost of its military bases in the separatist entity, with an estimated force of about 4,000 men. In January 2015, negotiations were under way to conclude with South Ossetia a treaty along the lines of that existing with Abkhazia

Russia also supports the budget and the economy of *Transnistria*, including by the free delivery of natural gas and the financing of social programs. In 2014, Moldova paid $374 per 1,000 cubic meters of Russian natural gas but in November of the same year, Gazprom and Moldovagaz (50 percent owned by Gazprom!) signed an agreement providing for a reduction of the gas price to $332 with a projected volume of gas deliveries, including to Transnistria, of 3 billion cubic meters. Tiraspol, however, avoids running high budget deficits because it is not paying for the gas it receives and making money from its sale as well as the electric energy produced with it. Moldovagaz owes nearly US$5 billion to Gazprom, including fines for culpable payment delays, but US$4.6 billion of this sum represents Transnistria's arrears, only US$400 million are the debts owed by Moldova. Costs accrue to Russia also because of its military presence in Transnistria, with a force numbering about 1,500 men.[72] The separatist republic, however, furnishes one of the very few examples of a projected reduction of the costs of empire. Tiraspol was expected to receive the equivalent of $100 million in

2015. However, the Kremlin will not pay that sum because of its "dissatisfaction with the numerous charter flights of the president of Transnistria, Yevgeny Shevchuk, and Russia's economic difficulties."[73]

THE CRIMEA

Prior to Moscow's annexation, Kiev had subsidized two-thirds of Crimea's budget. Now, Russia has assumed this burden and has promised to bring pensions and the standard of living up to Russian levels. In March 2014, Russian finance minister Anton Siluanov claimed that, for the current year, allocations for Crimea's and Sevastopol's integration into Russia "will not exceed 240 billion rubles" ($6.8 billion).[74] Almost miraculously, his cost estimates for that purpose for 2014, "including for building the bridge across the Kerch strait" to the peninsula, decreased to 150 billion rubles ($4.2 billion) and for 2015 to 100 billion ($2.8 billion).[75] However, according to other government estimates, the cost of building the bridge alone was calculated at $6.2 billion.[76] The same amount will most likely have to be spent on the construction of pipelines at the bottom of the Kerch Strait for the water supply of the peninsula. It is true that Russia also stands to gain from the acquisition of valuable property and natural resources in Crimea. But Ukraine is also counting the costs, and has vowed to hit Russia with lawsuits running into hundreds of billions of dollars—a major reason in addition to sanctions why foreign investors are likely to shun the peninsula and why the costs for Russia of supporting the Crimea will remain high.[77]

In a study of the "Burden of Empire," former Duma deputy and Putin critic Vladimir Ryzhkov makes a distinction between Russia's "colonial" possessions and "dominions," the former being Abkhazia, South Ossetia, Transnistria, and the Crimea, the latter including Belarus, Armenia, Tadzhikistan, and Kyrgyzstan. Summarizing the neo-imperial burden of the former, his calculations are that Russia is providing assistance amounting to approximately $1 billion per year to Transnistria and $350 million annually to Abkhazia; since 2008 it has paid over 1 billion to South Ossetia; and its annual costs for bringing Crimea up to par with Russia and building the bridge across the Kerch strait, excluding outlays for military, could reach 350–400 billion rubles annually ($5.2–6.0 billion).[78]

BURDEN OF THE "DOMINIONS"

Russia has subsidized Belarus for many years in the amount of $64 billion annually. For the years 2014–2015, it has allocated $1.2 billion to Kyrgyzstan. In Armenia, Moscow incurs expenditure for the maintenance of a ground forces' base in Gyumri and an air base in Erebuni near Yerevan, with troops of up to 5,000 men, as well as for the supply of weapons and natural gas at preferential prices. Assistance to Tajikistan, which hosts the largest Russian military base abroad, amounts to about $20 million per year. Now, after the United States and NATO withdrawals from Afghanistan, Russia's assistance to the country and its military presence there may well increase. [79]

DEMOGRAPHIC PROBLEMS AND THE "BRAIN DRAIN"

Much of the news about Russian demography over the past five years has been positive. Life expectancy has reached 71 years of age in 2013, up from 67 in 2007, due in part to receding deaths from alcohol poisoning, murder, and suicide. Last year, Russia recorded its first year of natural population growth since the Soviet Union collapsed in 1992, with the number of births exceeding the number of deaths by a small margin (24,013). Like virtually every other country in North America and Europe, however, Russia faces a future in which a smaller number of workers will have to provide for a larger number of retirees. There are, beyond that, many other negative factors that are specific for Russia.

First, due largely to the "demographic hole" of the 1990s, the general trend toward a shrinking labor force is happening *rapidly* and it is happening *now*. [80] Second, in contrast to other countries with low life expectancy, the figures in Russia are not due primarily to deaths at and in the first years after birth but to deaths of people at *working age*—a fact that applies in particular to men, whose life expectancy has also increased but still stands at a—for industrialized countries—unparalleled 65 years. Third, even now the managers of Russian firms and, even more so, foreign investors in the country complain of the lack of *qualified* workers. Fourth, one of the consequences of the Kremlin's shift, domestically, from modernization to mobilization and, internationally, from international cooperation to isolation, is the "brain drain"—the increasing tendency among the "best and the brightest" to leave the country or those, who are already abroad, not to return.

Over the past decade, Russia lost about a million and a half people from the middle class, and these are the most educated, the most successful, and the most enterprising. [81] Levada Center surveys show that half of the middle class have thoughts of leaving, and about 4–6 percent of them have already taken specific steps to this end by researching resettlement opportunities, writing to a future employer abroad, and/or applying for a visa. Significantly, many of them are among those who have been successful in Russia and understand that under current conditions they may not be able to protect their assets or their relatives in the absence of political protection, especially judicial protection. They are not protesting loudly in the squares; they are simply leaving. [82]

CONCLUSION

In October 2011, Putin categorically stated: "The Soviet Union—this, too, is Russia, only under a different name." Since then, in his third term as president, matters have developed so quickly and dramatically that one might be tempted to reverse his statement to read: "Russia—this, too, is the Soviet Union, only under a different name." Such a state of affairs has not been reached and it will not be. Marxism - Leninism as an ideology is dead , and to restore the Soviet Union as a constitutional entity with fifteen Union Republics is simply unthinkable. Nevertheless, important structural elements of the Soviet system that existed under CPSU party secretaries Brezhnev, Andropov, and Chernenko have been incorporated into what has been labeled the "Putin system." These include, in domestic politics, government control of the economy and the society, the importance of military factors in politics, economy, and the society, and in foreign policy the cultivation of a siege mentality.

In his comparative study of the rise and fall of great powers, Paul Kennedy has advanced the theory that decline sets in when expenditures on internal and external security exceed the economic possibilities of the state. The Soviet Union was one of his case studies .[83] Perceptive Russian critics, like Kudrin, have pointed out that current Russian policies were replicating Soviet policies of overextension, and even Putin and Medvedev, in a rare moment of taking "an objective and realistic look at the situation," acknowledged that unless radical and comprehensive changes were made, the very "existence" and "survival" of Russia were at risk.[84] Such changes were never attempted. Not only did the "modernization" rhetoric, when Medvedev was president, fail to be transformed into substance but the rhetoric itself was scrapped by Putin once he resumed office as president.

In December 2011, a few months before his return, Putin had enunciated the goal for Russia to accelerate economic growth to 6–7 percent.[85] That target is being missed by a wide margin. In September 2014, Medvedev was to deplore: "We focused on significantly higher growth rates. Now we are proceeding from the fact that the economy will grow 0.5 percent this year, possibly a little more; next year—around 1 percent."[86] The latter figures are considerably below the 3 percent growth constituting, as calculated by Kudrin, the threshold of stagnation for Russia. The premier took a philosophical attitude to this state of affairs: "The [projected increase] is small and not very good but the world is also in a fairly complicated situation."[87] By January 2015, however, the government no longer projected growth of the economy but its *decline*, amounting to 3 percent. Independent analysts predicted a GDP contraction of 4–5 percent.[88]

There is little evidence that the top leadership realizes or wants to acknowledge that its policies are the direct cause of stagnation and decline and that these, in turn, are significantly compounded by its foreign policy. As long as this is true, Russia's slide downhill will inexorably continue.

NOTES

1. Putin, then still president, in his speech at the enlarged session of the state council where he introduced a "strategy" for Russia's development until 2020; В. Путин, "Выступление на расширенном заседании Государственного совета 'О стратегии развития России до 2020 года," *Kremlin.ru*, February 8, 2008, http://archive.kremlin.ru/appears/2008/02/08/1542_type63374type63378type82634_159528.shtml.

2. President Medvedev in his annual "state of the nation" address to the federal assembly, "Послание Федеральному Собранию Российской Федерации," *Kremlin.ru*, 12.11.2009, http://kremlin.ru/transcripts/5979.

3. Lilia Shevtsova, *Russia: Lost in Transition* (Washington, D.C.: Carnegie Endowment, 2007).

4. Literally, Russia was merely "concentrating." Е.М. Примаков, "Россия в мировой политике: к 200-летию А.М. Горчакова," *Дипломатический вестник*, No, 7 (July 1998), http://www.mid.ru/bdomp/dip_vest.nsf/99b2ddc4f717c733c32567370042ee43/2c7c5a708d42786dc3256889002a0d7e!OpenDocument.

5. The statistical data provided subsequently are those from the Russian official Federal Statistical Service, Rosstat, http://www.gks.ru/wps/wcm/connect/rosstat_main/rosstat/ru/statistics/accounts/.

6. See O'Neill's interview with Beth Kowitt, "For Mr. BRIC, Nations' Meeting a Milestone," *Fortune*, June 17, 2009.

7. Putin in his speech presenting his Strategy for Russia's Development until 2020; Путин, "О стратегии развития России до 2020 года" (fn. 1).

8. Speech by Russian finance minister Andrey Kudrin in Davos on 23.1.2008, "Russia Is an 'Island of Stability'," Youtube.com, http://www.youtube.com/watch?v=haNGcSVVWbA.

9. "Медведев пообещал превратить Москву в мировой финансовый центр," *Lenta.ru*, June 7, 2008, http://lenta.ru/news/2008/06/07/moscow/.

10. И. Шувалов, "К концу года Россия станет шестой экономикой мира," *RosBusinessConsulting*, June 8, 2008, http://top.rbc.ru/economics/08/06/2008/180593.shtml.

11. For one of a plethora of reports see Independent Task Force Report, *Russia's Wrong Direction: What the United States Can and Should Do* (New York: Council of Foreign Relations, 2006), http://www.cfr.org/iran/russias-wrong-direction/p9997.

12. Putin's Munich 2007 speech (in Russian); https://www.youtube.com/watch?v=ZkS2xwhYvkM.

13. The subsequent data according to various publications of data by the Russian Statistical Agency, Rosstat, http://www.gks.ru/ (fn. 6).

14. The summary draws on Sergey Dubinin. This is available online at: http://dialog-europe-russia.org/events/201102/materials/material_dubinin.pdf. Dubinin is a Member of the Board of Directors of the financial services group VTB Capital.

15. Путин, "О стратегии развития России до 2020 года" (fn. 1).

16. Путин, "О стратегии развития России до 2020 года" (fn. 1).

17. Путин, "О стратегии развития России до 2020 года" (fn. 1).

18. The sources used here to recount Medvedev's scathing criticism of the current state of affairs and the requirements for "modernization" are his "state of the nation" address to the federal assembly in 2008, "Послание Федеральному Собранию Российской Федерации," *Kremlin.ru*, November 5, 2008, http://archive.kremlin.ru/appears/2008/11/05/1349_type63372type63374type63381type82634_208749.shtml; the article titled "Go Russia!," published online in September 2009, "Россия, вперёд! Статья Дмитрия Медведева," *Kremlin.ru*, September 10, 2009; http://www.kremlin.ru/news/5413; and the annual "state of the nation" address in 2009, "Послание Федеральному Собранию Российской Федерации," *Kremlin.ru*, November 12, 2009, http://kremlin.ru/transcripts/5979.

19. "Speech at the Inauguration Ceremony as President of Russia," *Kremlin.ru*, May 7, 2008; http://archive.kremlin.ru/eng/speeches/2008/05/07/1521_type82912type127286_200295 .shtml.

20. "Послание Федеральному Собранию," 2009 (fn. 18; italics mine).

21. Ibid. (italics mine).

22. On the history of the "innovation centre's" foundation and its projects in Russian see *Skolkovomedia.ru*, http://skolkovomedia.ru/; for corresponding information in English see *I-gorod.com*, http://www.i-gorod.com/en/about/.

23. "Послание Федеральному Собранию," 2009 (fn. 18).

24. Ibid. The program for the effective utilization of foreign policy factors was to be performed "on a systemic basis" (на системной основе; see *verbatim* below, the next footnote, the term used in the title of the foreign ministry's document). It is unclear, however, what that "system" is all about.

25. "Программа   еффективного   исползования   на   системной   основе внешнеполитических   факторов   в   целях   долгосрочного   развития   Российской Федерации, " May 11, 2010. Homepage of Russky Newsweek http://www.runewsweek.ru/country/34184/ (accessed 10.10.2010). The website, however, is no longer available since Russky Newsweek ceased publication. The document, however, can be accessed under http://perevodika.ru/articles/13590.html. The foreign ministry, as far as this author is aware, never published the document but also did not deny its existence.

26. "Послание Федеральному Собранию," 2009 (fn. 18). Further elaborations on that theme were provided in a televised speech in December 2009; Итоги года с Президентом России, *Kremlin.ru*, 24.12.2009, http://kremlin.ru/news/6450.

27. Putin at a congress of Business Russia, a public association that unites the country's medium-sized businesses, http://en.ria.ru/business/20111221/170407718.html.

28. http://commons.wikimedia.org/wiki/File:Russian_economy_since_fall_of _Soviet_Union.PNG.

29. The whole sentence reads: "We are on the brink of stagnation—economic growth in Russia of less than 3 percent is stagnation." As quoted by Douglas Busvine and Darya Korsunskaya, "Russia on the Brink of Stagnation–Kudrin," *Reuters*, September 21, 2012, http://www.reuters.com/article/2012/09/21/us-russia-summit-kudrin-idUSBRE88K0KM20120921. He made this statement in September 2012, that is, exactly one year after he had been ousted as finance minister.

30. Putin at the Congress of the United Russia party in preparation for the upcoming parliamentary elections of December 4, 2011, "Съезд партии 'Единая Россия'," *Kremlin.ru*, September 24, 2011, http://kremlin.ru/news/12802.

31. "Свист в 'Олимпийском' обрушил основы политической системы," *Ari.ru*, November 22, 2011, http://ari.ru/ari/2011/11/22/svist-v-olimpiyskom-obrushil-osnovy-politicheskoy-sistemy.

32. As reported by Ellen Barry, "Rally Defying Putin's Party Draws Tens of Thousands," *Newyorktimes.com*, December 10, 2011, http://www.nytimes.com/2011/12/11/world/europe/thousands-protest-in-moscow-russia-in-defiance-of-putin.html?pagewanted=all&_r=0.

33. At a rally in September 2012 that, according to witnesses, attracted at least 50,000 people; Thomas Grove and Gabriela Baczynska, "Anti-Putin Protesters Show Their Strength in Russia," *Reuters.com*, September 15, 2012, http://www.reuters.com/article/2012/09/15/us-russia-protest-idUSBRE88E06R20120915. The constitutional change, signed by Medvedev on December 30, 2008, provided for the presidential term in office of six rather than four years. Thus, if Putin won the elections of 2012 and 2018, he could remain president until 2024.

34. As quoted by Charles Clover, "A Return to Arms: Moscow Is Spending $755bn Over 10 Years to Bolster Its Military Might," *Ft.com*, October 1, 2013, http://www.ft.com/intl/cms/s/0/82d3917e-2a80–11e3–8fb8–00144feab7de.html. For another portrayal of Kudrin's resignation and its significance see "Bloomberg View: Is Vladimir Putin Going Back to the U.S.S.R.?", *Businessweek.com*, June 14, 2012, http://www.businessweek.com/articles/2012–06–14/bloomberg-view-is-vladimir-putin-going-back-to-the-u-dot-s-dot-s-dot-r-dot. Kudrin was forced to resign from his position as finance minister in September 2011. He himself was gracious enough to say that he had gone voluntarily. But the Kremlin rejected this portrayal as incorrect.

35. "Новый интеграционный проект для Евразии—будущее, которое рождается сегодня," *Izvestia.ru,* October 3, 2011, http://www.izvestia.ru/news/502761.

36. President Medvedev at a press conference in Svolkovo, "Ukrainian Integration with Europe Could Hamper Ties with Customs Union–Medvedev," *Rian.ru,* May 18, 2011, http://en.rian.ru/world/20110518/164092502.html (italics mine).

37. According to decisions adopted in July and August 2014. On September 8, the EU tightened the financial sanctions policy and shortened the maturity period from 90 to 30 days.

38. Analysis by the Fitch rating agency, "Support, Low Refi Risk Limit Russian Bank Sanctions Hit," *Fitchratings.com,* August 1, 2014, https://www.fitchratings.com/gws/en/fitch-wire/fitchwirearticle/Support,-Low-Refi?pr_id=843634.

39. The subsequent calculations are those of Anders Åslund of the Peterson Institute of International Economic Studies, "Are Russia's Usable Reserves Running Dangerously Low?" *Piee.com,* November 20, 2014, http://blogs.piie.com/realtime/?p=4624.

40. Ibid. According to Moscow economist Sergei Pukhov, not taking into consideration the problem of liquidity, reserves by the end 2015 could be down to $200 billion; as quoted by Bill Powell, "Will Sanctions on Russia Tip the World Into Recession?," *Newsweek.com,* August 5, 2014, http://www.newsweek.com/2014/08/15/will-sanctions-russia-tip-world-recession-2630 16.html.

41. See the statements of Putin and Medvedev (fn. 1, 2).

42. "Crude Oil and Commodity Prices," Statistical series, *Oil-price.net,* http://www.oil-price.net/.

43. "ЦБ: отток капитала из РФ в 2014 г составил $151.5 млрд, *Ria.ru,* January 16, 2015, http://m.ria.ru/economy/20150116/1042939274.html. In November, the Central Bank had estimated the outflow "only" at $130 billion; "Центробанк России признал, что из РФ за год 'убежит' почти 130 миллиардов долларов капитала," *Odnako.su,* November 10, 2014, http://odnako.su/news/finance/-208958–centrobank-rossii-priznal-chto-iz-rf-za-god--ubejit--pochti-130–milliardov-dollarov-kapitala/.

44. Press releases of the Central Bank of Russia, various issues: Центральный банк России, Пресс центр Пресс-релизы, http://www.cbr.ru/Press/?PrtId=month_archive.

45. Центральный банк Российской Федерации, "О ключевой ставке Банка России," *Cbr.ru,* January 30, 2015, http://www.cbr.ru/press/PR.aspx?file =30012015_133122dkp2015–01–30T13_15_49.htm.

46. "Russland kehrt zur staatlichen Wirtschaft zurück–'Wedomosti'," *Ria.ru,* November 6, 2013, http://de.ria.ru/trade_and_finance/20121106/264878636.html.

47. "Russia Jumps 20 Places in Ease of Doing Business Ranking," *Rbth.com,* October 29, 2013, http://rbth.com/news/2013/10/29/russia_jumps_20_places_in_ease_of_doing_business _ranking_31246.html. For the latest data of the World Bank on Russia see http://www.doingbusiness.org/data/exploreeconomies/russia.

48. According to the head of the State Duma's defense committee, Admiral Vladimir Komoyedov, as quoted in "Russian Defense Budget to Hit Record $81 Billion in 2015," *Themoscowtimes,* October 16, 2014, http://www.themoscowtimes.com/business/article/russian-defense-budget-to-hit-record-81bln-in-2015/509536.html. U.S. dollar figures at the February 10, 2015, exchange rate. However, when Komeyedov provided these figures, the 3.3 trillion rubles for "national defense" were, indeed, as stated in the article, worth $81 billion. Because of the huge shrinkage of the value of the ruble, some of the subsequent figures are in percent of GDP rather than in current rubles. Current U.S. dollar values would understate the actual burden of military expenditures on the economy.

49. "Russia's Finance Ministry Proposes 10 percent Budget Cuts, Except Defense Spending," *Itar-tass.com,* January 14, 2015, http://itar-tass.com/en/economy/771059; "Антикризисный план - что в нем?", *Российская газета, Rg.ru,* January 28, 2015, http://m.rg.ru/2015/01/28/plan.html. The "anti-crisis plan," worth about $35 billion, was signed by prime minister Medvedev on January 28, 2015.

50. Statement and data by Oleg Bochkarev, deputy chairman of the board of the Military Industrial Commission, "ВПК: расходы на оборонную отрасль не будут сокращены независимо от экономической ситуации," *Itar-tass.com,* December 19, 2014, http://itar-tass.com/armiya-i-opk/1658891. U.S dollar figure at the February 10, 2015, exchange rate.

51. Владимир Мухин, "Милитаризация угрожает ввп. Рост военных расходов в россии ударит по экономике и благосостоянию населения, *Несависимое военное обозрение,*" *Nvo.ng.ru,* July 23, 2014, http://nvo.ng.ru/armies/?id_user=Y&PAGEN_1=12. U.S dollar figure at the February 10, 2015, exchange rate.

52. According to Dmitry Rogozin, deputy prime minister and chair of the government's military-industrial commission. For details of the likely consequences of Western sanctions and the rupture of ties with the Ukrainian arms industry see Julian Cooper, "Sanctions Will Hit Russia's Rearmament Plans," *Themoscowtimes,* August 12. 2014, http://www.themoscowtimes.com/opinion/article/sanctions-will-hurt-russia-s-rearmament-plans/505006.html, and Natalya Pechorina, *Russian-Ukrainian Defense Industry Cooperation in 1992–2013,* Center for the Analysis of Strategies and Technologies (CAST), Moscow), October 2014.

53. For one of many examples see "Владимир Путин: 'Россия будет наращивать возможности ВКО,'" *Национальная оборона,* No. 11 (November 2014), http://www.nationaldefense.ru/includes/periodics/maintheme/2013/0705/193911209/detail.shtml.

54. Концепция национальной безопасности Российской Федерации, *Независимое военное обозрение.* http://nvo.ng.ru/concepts/2000–01–14/ 6_concept.html.

55. In a speech in Nizhny Novgorod, ITAR-TASS (in Russian), March 21, 2000.

56. What needed to be done to achieve this (miracle), however, was to "improve the procedures for awarding government contracts, accelerate innovation, recruit younger specialists, tighten quality controls, amend provisions for enterprise bankruptcy, prevent the illegal transfer of high technology abroad, and make better use of foreign exchange earnings from arms exports" (ibid.). For confirmation of Putin's ideas with further verbatim quotations see Виталий Денисов, "Оборонный заказ увеличится в полтора раза," *Красная звезда,* January 28, 2000. For Putin's recent views on this subject see also Pavel Felgenhauer, "Putin Plans to Rearm Russia Against the West with Western Help," *Eurasia Daily Monitor,* Vol. 9, Issue 161, September 6, 2012, http://www.jamestown.org/single/?tx_ttnews percent5Btt_news percent5D=39806&no_cache=1. Ilya Ponomarov, a Duma deputy for the Just Russia party, is representative of many other Russian politicians who point to the United States as supposedly a successful model for the use of military industry as a locomotive for the whole economy; see "Drawing Lessons From the U.S. Defense Sector," *Themoscowtimes,* January 30. 2013, http://www.themoscowtimes.com/opinion/article/drawing-lessons-from-the-us-defense-sector/474732.html .

57. Prime minister Putin at a session of the Supreme Soviet of the constitutional Union Russia-Belarus on 25.11.2011 in Moscow; "Путин: Белоруссия будет получать газ по 164 доллара за кубометр," *Vesti.ru,* 25.11.2011, http://video.mail.ru/bk/vesti.ru/ecomony/58563.html; see also "Russian Prime Minister Vladimir Putin Says Moscow is Slashing the Price Minsk Has to Pay for Gas to Less than Half the Average Paid by Other European States," Radio Free Europe / Radio Liberty, *Rferl.org,* 25.11.2011, http://www.rferl.org/articleprintview/24402392.html.

58. For a survey of price differentials in 2014 see Glenn Kates and Li Luo, "Russian Gas: How Much Is That?," *Rfer.org,* July 1, 2014, http://www.rferl.org/content/russian-gas-how-much-gazprom/25442003.html.

59. The analysis of the effects of the adjustment of tax rates in the oil export business draws on Alexey Kobylyanskiy, "New Oil Tax Laws in Russia Could Backfire," *Global Risks Insights,* November 11, 2014, http://oilprice.com/Energy/Crude-Oil/New-Oil-Tax-Laws-In-Russia-Could-Backfire.html. Excepted are the data for Belarus which are from "Belarus to Greatly Reduce Oil Export Duties to Match Russia's," *Belta.by,* December 29, 2014, http://eng.belta.by/all_news/economics/Belarus-to-greatly-reduce-oil-export-duties-to-match-Russias_i_78483.html.

60. Ibid. (Kobylyanskiy).

61. Ibid. U.S. dollar figures at the February 10, 2015, exchange rate.

62. According to Gazprom in late November 2010; South Stream приравняли к Nabucco по стоимости километра трубы, *Коммерсантъ,* December, 1, 2010.

63. Approximately €10 billion for infrastructure in Russia, another €10 billion for the offshore section plus €6.6 billion for the gas pipeline running through European countries; see

Szymon Kardas and Ewa Paszyc, "At Any Price: Russia is Embarking on the Construction of South Stream," *East Week*, No. 98, December 1, 2012, http://www.osw.waw.pl/en/publikacje/osw-commentary/2012–12–07/any-price-russia-embarking-construction-south-stream.

64. Jim Yardley and Jo Becker, "How Putin Forged a Pipeline Deal That Derailed," *Nytimes.com*, December 31, 2014, http://www.nytimes.com/2014/12/31/world/europe/how-putin-forged-a-pipeline-deal-that-derailed-html?_r=0.

65. Florian Hassel, "Aus South Stream wird Seepipeline," *Süddeutsche Zeitung*, August 22, 2014, p. 7. U.S. dollar figure according to the February 10, 2015, exchange rate.

66. "New gas pipeline towards Turkey," Gazprom press release, *Gazprom.com*, December 2, 2014, http://www.gazprom.com/press/news/2014/december/article208505/.

67. Ivan Sukhov, "Abkhazia's Crisis Sets a New Precedent," *Moscow Times*, June 5, 2014, and "Russia, Abkhazia, South Ossetia To Form Yet Another Anti-NATO," *Eurasianet.org*, September 4, 2014, http://www.eurasianet.org/node/69801, and Thomas de Waal, "Deeper with Russia," *Eurasia Outlook*, *Carnegie.ru*, 20.11.2014, http://carnegie.ru/eurasiaoutlook/?fa=57274. U.S. dollar figures according to August 2014 exchange rates.

68. "The Hidden Costs of a Russian Statelet in Ukraine," *Theatlantic.com*, March 4, 2014, http://www.theatlantic.com/international/archive/2014/03/the-hidden-costs-of-a-russian-state-let-in-ukraine/284197/. U.S. dollar figures according to February 2014 exchange rates. Only half of the $350 million was actually spent, however, because of mismanagement and corruption.

69. "Abchasien schließt Bündnis mit Moskau," *Frankfurter Allgemeine Zeitung*, November 26, 2014, p. 2. Like Putin, Khadzhimba is a former KGB officer. On January 23, 2015, the Russian Duma ratified what it called a "Treaty on Alliance and Strategic Partnership."

70. "How Putin is Going to Save on the Crimean Autonomous Republic," *Euromaidanpress.com*, March 7, 2014, http://euromaidanpress.com/2014/03/08/how-putin-is-going-to-save-on-the-crimean-autonomous-republic/. U.S. dollar figures according to the exchange rate of December 31, 2009.

71. "South Ossetia: The Burden of Recognition, International Crisis Group," Europe Report No. 205, *Crisisgroup.org*, June 7, 2010, http://www.crisisgroup.org/~/media/files/europe/205%20south%20ossetia%20-%20the%20burden%20of%20recognition.ashx

72. The analysis of Russia's subsidization of Transnistria is based on the following sources: "Moldovagaz and Gazprom Prolong Gas Supply Contract for 2014," *Infotag.md*, December 26, 2013, http://www.infotag.md/economics-en/182643/; Paul Ivan, "Transnistria—Where to?", *Epc.eu*, March 13, 2014, http://www.epc.eu/pub_details.php?cat_id=3&pub_id=4257; and "Moldova to Submit Repayment Schedule for $400–Million Gas Debt," *Sputniknews.com*, November 11, 2014, http://sputniknews.com/business/20141120/1014941338.html. According to the Moldovan ambassador in Ukraine, Transnistria is paying about one sixth of the price for Russian gas that Moldova is paying: "Посол Молдовы: Россия держит в Приднестровье склады с боеприпасами—в двух километрах от границы с Украиной," *Glavkom.ua*, September 29, 2014, http://glavcom.ua/articles/22794.html. It is unclear, however, whether this is a hypothetical or a real payment.

73. According to a source of the Transnistrian regime; "Россия впервые отказалась финансировать Приднестровье," *Novayagazeta.ru*, January 26, 2015, http://www.novayagazeta.ru/news/1691121.html.

74. "Силуанов: Расходы на поддержку Крыма и Севастополя в 2014 году не превысят 240 млрд рублей," *Rosbalt.ru*, March 26, 2014, http://m.rosbalt.ru/main/2014/03/26/1248989.html. Exchange rate of March 26, 2014.

75. "Правительство РФ выделит Крыму из резервов 250 млрд руб в 2014–2015 гг," *Ria.ru*, July 18, 2014, http://ria.ru/crimea_today/20140718/1016528028.html. Exchange rate of July 18, 2014.

76. "Cost of Kerch Strait Bridge to Crimea Valued at More Than $6 Billion," *Itar-tass.com*, September 1, 2014, http://en.itar-tass.com/russia/747587.

77. For a comprehensive compilation and analysis of the data see "Factbox—Costs and Benefits from Russia's Annexation of Crimea," *Reuters.com*, April 8, 2014, http://uk.reuters.com/article/2014/04/08/uk-ukraine-crisis-crimea-costs-factbox-idUK-BREA370NY20140408.

78. Владимир Рыжков, "Бремя империи," *Echo.msk.ru*, June 11, 2014, http://m.echo.msk.ru/blogs/detail.php?ID=1338210. Exchange rate of February 10, 2015.

79. All data on the "dominions" are by Ryshkov, ibid.

80. Details and subsequent analysis of the labor force problem are based, in part, on Mark Adonis, "Russia's Workforce is Shrinking," *Forbes.com*, June 21, 2014, http://www.forbes.com/sites/markadomanis/2014/06/21/russias-workforce-is-shrinking/; Rosstat, the Russian Statistical Service, Федеральная служба государственной статистики (Росстат), http://www.gks.ru/; and "Russian Male and Female Life Expectancy," http://commons.wikimedia.org/wiki/File:Russian_male_and_female_life_expectancy.PNG.

81. According to Lev Gudkov, director of the Levada polling center, "Emigration on the Rise," *Rian.ru*, October 26, 2012, http://en.rian.ru/papers/20121026/176938418.html.

82. Ibid.

83. Paul Kennedy, *Rise and Fall of the Great Powers: Economic Change and Military Conflict From 1500 to 2000* (New York: Random House, 1989).

84. Putin and Medvedev (fn. 1, 14 and 18).

85. Putin at a congress of Business Russia, a public association that unites the country's medium-sized businesses, http://en.ria.ru/business/20111221/170407718.html.

86. Medvedev in an interview with Russian newspaper Vedomosti, "Интервью — Дмитрий Медведев, председатель правительства России, *Vedomosti.ru*, September 8, 2014, http://www.vedomosti.ru/library/news/33117591/est-veschi-postrashnee-ogranicheniya-post-avok-dmitrij.

87. Ibid.

88. "Russian government sees 2015 GDP down 3 percent, more optimistic than other forecasts," *Reuters.com*, January 31, 2015, http://www.reuters.com/article/2015/01/31/us-russia-crisis-economy-forecasts-idUSKBN0L40GK20150131.

BIBLIOGRAPHY

De Waal, Thomas. "Deeper with Russia." *Eurasia Outlook. Carnegie.ru*, accessed November 20, 2014. Available online at: http://carnegie.ru/eurasiaoutlook/?fa=57274

Hassel, Florian. "Aus South Stream wird Seepipeline." *Süddeutsche Zeitung*. August 22, 2014.

Kardas, Szymon and Ewa Paszyc. "At Any Price: Russia is Embarking on the Construction of South Stream." *East Week*, No. 98, December 1, 2012. Available online at: http://www.osw.waw.pl/en/publikacje/osw-commentary/2012-12-07/any-price-russia-embarking-construction-south-stream.

Kennedy, Paul. *Rise and Fall of the Great Powers: Economic Change and Military Conflict From 1500 to 2000*. New York: Random House, 1989.

Shevtsova, Lilia. *Russia: Lost in Transition*. Washington, D.C.: Carnegie Endowment, 2007.

Independent Task Force Report. *Russia's Wrong Direction: What the United States Can and Should Do*. New York: Council of Foreign Relations, 2006. Available online: http://www.cfr.org/iran/russias-wrong-direction/p9997.

Sukhov, Ivan. "Abkhazia's Crisis Sets a New Precedent." *Moscow Times*, June 5, 2014. See also: "Russia, Abkhazia, South Ossetia To Form Yet Another Anti-NATO," *Eurasianet.org*, September 4, 2014.

Yardley, Jim and Jo Becker. "How Putin Forged a Pipeline Deal That Derailed." *New York Times*. December 31, 2014. Available online: http://www.nytimes.com/2014/12/31/world/europe/how-putin-forged-a-pipeline-deal-that-derailed-html?_r=0.

Chapter Ten

France

Another Sick Man in Europe?

Benoit d' Aboville

On November 17, 2012, the *Economist* published a 14-page special report on France under the title "The time-bomb at the heart of Europe." This reflected a commonly held view in Brussels that the French economy, compared with its main European partners, is not only a laggard in restoring growth after the crisis, but that the current social-democratic government in Paris remains unable, in spite of repeated promises, to embrace the structural reforms which most experts deem necessary.

Meanwhile a pervasive feeling of malaise and a crisis of identity are setting in within France: there is no clear indication where the country will go in the coming years. At the political level, the EU and its indecipherable institutional setup is presented as the scapegoat for all the current French ills. More specifically, the euro is increasingly branded by politicians, from the extreme right of Jean Marie Le Pen to the extreme left of Melanchon, as the true villain, not only responsible for the decline of France's industries but also for allowing the consolidation of Germany's political leadership on the continent. Paradoxically, the EU clearly makes it easier for the country to avoid painful reforms. France fully benefits from a depreciated euro, and a European Central Bank monetary policy that allows for low interest rates. The French State is therefore able to continue to borrow cheaply on the world's financial markets to finance a runaway deficit.

From 2003 to 2010, Italy and Spain (not to speak about Greece, which is a different case) went on a spending binge, thanks to the ample supply of cheap liquidities available. Then the party had to stop as fiscal conservatives in Germany and northern Europe became alarmed of the consequences for the entire monetary zone and the cost of the financial transfers implied for its preservation. The uneasy question for the coming years is whether that scenario is applicable to France—the second economy of the EU— and whether the economic and political costs of bringing the French economy into the Maastricht criteria will be acceptable both to France's entrenched political elite and to its population in general. The elites still seem inadequately fearful while the general population grows more and more concerned.

FRENCH COMPETITIVENESS IN EUROPE AND THE FEAR OF ECONOMIC DECLINE

After almost 13 years of global economic crisis, whose impact in France was cushioned by its extensive social net, the return of growth in Europe is slowly brigthening French economic prospects. With a GNP growth that could reach 1.2 percent in 2015 and 1.8 percent in 2016, the hope is that the severe unemployment, especially amongst the younger workers, will diminish. However those results could have to wait: unempoyment will still be around 9.6 percent in 2017 and the trade deficit will again increase. While Spain and Italy are, at last, picking up growth again after several years of austerity, French industry continues to lose competitivity, not only against Germany, but also against other EU partners.

At a time when the euro's value fell by 20 percent and the oil price was cut by half in one year, the French trade balance is still worsening. If luxury products, aerospace industries, and arms are still doing quite well, the overall results of external trade are worrying. French exports stagnated at a 1 percent growth rate in 2014 after negative growth of 1.2 percent in 2013. Some traditional strengths of French exports are even vanishing: agricultural products, for example, fell in 2014 by 10.5 percent. Thus, the external trade balance for 2015 will show a puny growth of 60.8 billion relative to a deficit of 55.8 billion from the previous year. Between 2003 and 2014, a decade of crisis has resulted in an accumulated trade deficit amounting to 513 billion euros. The industrial sector shifted from an external surplus to a deficit as early as 2005. It was accompanied by a dramatic fall of the numbers of workers employed in industry. In reality, the decline started around 2002, well before the economic crisis. French industry was employing 5.5 million people in 2003, but by 2013, industrial employment had dropped to only 3.26 million while the process of deindustrialization continued unabated.

In 2013, President Hollande famously announced that the "curve of unemployment will be inverted soon," France's equivalent of the "light is at the end of the tunnel" promise. The reverse trend is what actually occurred, despite the introduction of state subsidized jobs. France maintains in 2015 an unemployment rate of 10.6 percent and 3.53 million unemployed while employment rates in Germany and the United Kingdom are 6.4 percent and 5.5

percent, respectively. The most worrying aspect of the situation is that the unemployment rate in France is reducing much more slowly than in the other EU countries. With the exception of Finland and Greece, France is the only country where the unemployment rate continued to increase in 2014, while it has been declining by an overall 0.5 percent throughout the eurozone. Even in Spain, where unemployment remains dramatically high at 22.7 percent, it has now been slighty reduced by half a point. GNP growth in France will remain at a modest 1 percent to 2 percent in 2015. Meanwhile the active population is estimated to grow from between 3 percent and 5 percent, while the decline in unemployment is not expected to start before the end of 2016. As 2017 is a presidential election year the unemployment numbers will be a key factor. Especially, as current polls show that 74 percent of the population— particularly amongst workers and young people— have declared a loss of confidence toward the government and the current president.

THE CURRENT SOCIAL AND POLITICAL MALAISE

France's declining economic performance, now that the world recession can no longer be presented as an overall explanation, is one obvious element of the current political and social malaise. It is however not the only factor of a widening identity crisis, now firmly entrenched in the current public debate. The "declinist" school of thought, as the French press refer to it, has been well represented since 2013 by a large number of books and articles, coming from both political sides, right and left. The diagnosis is surprisingly homogenous amongst French and international experts and is now becoming part of the dominant "conventional wisdom" about "French malaise:" too much state interference in the economy and the society, an increasing competitivity gap resulting from social rigidities, punitive taxation given a political inability to reduce public expenditures, and a confused debate on immigration fueled, in France as in other European countries, by populist politicians.

France remains a country where the share of the GNP represented by the state and social security expenditures hovers above 56 percent—one the highest rate amongst industialized countries. The French government is therefore poorly equipped to encourage the flexibility and agility required by the world globalization process and the revolution of the numerical economy. Moreover, successive French governments have been obsessively tied to macroeconomic assumptions. Given the economic crisis, they thought that they should adopt a resolutely Keynesian approach, boosting demand, forgetting that the central problem of the French economy was not low demand but insufficient supply. This old weakness results from many factors, including the failure of the educational system. But the lack of competitivity can also be attributed to excessive social costs, high taxes, and social rigidity.

The increasing competitive gap of the French economy, compared with Northern Europe and Germany, has been attributed by OECD studies in part to the sorry state of labor relations and the extreme polarization of the societal debate. Both as a result and a cause, the crisis of representation within the labor unions, whose membership is dwindling, has recently grown worse. Unions have been politically divided since 1945, and since the 1980s, ruled by a bureaucratic leadership torn between arcane political and personal rivalries. Their rigidity is matched by the timidity of the government and the employers' confederations, which prefer to raise salaries in order to maintain social peace rather than to push for reforms. Everybody continues to look with envy to the way Chancelier Schröder was able, from 2003 on, to implement successfully in Germany the Hartz packages of labor reforms. In France, even modest steps related to raising the pension age have been an exception. But both the left and the right suffer from the political hesitations of the past 15 years of successive governments. All have avoided engaging with the politically sensitive but much needed reforms of the social laws and overall reform of the public pension schemes. In the last ten years each attempt to bring more flexibility to the recruitment of the workforce has been defeated, sometimes as the result of street demonstrations and strikes, most of the time from the lack of political courage. Moreover, when some changes have been eventually been pushed through the Parliament, they became loaded with so many compromises and amendments that the result has been more rigidity and bureaucratic interference. France remains still the *"société bloquée,"* already described at the end of the 1970s.

This political impasse is also reflected in the arcane complexity of the French tax code and the general trend to increase the tax burden on the middle classes, while at the same time reducing the tax base in order to exempt, for political reasons, the lowest incomes. In the past fifteen years, France has not known one single balanced budget. As recently recognized by its Finance Minister, a political threshold of tolerance for the pursuit of the present tax policies has been reached. France is now on the verge of a "tax revolt." Consequently, the current and future governments in Paris, unlike their predecessors, will no longer be able to increase significantly their revenues, by relying only on the tax dividend of a slow return to growth. For the last three years, discussions with the Commission in Brussels and the other partners have been framed by this economic context. France asks for a "growth Pact" and economic stimulation at the European level while Germany and the Commission demand fiscal discipline. Under the pressure of the EU, Paris has been obliged to announce that by 2016 France will, after several unfulfilled pledges, implement the goal of a reduced state deficit within the European norm of 3 percent.

Meanwhile, some overtly political tax measures like the wealth tax (*"Import de Solidarité"*) and the Hollande electoral pledge of a 75 percent tax on highest salaries have led to a not inconsequential flight of upper class and managerial people outside of France, in addition to a number of delocalizations of companies and bank headquarters. The UK remains a favorite destination and London's French population makes one of the five most populated French cities. From 1995 to 2013, the numbers of French citizens established abroad has doubled from 0.8 million to 1.6 million. While obviously only a small part of them are "tax exiles," an increasing number of young educated people are seeking to start their professional careers abroad in order to avoid the ridigidy of the French entreprise culture and what they consider the lack of economic perspectives. The numbers are globally small and could be also interpreted as indications of a healthy participation of French firms in the global economy (even if the number of French multilateral entreprises belonging to the world top ten has recently declined).

But more worrying, this current migration can also be read as a telling sign of the current negative mood of the younger educated generation, doubtful about the prospects of current French economy to meet the challenges of globalization. Especially, considering that the demographic dynamism of France, when compared with the aging of the population in Germany and Italy, still remains one of France's greatest assets. Polls show that today's youth consider themselves to be a "sacrificed generation" when compared with their elders, who enjoyed both the prosperity of the "Thirty Glorious Years" of economic expansion and social modernization. According to the same polls this sacrificed generation is amongst the category of the population most likely to vote against the current government and, surprisingly, a fair proportion of them are tempted to vote for the *Front National*, as a protest vote, even if they don't share its policies.

The current French malaise encompasses many interacting elements: a loss of confidence toward all institutions, the debilatating weakness of the social intermediaries such as the labor unions and churches, the anguish about immigration, and the break-up of what was up to now considered as a fairly stable social compact. A growing anguish about the weakening of French influence within Europe and in the world also plays its part. France was accustomed to see the EU as a kind of lever, which could insure the continuation of its role at the international level. Yet the ambition of *"Europe puissance"* has, for the time, vanished. Instead, the strong role of the state, to which the French are accustomed, is now being challenged by the shift of capabilities to the European Union and to global market forces. It is not an accident if the national policies which are, so far, meeting the greatest degree of consensus within the French public opinion are those linked with defense and the fight against terrorism, which are seen as the remaining regalian competencies of a national state buffeted by adverse global forces.

Unlike decentralized European countries like Germany or Italy, France has too strongly identified itself with a centralized state during its past not to suffer from a deep crisis of identity today. This crisis is increased by uncertainty about where the EU is going: where are its ultimate geographical limits, and what will be the international role of Europe? The historian, Pierre Nora, wrote recently that this identity crisis is related to the fact that "France is presently living the transition from one model of nation to another." But to accept such a transition, the country must have a sufficient degree of confidence in its governing elites.

THE SPLIT BETWEEN THE PEOPLE AND THE ELITES: THE EUROPEAN SCAPEGOAT

In the last ten years, the feeling that the political elites were unable to manage the country and give direction to it has translated into a growing rejection by roughly half of the voters. Europe has been the convenient scapegoat, whether the issue was the enlargement of the EU, the "social dumping" of the lower salaries of the newest eastern members of the EU, or the "austerity" imposed by Brussels. The narrow approval of the Maastricht Treaty in 1992 by 51 percent of the voters was followed on April 2002 by the stunning elimination of the socialist candidate and Prime Minister Lionel Jospin in favor of Jean Marie Le Pen on the first ballot of the presidential election. It was a clear sign of a protest vote, which subsequently led the elected President, Jacques Chirac, to adopt a cautious approach to reforms and to the EU.

The rejection of the European Constitution in 2005 by 54.7 percent also created a deeper political shock, not only in Europe—but also within the French ruling class. If French political parties had been divided within themselves, the overwhelming majority of the media and other political and economic elites were strongly in favor of a text drafted under the authority of former president Giscard d'Estaing. Devoid of significant new approaches, thanks to clever British diplomatic footwork, and emasculated by most national governments eager to limit the abandoning of national sovereignty, it was more of a compendium of previous treaties than a decisive step into a European political union. Post electoral analysis showed that more than half the negative votes were expressed on account of domestic considerations, not about Europe, or even the actual text, which was not even read.

It showed a France sociologically split in two. On one side, the upper classes, the economic managers, and the retired older people, who in France have benefited from the solicitous attention of successive governments, and on the other side, the increasingly vulnerable lower middle class, the unemployed, and the inhabitants of the poorer rural areas of the country, where public services and economic activities have been slowly dwindling. The desertion of the middle classes worried by the economic crisis and the downgrading of their status (62 percent voted against) was a confirmation of a trend that has been confirmed in all the following French elections since.

At the same time, the negative vote in the Netherlands was motivated by completely different reasons that have left Brussels in a state of paralysis and confusion. It was only through the subterfuge of the 2009 Lisbon treaty that the EU could go back to normal work. However, it was only possible through a discreet parliamentary approval cleverly engineered by President Sarkozy. Denying another vote (as in Ireland) reinforced the accusation of the democratic illegitimacy of EU norms and directives, a favorite theme of anti-European groups in France, ranging from nationalist right to extreme left.

Those disaffected categories of the society, which have used the EU as a scapegoat for venting their social and political frustrations, are also the most alarmed by immigration, especially of Muslims from North Africa and the Sahel (they represent about 5 million people, less than 8 percent of the general population and two-thirds of which are concentrated in cities of more than 200,000 inhabitants). Their integration into the general French population, especially given the religious factor, is considered to be more difficult than the previous waves of European immigants of the 1930s (mostly Catholic Poles or Italians). Under the constant drumming of the Front National propaganda, part of those electors are led to suspect that the governing elites, conveniently living in lilywhite areas, are silently abandonning the traditional French policy of assimilation, in favor of a more communitarian approach, less demanding toward the new categories of entrants. The mainstream parties are embarrassed and divided on the answers but not willing to abandon the electoral issue to the Front National.

In 2005 the populist vote was made up of a scattering of groups belonging from the extreme right Front National, the extreme left, and ecologists. Ten years later, the Front National under Marine Le Pen has been able to coalesce the anti elite frustration. Expanding their electoral base from 15 percent to 18 percent by 2004, the Front National has succeeded in doubling its vote, reaching 25 percent of the votes in the May 2014 European parliamentary elections. The "losers" from modernity and globalization have felt abandoned by the established main parties, and have taken out their revenge on the UMP and the Socialist Party (which Marine Le Pen unites in common scorn as "UMPPS"). The result has been an increasing timidity toward reforms by the political establisment and prudence, amounting to silence, on the broader European issues.

THE EURO PARADOX AND HARD CHOICES ABOUT REFORM

Most European debates have traditionally been about the balance of power within the institutional framework of the European Council. France, maintaining, until 2000 a voting parity with Germany, as well as a close political alliance, was considering itself to be in a solid and comfortable position. The Nice European Council in December 2000 had to modify the voting arrangements within the EU in order to take into account the new demographic weight of the reunified Germany, as well as the EU enlargement. France, its institutional weight formally reduced, felt, at the time, a loser to Germany within the EU.

However, it was the increased focus on the management of the common currency which had the most important effects: it shifted the debate within the EU, from the institutional debates on the political aims of the Union to the more narrow, but still intensely political issues of the discipline of the common currency, to be enforced by the EU Commission. Measuring the importance for France of this major political evolution of the EU requires going back to the origins of the euro.

The inability to contain the speculative assaults against the French franc, during the the currency crisis of 1993, involved also the British pound. Mitterrand obtained from Kohl a widening up to 15 percent of the European Monetary System's margin of currency rate variations. This amounted to a de facto French devaluation. It was a major failure of the "currency snake," itself a major component of the Single European Market.

Well before the fall of the Berlin wall, in June 1988 at the Hanover European Council, a decision of principle was therefore taken to study the feasibility of a common currency. For the French, the aim was mainly economic: to prevent a repetition of those devaluations which have plagued the single European market since the early 1980s, in particular, allowing Spain and Italy to make big inroads into the French markets and disrupting the price mechanisms under the Common Agricultural Policy.

In the fall of 1989, in the perspective of imminent German reunification, political considerations became overwhelming. Mitterrand was aiming at anchoring the new Germany to Europe and preventing a transformation of the EU into a mark zone. Kohl was also seeing the entreprise, which was adamantly opposed by the Bundesbank, as a first step toward a European political union. Subsequently, despite difficult negotiations the French succeeded in having accepted the principle of the creation of the euro, but under mostly German conditions, including the independance of the European Central Bank, built on the model of the Bundesbank, as well as severe criteria on fiscal deficits. This "*Dreikommanull*" was politically easy to publicize in Germany and reassured public opinion about a runaway debt. There was a solemn pledge that EMU would not lead to financial transfers. Each country was to be responsible on a national basis for its good economic management (fiscal policy) and the ECB was to be in charge of fighting inflation (monetary policy). There was neither a full anticipation of the disruptive effect of the liberalization of world financial flows, nor of the consequences of a widening of the productivity gap between the participating countries, instead of the convergence expected.

By separating the monetary aspect from the budgetary policies—thereby renouncing an integrated economic policy, and forgetting about financial solidarity, the governments were able, at the time, to make the euro process acceptable politically, but left incomplete the actual common currency process. For France, the first test of implementing the budgetary deficit criteria was in April 2002, one year before the deadline agreed for implementing the Maastricht criteria. The previous year, the attack on the Twin Towers in New York had led President Chirac to seek an increased military budget for France. The EU experts became worried about French implementation of the 3 percent budget criteria and at the end of 2003 the Commission launched a procedure against Paris by asking for rectification of the budget. But Brussels failed. Seeking political parity, the Commission made the mistake of launching a parallel procedure against Germany, which infuriated Chancellor Schröder. Italy, anticipating their own problem, joined France at the November 2003 meeting of the Finance ministers. With the help of Jean Claude Juncker of Luxembourg, who argued that it was politically impossible for the EU to put simultanously the three major economies of the EU on the defensive, the anticipated sanctions were abandoned. The President of the Commission Romano Prodi was himself not in a position to intervene, having said publicly that the criteria were "stupid because they were too rigid."

While Paris was satisfied that it would be immune to every financial crisis, the financial markets began to target smaller countries of the euro zone. They could borrow on world financial markets at rates close to those of the best economic performer of the zone, Germany, with their "spread" reduced to a minimum. Ireland and Portugal became the first tests. One year thereafter, the world monetary crisis, brought on by the Lehman Brothers bank crash, hit the European banks. Meanwhile, Greece chose, after the socialist government victory in 2009, to recognize officially the falsification of its financial data.

The ensuing euro crisis became the test of two contending approaches. For German Chancellor Merkel, the faltering country should first help itself through austerity measures, if only to prevent another precedent for giving way to "moral hazard." By contrast, French President Sarkozy thought one should forget, temporarily, about the legalities of the treaties and, for the sake of the euro zone stability, help the culprit. In May 2010 EU mechanisms were used to provide Athens with first aid. Berlin demanded that the IMF also participate. However, in October 2010, in Deauville, Sarkozy and Merkel let it be known that the euro countries in crisis should not be considered as committed to reimburse in full their sovereign debts and that the markets should also participate in debt rescheduling. To avoid the worsening of the crisis, it was decided a few days later that the banks would have to accept a discount of 21 percent on their Greek debt, and that all the euro countries would also participate in the rescue. For the first time it was recognized that the European Stabilization Mechanism would intervene on the debt market. Italy and Spain would soon benefit from its interventions. Even if the European loans for such debt stabilization were not deemed officially as financial transfers between euro countries, a taboo had therefore been broken. At a dramatic G-20 summit in Nice in November 2011, not only the fall of George Papandreou and Silvio Berlusconi was engineered by their fellow European colleagues but also the amount of eurofunds available was increased tenfold. One year later it was agreed that the European Stability Mechanism could also help to recapitalize banks in difficulty. In exchange a European supervision of the European banks under the ECB supervision was approved.

As a counterpart to this change of approaches, a new budgetary Pact was approved in December of the same year, with the assent of France and Italy, the two countries most likely to have difficulties implementing it. Given this new course of the common currency management, in June 2012, Mario Draghi, the head of the ECB, surprised world financial markets by announcing that the Bank, now acheiving the status of the only federal institution within the EU, would "do whatever it takes to preserve the euro," and presumably to prevent the default of a European euro member. Subsequently he launched the European equivalent of the American Federal Reserve's monetary "quantitative easing."

Thus, over the fifteen years of the extended euro crisis, the whole context of the EU policies has been deeply transformed. For Paris, the new euro policies reflected economic and financial realities, far from the rigid legal rules, which prevailed at the start of the process. A general lowering of world interest rates and a fall in oil prices followed it. Paris was therefore able to boast about an "alignment of the stars" which had potential to last for a long time.

LOOKING AHEAD FOR THE 2017 PRESIDENTIAL ELECTION

The risk, however, is that in anticipation of the 2017 presidential election the French government will maintain its "double language." To Germany and the other euro countries it seeks to renew its commitment to get back within the criteria of the European Budgetary Pact by betting on the return to economic growth. To the French electorate and especially to a divided socialist party, reform will be seen to have limited social impact and incremental implementation.

Whether the other European countries and the financial markets will agree to that political compromise remains an open question. The prospect of a possible rise of world interest rates, given the perspective of an end to

America's monetary "quantitative easing," would be a great problem for France's budgetary balance as the reimbursement of sovereign debt is already weighing heavily. The present possibility for the French state to continue to borrow on the cheap and to benefit from the euro safety net is therefore presently an inducement for the taking a slow road to reform. The short-term political benefits are attractive to politicians looking to the 2017 election. But it only delays the problem of the political risk of reform. The mid and long term risks for France could be to enter further on the slippery process of decline. However, the refusal to become a second-class country in Europe is deeply entrenched in the general population and there is a consensus on the severity of the choices ahead. For the first time in twenty years, polls indicate that the majority of public opinion is ready to endure the costs of reforms. France has often been challenged by reform in its long history. Sometimes the challenges have been well met, and sometimes not. But abating the spectre of decline requires a grand solution to France's political and economic stagnation. The people are ready. Thus, there is only one question: will the political elites listen? [1]

NOTE

1. Downloaded by [FNSP Fondation National des Sciences Politiques] at 01:45 15 January 2014, US Strategy in a Post-Western World, 127.

BIBLIOGRAPHY

Baverez, Nicolas. *La France Qui Tombe* . Paris: Perrin, 2003.
Bourlanges, Jean-Louis. "Identité Européenne Et Ambition Française." *Commentaire* Numéro 147.3 (2014): 484.
Erlanger, Steven. "A Proud Nation Ponders How to Halt Its Slow Decline." *The New York Times*. The New York Times, 24 Aug. 2013.
Julliard, Jacques, and Jean-Claude Michéa. *La Gauche Et Le Peuple*. N.p.: Flammarion, 2014.
Julliard, Jacques. *Le Malheur Français*. Paris: Flammarion, 2005.
Marsh, David. *The Euro: The Battle for the New Global Currency*. New Haven, CT: Yale UP, 2011.
"The Time-Bomb at the Heart of Europe." *Economist (US)* 17 Nov. 2012.
Tribalat, Michèle. "Intégration, La Fin Du Modèle Français." *Commentaire* Été.2 (2015): 331.
Verdier-Molinié, Agnès. *On Va Dans Le Mur...* Paris: Albin Michel, 2015.

Index

About the Contributors

David P. Calleo is Dean Acheson Professor and University Professor at Johns Hopkins University.

Aaron Zack is professor of politics at Baruch College of the City University of New York.

Benjamin M. Rowland is a former investment banker and economic policy consultant, and a retired staff member of the World Bank.

Gabriel Goodliffe is professor at Instituto Tecnologico Autonomo de Mexico.

Thomas Row is professor at the Diplomatic Academy, Vienna, and senior adjunct professor at SAIS Europe.

Stephen F. Szabo is executive director of the Transatlantic Academy of the German Marshall Fund, and professorial lecturer at SAIS.

Hannes Odomeit is emeritus professor at the College of Europe, Warsaw.

Mark Gilbert is professor at SAIS Europe.

Lanxin Xiang is professor at the Graduate Institute of International Studies, Geneva.

Dana H. Allin is senior fellow for U.S. Foreign Policy and Transatlantic Affairs and editor of Survival at the International Institute of Strategic Studies, London, and professor at SAIS Europe.

Benoît d'Aboville, a former French diplomat and ambassador, is currently associate professor at SciencesPo/PSIA in Paris and vice president of the Fondation pour la Recherche Stratégique.